the first emancipation
the abolition of
slavery in the North

the first emancipation
the abolition
of slavery
in the
North

ARTHUR ZILVERSMIT

The University of Chicago Press
CHICAGO AND LONDON

ISBN: 0–226–98331–5 (clothbound) ; 0–226–98332–3 (paperbound)

Library of Congress Catalog Card Number: 67–15954

THE UNIVERSITY OF CHICAGO PRESS, CHICAGO 60637
The University of Chicago Press, Ltd., London

© *1967 by The University of Chicago*

Published 1967

Fourth Impression 1970

Printed in the United States of America

TO THE MEMORY
OF MY FATHER
MARCUS ZILVERSMIT

preface

During one of the many debates on Negro slavery that agitated New York in the years after independence, an opponent of a proposed constitutional ban on slavery suggested that such a clause would be highly inexpedient. If New Yorkers did not mention slavery in their constitution then future generations might forget that it had ever existed in the state.[1] This prediction has proved accurate. The slaves of the northern states are remembered in our histories as comprising only a few domestic servants who were freed shortly after the restraining hand of Great Britain had been forcibly removed. Forgotten is the fact that slavery existed in all the northern colonies and that it continued to be an important economic and social institution for several decades after independence. Yet the story of slavery and its abolition in the northern states deserves to be remembered, not because it is necessary to assign guilt and to distribute blame, but because the North managed to solve the great American dilemma of how to deal with human bondage in a society dedicated to both human equality and property rights. The triumph of gradual abolition in the North was really a triumph for popular government. On the other hand, the peaceful, gradual abolition of slavery in one section, accompanied by its increasing strength in another, was to put American democracy to its greatest test in 1861.

Why did gradual abolition succeed in the North? Was it merely a confirmation of the unprofitability of slavery in the northern states or was it abolished despite its con-

---

[1] Nathaniel H. Carter and William L. Stone, *Reports of the Proceedings and Debates of the Convention of 1821* (Albany, 1821), p. 497.

tinuing profitability? How were the abolitionists able to persuade the states to abolish slavery and how did northern slaveholders react to these attempts to deprive them of their property? The hope of answering these questions prompted this study.

The problem of the abolition of slavery in the northern states was suggested to me by Kenneth Stampp's insightful study, *The Peculiar Institution.* I was fortunate to have Professor Stampp's guidance in writing the doctoral dissertation from which this study has emerged. I am grateful to a number of scholars who have given me the benefit of their criticisms at various stages: Russell H. Bastert and Frederick Rudolph of Williams College; and Norman Jacobson, Leon Litwack, and Charles Sellers of the University of California. I am deeply indebted to my friend Jack M. Holl of Williams for his imaginative and incisive criticism of the entire manuscript.

I am indebted to the University of California for its Honorary Traveling Fellowship, which facilitated access to research materials. Miss Bessie Wright has earned my gratitude by her excellent typing of the manuscript and I am indebted to Miss Barbara Trebelhorn for editorial assistance. The Williams College Class of 1900 Fund paid for typing the manuscript. I appreciate the courtesies extended to me at the libraries of the following institutions: Columbia University, Haverford College, Historical Society of Pennsylvania, New Jersey Historical Society, New Jersey State Library, New-York Historical Society, New York Public Library, Rutgers: The State University, Union Theological Seminary, Williams College. Finally, I thank my wife Charlotte, for without her advice, support, and encouragement at every stage I could not have produced this study.

contents

CONTENTS

the first emancipation
*the abolition of
slavery in the North*

Negro slavery   **1**
in the North

Negro slavery made its appearance soon after the founding of the northern colonies. Faced with a chronic labor shortage, colonists and promoters hoped that the importation of Negroes would make their ventures profitable. In 1644, for instance, it was suggested that one way of arresting the decay of the Dutch colony of New Netherlands would be to send "as many Negroes" as could be sold "at a fair price," since "Negroes would accomplish more work . . . , and at less expense, than farm servants, who must be bribed to go thither by a great deal of money and promises."[1]

NEGRO POPULATION

By 1715 slavery was well established in the northern colonies. There were probably 12,500 Negroes (virtually all slaves) in the New England and middle colonies, and one out of every five slaves on the continent was owned by a northern master. The density of Negro population varied considerably. New England's lack of currency, its predominate pattern of small-scale agriculture, and the region's marked hostility to all foreigners—black and white—served to keep its slave population small. Although New Englanders took an early lead in the slave trade, they found it more profitable to sell their cargoes in the plantation colonies. If the southern markets were glutted, however, or if some of the Negroes were too weak for plantation labor, they were brought back for sale in the New England market.[2]

[1] Edmund B. O'Callaghan (ed.), *Documents Relative to the Colonial History of the State of New-York* (11 vols.; Albany, 1856–61), I, 154.

[2] Evarts B. Greene and Virginia D. Harrington, *American Population Before the Census of 1790* (New York, 1932), p. 4; James Brown to Obadiah Brown, January 28, 1736, James B. Hedges, *The Browns of Providence Plantations* (Cambridge, Mass., 1952), p. 71.

Many rural New Englanders had little contact with slavery; in 1764 fewer than one out of eight Massachusetts families owned slaves. Even in New England, however, there were regions where slavery was commonplace and firmly woven into the fabric of the community. In Rhode Island in the beginning of the eighteenth century, slaves outnumbered indentured servants nearly eight to one, and fifty years later Negroes still accounted for nearly twelve per cent of the colony's population. Slaves were especially numerous in the Narragansett region; nearly one-third of the population of South Kingstown was Negro in 1755. Moreover, large slaveholdings were common; Governor William Robinson owned twenty Negroes and another Narragansett planter, Robert Hazard, disposed of twenty-four Negroes in his will. Eastern Connecticut was the only other New England region where large-scale slaveholdings were common—the New London area was over six per cent Negro in 1774.[3]

The Negro population of colonial New England never exceeded sixteen thousand. On the eve of the Revolution, Connecticut had more Negroes than any other New England colony—6,464 (just over three per cent of the population) ; but the highest proportion of slaves was found in Rhode Island, where Negroes represented over six per cent of the population. In colonial Massachusetts the Negro population never exceeded a fraction over two per cent. New Hampshire and Vermont had very few slaves.[4]

Slavery took deeper hold in the middle colonies. Patrick M'Robert, who visited New York in 1774, was shocked at the number of slaves: "It rather hurts the Europian eye to see so many negro slaves upon the streets, tho' they are said to deminish yearly here." For New Yorkers contact with large numbers of black slaves was no novelty. Owning slaves was a widespread, common, and accepted practice in colonial New York. Throughout most of the colonial period the Negro population of New York was about fourteen per cent. A high

[3] Lorenzo J. Greene, *The Negro in Colonial New England* (New York, 1942) , pp. 97–98, 85–88; William B. Weeden, *Early Rhode Island* (New York, 1910) , pp. 143, 172, 285, 288; Greene, *Negro in New England,* pp. 91–93, 97–98.

[4] Greene, *Negro in New England,* pp. 31–35, 74, 77–78, 81, 87, 90.

proportion of Negroes lived in the counties surrounding the port of New York—mid-eighteenth-century Kings County (on Long Island) was over one-third Negro; and at the outbreak of the Revolutionary War, over twenty per cent of the population of Queens and Richmond counties was made up of Negro slaves.[5] A Hessian officer traveling through upstate New York saw many houses that had a "negro family living nearby in an out-house." Slaveholding was even more common in New York City. In 1738 over one-half the families of Kings County owned slaves. Furthermore, Kings County slaveholdings were relatively large—out of 169 slaveholding families, thirty-three owned five or more. Most New York masters, however, owned only one or two slaves; Lewis Morris, who owned twenty-nine slaves over fourteen years old, was clearly exceptional.[6]

New Jersey's slaves accounted for approximately eight per cent of her population throughout the colonial period, but Negroes were not evenly distributed within the colony. New Jersey consisted of two distinct regions: East Jersey, settled by the Dutch and economically tied to New York City, had many more Negroes than West Jersey, whose Quaker settlers had small farms and were in the commercial orbit of Philadelphia. Thus the pattern of slavery in East Jersey was similar to that in New York; about twelve per cent of its population was Negro. In West Jersey slaves accounted for only four or five per cent of the inhabitants. Just prior to the Revolution, there were approximately 11,000 slaves in New Jersey.[7]

[5] Carl Bridenbaugh (ed.), "Patrick M'Robert's Tour Through Part of the North Provinces of America," *Pennsylvania Magazine of History and Biography,* LIX (1935), 142; figures derived from Edmund B. O'Callaghan (ed.), *Documentary History of the State of New-York* (4 vols.; Albany, 1849–51), I, 689–97.

[6] William Stone (trans.), *Letters of Brunswick and Hessian Officers During the American Revolution* (Albany, 1891), p. 142; O'Callaghan, *Documentary History,* III, 852–53, IV, 188–200.

[7] The last complete census of colonial New Jersey reported the presence of 4,606 Negroes in 1745. An incomplete census, made in 1772, showed there were 3,714 Negroes in West Jersey, but since the unreported counties accounted for approximately two-thirds of New Jersey's Negro population in 1745 and 1784, it can be assumed that the total number of slaves in the colony shortly before the Revolution was about 11,000. Simeon Moss, "The Persistence of Slavery and Involuntary

In the absence of census data, Pennsylvania's slave population can only be guessed on the basis of several contradictory estimates. Contemporary calculations went as high as 100,000 Negroes in 1774 (which would have made the colony one-third Negro) and as low as 2,000 the next year (which would mean that less than one per cent of the population was slave). According to the most recent compilation of colonial population data, there were nearly 6,000 Negroes in Pennsylvania in 1770, and throughout the colonial period Negroes accounted for about two-and-one-half per cent of the total population.[8] If these figures are correct, the number of slaves in Pennsylvania was much closer to the figures for the New England colonies than for New York and New Jersey. Yet Pennsylvania's slave code hewed closely to that established in the other middle colonies.

The pattern of slaveholding in New Jersey and Pennsylvania was much the same as in New York; there were many masters who relied on a few Negroes, but large holdings were common in some areas. As early as 1685 Colonel Lewis Morris employed sixty or seventy Negroes on his plantation and iron mill in Shrewsbury, New Jersey. Mark Bird, a leading iron manufacturer of Berks County, Pennsylvania, owned fourteen adult Negroes in 1780. In York County, largely settled by Germans, three-and-one-half per cent of the propery owners were assessed for slaves in 1780. But whereas one township in the county reported no slaves, over sixteen per cent of the property owners of another township owned slaves.[9] Despite the fact that a few Pennsylvania masters had

Servitude in a Free State (1695–1866)," *Journal of Negro History*, XXXV (1950), Table I, 310, Table III, 311; Thomas F. Gordon, *A Gazeteer of New Jersey. . . .* (Trenton, N.J., 1834), p. 29; Greene and Harrington, *Population Before 1790*, p. 112; *New Jersey Gazette*, December 6, 1784.

[8] Greene and Harrington, *Population Before 1790*, p. 114; U.S. Bureau of the Census, *Historical Statistics of the United States, Colonial Times to 1957* (Washington, D.C., 1960), p. 756.

[9] Georges Scot, *The Model of the Government of the Province of East New-Jersey in America. . . . ,* reprinted by William A. Whitehead, in *East Jersey Under the Proprietary Governments* (2d ed., Newark, N.J., 1875), pp. 128–29; Paul N. Schaefer, "Slavery in Berks County," *Historical Review of Berks County*, VI (1941), 112–13; figures derived from *Pennsylvania Archives*, 3d ser., XXI, 165–324.

large holdings, most masters, as in New York, had only one or two Negroes.

Although the slave population of the North was relatively small, Negro slavery was a common and accepted practice here as well as in the South. In general, northern masters owned only a few Negroes, but there were areas in the North where the plantation system was reproduced on a small scale. Almost everywhere in the North a visitor could see farmers cultivating their fields with the aid of one or two Negroes, and in some places he might see large plantations worked by a dozen slaves.

TREATMENT OF NEGROES

Although most northern slaves probably escaped the barbarous treatment endured by the Negroes who worked the West Indian plantations, their lives were undeniably harsh. Life as a slave often began with kidnapping in Africa and with the terror of the crowded hold of a slave ship. The newly imported slave found himself in an inhospitable climate, without friends and unable to understand what the white man wanted. As runaway slave advertisements testify, many of them escaped their new masters before they had learned to speak English. Other slaves were brought to the North after they had been enslaved elsewhere, either in the island colonies or on the southern plantations. These Negroes were again parted from friends and family.

In the early years of the eighteenth century, many masters thought of their slaves as little better than beasts of burden. According to an early antislavery writer, New Jersey masters dressed their slaves in rags and forced them to go barefoot in the cold of winter. They showed their contempt for their Negroes by naming them Toby, Mando, Mingo—names ordinarily reserved for dogs and horses.[10]

Since they regarded Negroes as subhuman, many masters strenuously resisted the attempts of the Society for the Propa-

[10] John Hepburn, *The American Defence of the Christian Golden Rule, or an Essay to Prove the Unlawfulness of Making Slaves of Men* (1715); reprinted in American Antiquarian Society, *Proceedings*, LIX (1949), 122.

gation of the Gospel in Foreign Parts (SPG) to convert the slaves. Elias Neau, who served as catechist to the Negroes of New York, complained in 1708 that despite the passage of a law that denied that Negroes became free when they were baptized, some masters still refused to send their slaves to school to be prepared for baptism. Those Negroes who asked for permission to attend his school were "either threatened to be sold to Virginia or else to be sent into the Country." A Rye, New York, clergyman reported that some of his parishioners were "so profane as to say that they do not think that baptism will be of any service" to the Negroes and some Long Island masters maintained that "a Negro hath no soul." Elias Neau was one of the few white men who would "condescend familiarly to discourse with the poor slaves," who, since they were "put to the vilest drudgeries," were "esteemed the scum and offscourings of men." Neau himself was despised because of his work with the slaves. He could often be observed "creeping into Garrets, Cellars and other nauseous places, to exhort and pray by the poor slaves when they are sick." The Reverend John Sharpe reported in 1713 that New York masters paid little attention to their slaves' religion and that most of the Negroes were married outside of the church and were buried by other slaves with "Heathenish rites . . . performed at the grave." [11]

Delaware and Pennsylvania masters were also reluctant to have their slaves instructed and baptized. The Reverend George Ross confirmed reports of the neglect of Negro education, which he attributed "to the conduct of those slaves who after their initiation grew turbulent and boisterous aiming at a freedom which though no part of their Christian privilege, it appeared they had most at heart." This made the whites suspicious of the sincerity of the Negroes "who had no other benefit in view . . . but an exemption from a yoke, which is not in the least inconsistent with true Christian liberty." As late as 1755, residents of Dover, Pennsylvania, threatened to

[11] Frank J. Klingberg, "The S.P.G. Program for Negroes in Colonial New York," *Historical Magazine of the Protestant Episcopal Church*, VIII (1939), 309, 315, 341, 350; "Rev. John Sharpe's Proposals, Etc.," (*Collections of the New-York Historical Society*, 1880), pp. 348–350, 355.

tie and whip their slaves if they went to church or answered to their Christian names.[12]

The British were disturbed by the refusal of the colonists to allow their slaves to be baptized and repeatedly urged colonial governors to secure laws to facilitate the conversion of Negroes and Indians. The governor of New York reported in 1699 that such a bill "would not go downe with the Assembly;" they have a notion, he explained, "that the Negros being converted . . . would emancipate them . . . [and] they have no other servants in this country but Negros." It was not until 1706 that the New York Assembly complied with the crown's wishes and passed a law denying the "Groundless opinion" that baptism emancipated Negroes. New Jersey provided for slave baptism in 1704, but the law also permitted the branding of any Negro convicted of theft and the castration of a slave who by force or "perswasion" had sexual intercourse with a white woman. The crown disallowed the law since it provided punishments that were "never . . . allowed by or known" in the laws of England.[13] The slave baptism sections of the law were never reenacted, and New York remained the only northern colony to comply with this royal request.

Even when the law encouraged slave baptism, however, bringing religion to the slaves could lead to practical problems. As a Westchester County, New York, minister ruefully noted, Negroes would not or could not "live up to the Christian covenant in one notorious instance at least, viz. matrimony." They married according to heathen rites and were casual in breaking marital ties. But if the church tried to provide religious marriages for slaves, then the masters would "object and say it is not lawful to part man and wife, and how can we sell one of them?" Another minister agreed that slave marriages would lead to "difficulties and inconven-

[12] Frank J. Klingberg, "The African Immigrant in Colonial Pennsylvania and Delaware," *Hist. Mag. Episcopal Church*, XI (1942), 132–133, 147.

[13] *N.Y. Documents*, III, 374, 547; IV, 510–511; *Colonial Laws of New York. . . .* (4 vols.; Albany, 1894), I, 597–98; *Anno Regni Reginae Annae . . . Tertio* [Acts Passed by the Second Assembly of New Jersey, December, 1704] (New York, 1704), pp. 18–19; *N.Y. Documents*, V. 157.

iences"; whether the husband and wife were in the same or different families. If they were both held by the same master, then he was obliged "either to keep or sell both, let his necessities be ever so pressing." If the slaves had different masters, as was "most usual," then when one master left the neighborhood, the families were separated (as happened in the case of the minister's own Negro woman) and it was "almost impossible, to keep them faithful" under these circumstances.[14]

The slave family, then, was a precarious institution subject to the needs and wishes of the master. Contemporary advertisements show that in some instances masters sold husbands, wives, and children separately, and groups of slaves were frequently offered for sale with no mention of family ties. Some masters were explicit. In 1732 a New England master offered to sell his nineteen-year-old Negro woman and her six-month-old child either "together or apart." A New Jersey master showed more consideration. He proposed to sell a Negro man, woman, and child: "They being man and wife would make it most agreeable to sell them together; however, a few miles separation will not prevent the sale." The anomalous position of the family in a slave society was painfully apparent in an advertisement of a New Jersey master who offered a reward for the return of his nine-year-old Negro girl who "Was Stolen by Her Mother." [15]

The enforced separation of Negro families was often tragic. On a visit to Perth Amboy, New Jersey, in 1797 William Dunlap observed a slave woman whose master had separated her from her beloved child: "the Mother by her cries has made the town re-echo & has continued her exclamations for 2 hours incessantly & still continues them. I am sick, at oppression." The separation of slave families was not always the result of callous indifference. A New Jersey man sent his son the "boy" he had requested although he was

Sorry . . . to part with Him, but much more so that you are necessitated to Sel him. I presume you know not what other Shift

[14] Klingberg, "The S.P.G. in New York," pp. 339–40, 342.
[15] *New-England Weekly Journal*, May 1, 1732, in George H. Moore, *Notes on the History of Slavery in Massachusetts* (New York, 1866), p. 70; *New Jersey Gazette*, December 20, 1780; April 23, 1778.

to make or you wo[ul]d not do it . . . the boy is much afected at leaving the House and being Sold out of the famely; indeed all the famely Seem more affected than usual on Such ocasions.[16]

Some masters, when forced to sell their Negroes, did concern themselves with the happiness of their slaves. A New Jersey innkeeper who wanted to sell seven Negroes made it clear that "The man and wife and three children must not be parted, nor the mother and son; as they have lived long in one family together, it would be most agreeable if they could be fixed near each other." [17]

Although individual masters tried to preserve family ties, the slave family was unprotected by law, weakened by insecurity, and easily destroyed. The weakness of the family encouraged casual sexual relationships rather than permanent bonds. Masters did not necessarily disapprove of their slaves' attitude toward sex; Samuel Sewall accused masters of conniving at the fornication of their slaves to save themselves the expense of finding wives for them. Slaveowners might even encourage promiscuity. A traveler in New England in 1639 heard a Negro woman weeping outside his house and discovered that her master wanted to breed Negroes but that she refused to go to bed with a young Negro man; when her master ordered her to do so, she kicked her partner out of bed. "This she took in high disdain beyond her slavery, and this was the cause of her grief." A great deal of miscegenation occurred under slavery. A New Jersey master was said to have had children by each of three Negro women he owned. "Whenever he could dispose of these his own offspring, he sold them, in the same manner as he would have disposed of his hogs." [18]

---

[16] *Collections of the N.Y. Hist. Soc.*, (1929), I, 18; "Letter of Lieutenant-Colonel Elijah Clark to his Son Lardner Clark, Haddonfield, N.J., May 17, 1782," *Pa. Mag. of Hist.*, XXVIII (1904), 107–8.

[17] *Pennsylvania Packet,* March 18, 1780.

[18] Samuel Sewall, *The Selling of Joseph* (Boston, 1700); reprinted in "Diary of Samuel Sewall," (*Collections of the Massachusetts Historical Society*), 5th ser., VI, note, p. 18; Moore, *Slavery in Mass.*, p. 8; Edward R. Turner, *The Negro in Pennsylvania* (Washington, D.C., 1911), p. 31; Isaac Holmes, *An Account of the United States of America* (London [1823]), p. 328.

SLAVE CODES

The crown was not only concerned with slave baptism but was disturbed by tales of mistreatment, and it repeatedly urged royal governors to obtain laws to restrain masters from "Inhuman Severitys" and to provide the death penalty for the willful murder of a slave as well as "a fit penalty . . . for the maiming of them." The colonists, however, devoted their attention to working out a system for the control of their slaves—the black codes. All the colonies were anxious to pass laws to restrain slaves from running away. A Massachusetts law of 1680 forbade shipowners taking on board any Negro without the governor's consent. The Connecticut Assembly found in 1690 that "many persons of this Colony doe for their necessary use purchase negroe servants" who often "run away to the great wronge, damage and disapoyntment of their masters." To prevent this, any Negro found outside of the town limits was to be apprehended and returned to his owner. A Rhode Island law of 1703 prohibited Negroes and Indians (slave or free) from being on the streets at night. Violators were to be punished by whipping "not exceeding fifteen stripes upon their naked backs, except their incorrigible behaviour require more." [19]

The New York Assembly observed in 1702 that the number of slaves in the colony was steadily increasing and that these slaves were often "guilty of Confederating together in running away, or other ill-practices." Therefore, it prohibited unauthorized meetings of more than three slaves, the offending Negroes to be punished by up to forty lashes on the bare back. In 1705, during a war with France, New York enacted a more drastic fugitive slave law. Designed to prevent intelligence from reaching the enemy and to discourage slaves from taking advantage of the war to seek refuge in Canada, the law called for the execution of any slave found more than forty miles north of Albany. Various East Jersey statutes were designed to prevent freemen from concealing

[19] *N.Y. Documents,* III, 374, 547; Greene, *Negro in New England,* p. 128; *Public Records of the Colony of Connecticut* (15 vols.; Hartford, 1850–90), IV, 40; John R. Bartlett (ed.), *Records of the Colony of Rhode Island and Providence Plantations in New England* (10 vols.; Providence, 1856–62), III, 492.

fugitive slaves, and New Jersey's comprehensive slave code of 1714 required anyone finding a slave more than five miles from home without a pass to whip the offender.[20]

In a move to protect the community from petty thievery, most colonies enacted laws to prevent freemen from trading with slaves. An East Jersey law of 1683 took note of the fact "that Negro and Indian Slaves, . . . under pretence of Trade, . . . do frequently Steal from their Masters and others." Since it was "a known Truth, that without a receiver, the Theif would soon desert his practice," the law prohibited freemen from selling liquor or other goods to slaves, and slaves who attempted to sell goods were whipped. Thirteen years later, East Jersey set up special courts to try slaves for theft. Convicted slaves were to suffer corporal punishment "not exceeding forty stripes." A Pennsylvania law of 1706 provided that slaves who stole less than five pounds were to be whipped, but those who were convicted by special courts of greater thefts should be whipped, branded, and banished from the colony (which usually meant being sold to the plantation colonies). A Connecticut law of 1708 punished slaves who stole with up to thirty lashes; and a Rhode Island law of 1718 set up special courts for the trial of Negroes accused of purloining. This was the only instance in which New England law established special trial procedures for Negroes.[21]

New York and New Jersey had the most severe black codes of the northern colonies. New York provided a firm legal basis for slavery by making slaves of all children born of slave mothers (no other northern colony gave slavery this specific legal sanction). The New York law of 1702 specifically permitted masters "to punish their slaves for their Crimes

[20] *N.Y. Colonial Laws,* I, 519–21, 582–84, 880–81; III, 448–49; Aaron Leaming and Jacob Spicer (compilers), *Grants, Concessions and Original Constitutions of the Province of New Jersey* (Philadelphia, 1758), pp. 109, 340–42; William Bradford (printer), *Laws and Acts of . . . New-Jersey* ([New York], 1717), p. 19.

[21] Leaming and Spicer, *Grants and Concessions,* pp. 254–55; Turner, *Negro in Pa.,* p. 29; *Conn. Colonial Records,* V, 52; Jeffrey R. Brackett, "The Status of the Slave, 1775–1789," *Essays in the Constitutional History of the United States,* ed. J. Franklin Jameson (Boston, 1889), pp. 268–69.

and offences att Discretion, not extending to life or Member." The law further provided that a slave found guilty of striking a Christian freeman was to be jailed up to fourteen days and to suffer corporal punishment not extending to life and limb. Since slaves were property and could not "without great loss . . . be subjected in all Cases criminal, to the strict Rules of the Laws of England," special procedures were set up for the punishment of petty theft—the master was to make restitution and the slave to suffer corporal punishment. Slave testimony was only allowed to be used in cases of slave conspiracies. Following an "Execrable and Barberous" crime committed by an Indian and a Negro slave, who murdered their master, mistress, and five children, the assembly extended special trial procedures to capital crimes. Clearly designed to terrorize the slaves, the new law provided that a slave convicted of murder or of conspiracy to murder a free person was to "Suffer the paines of Death in such manner and with such Circumstances as the aggravation and Enormity of their Crime . . . shall merritt." What the assembly meant by "the paines of Death" was clear: the Negro woman implicated in the crimes that provoked the act was burned to death and the Indian slave was hung, after being "put to all the torment possible for a terror to others." [22]

The horror of a slave revolt soon convinced New Yorkers that the laws were still inadequate to control their barbarous slaves. In the spring of 1712 a group of slaves who conspired to revenge themselves by murdering their masters succeeded in killing nine people, wounding five or six more, and thoroughly alarming the residents of New York City. When they were caught, six slaves immediately committed suicide (a wise move, in view of what followed) and twenty-one were executed: "some were burnt others hanged, one broke on the wheele, and one hung live in chains." As the governor observed, "there has been the most exemplary punishment inflicted that could possibly be thought of." Many slaveowners immediately blamed Elias Neau's catechism school for encouraging the Negroes to revolt and seek their freedom,

[22] *N.Y. Colonial Laws*, I, 519–21, 597–98, 631; *N.Y. Documents*, V, 39; Kenneth Scott, "The Slave Insurrection in New York in 1712," *New York Historical Quarterly*, XLV (1961), 45.

but it was soon established that only two of the accused slaves had ever attended the school. One of them, who had been baptized, "dyed protesting his innocence and was (but too late for him) pityed and declared guiltless even by the prosecutors." Another Negro, who had wanted to be baptized but was refused this by his master, was hung alive in chains. The Reverend John Sharpe went to visit him five days after his punishment began.

He declared to me he was innocent of . . . [his master's] murder with a seeming concern for his master's misfortune. He was often delirious by long continuance in that posture, thro hunger, thirst and pain but he then answered directly to what I enquired and called me by my name so that I might conclude he had some intervals of the exercise of his reason.[23]

New York reacted to the Negro plot with a new, even more severe, law that added a whole list of crimes to those to be tried in special slave courts. If convicted, the slave was to suffer the death penalty, administered in a manner consistent with the enormity of the crime. A master could choose to have his slave tried by a regular jury (the choice was the master's and not the slave's and was merely a recognition of the master's property rights). The law severely limited the rights of free Negroes under the assumption that free Negroes could aid rebellious slaves. Severe as it was, this act was "much mitigated in its severities by the Council's amendments." Governor Robert Hunter realized that the Lords of Trade might consider the act too harsh but, he explained, "after the late barbarous attempt of some of their slaves nothing less would please the people." [24]

New Jersey's slave code, enacted in 1714, was also a product of the fear engendered by the New York Negro plot. The section dealing with murder and related crimes was almost identical with the provisions of the New York law, and it established special courts for the trial of slaves. To discourage masters from helping their slaves avoid punishment (to save themselves the loss involved in the destruction of their prop-

[23] *Ibid.*, pp. 43–74; *N.Y. Documents*, V, 341; "Sharpe's Proposals," pp. 352–53.

[24] *N.Y. Colonial Laws*, I, 761–67; *N.Y. Documents*, V, 356.

erty), masters were to be compensated for executed Negroes.[25]

In 1700 Pennsylvania established special courts to try Negroes for high crimes, but since the statute creating these courts allowed the castration of Negroes convicted of the attempted rape of white women, it met the same fate as the New Jersey law of 1704—the crown was unwilling to countenance such cruelty. Six years later, the assembly enacted a slightly altered version of the same law, changing the punishment for attempted rape to whipping, branding, and deportation. Since the execution of a slave was "so great a harship," masters might send Negroes accused of a capital crime out of the colony "to escape justice, to the ill example of others." Pennsylvania therefore followed the example of New York and New Jersey, compensating masters of executed Negroes. Pennsylvania's slave code, like those of the other middle colonies, prohibited Negroes from meeting in groups or carrying arms. [6]

Special slave courts established in New York and Pennsylvania lasted until after the Revolution. In New Jersey, however, slave trials were held in the regular courts of the colony after 1768, when the trial procedures established in the 1714 code were found to be "inconvenient." [27]

After the slave conspiracy of 1712, New Yorkers were increasingly alarmed by the dangers of a growing free Negro population. Most colonists thought the combination of the words "free" and "Negro" was anomalous and that by their mere presence, freed Negroes would incite slaves to seek liberty. The slave code of 1712 severely penalized free Negroes who concealed fugitive slaves: they could be fined ten pounds for every night they hid a fugitive—a penalty that probably meant reenslavement, since few freed Negroes had much money. In addition, the act barred any Negro freed thereafter from owning any lands or houses. Furthermore, the New York Assembly claimed that "the free Negroes of this Colony are an Idle slothfull people and prove

[25] Bradford, *N.J. Laws*, pp. 19–22.

[26] Turner, *Negro in Pa.*, pp. 26–29; William E. B. Du Bois, *The Philadelphia Negro* (Philadelphia, 1899), pp. 411–14.

[27] Samuel Allinson (compiler), *Acts of the General Assembly of the Province of New Jersey. . . .* (Burlington, N.J., 1776), pp. 307–8.

very often a charge on the place they are." Therefore, masters who wished to emancipate their slaves would have to post two bonds of at least 200 pounds each to guarantee that they would pay their ex-slaves twenty pounds per year for the rest of their lives. Across the Hudson, New Jerseyites came to similar conclusions about free Negroes, and the 1714 slave code contained the same language and provisions on manumission as the New York law, prohibiting free Negro land-holding and requiring masters to pay twenty pounds per year to every Negro they freed.[28]

These laws made manumission virtually impossible. It would be difficult to imagine that even the most charitable slaveowner could afford to place such a heavy burden on his estate for an indeterminate period. The shortsightedness of the policy soon became obvious. Governor Robert Hunter of New York, after hearing of a case in which a Negro, freed by his master's will, had been forced to remain in bondage because the executors refused to post the required bond, recommended changes in the law. The limitations on manumissions, he charged, cut off "all hopes from those slave[s] who by a faithful and dilligent discharge of their duty, may at last look for the reward of a manumission by their masters will." This would not only tend to make slaves careless of their master's interests but would "excite 'em to insurrections more bloody than any they have yet attempted, seeing that . . . death is made more eligible than life, for the longer they live, the longer they are slaves." The assembly was forced to agree that the regulations governing manumissions had proved to be "very Inconvenient, prejudicial" and would "very much Discourage and Dishearten" the slaves from serving their masters truly and faithfully. Accordingly, in 1717 the legislators eliminated the requirement for annual payments to freedmen, although benevolent masters would still have to post bonds to reimburse the community in case the emancipated Negroes became incapable of supporting themselves and had to rely on public charity. And to correct an obvious injustice, the new law allowed another person to post the required bonds if the executors of an estate

---

[28] *N.Y. Colonial Laws*, I, 764–65; Bradford, *N.J. Laws*, p. 22.

refused to do so. New Jersey's restrictions on manumission remained unchanged until 1769, when the legislature eliminated the requirement for annual payments and adopted a procedure similar to New York's.[29]

As early as 1702 Connecticut passed a law regulating manumissions, but its object was merely to prevent masters from escaping the responsibility for maintaining old or sick slaves by freeing them "after they have spent the principall part of their time and strength in their masters service." The law held masters responsible for the support of their slaves even after their manumission. Massachusetts enacted a similar statute a year later but made manumissions more difficult by requiring masters to post a £50 bond to secure the community in case their former slaves became public charges. Rhode Island required a £100 bond. Pennsylvania's manumission law, similar in language to those of New York and New Jersey, declared that "free Negroes are an idle and slothful people . . . [who] often prove burdensome to the neighborhood and afford ill examples to other Negroes." In effect, however, the law was more liberal and closer in spirit to those of the New England colonies. Masters who wished to manumit their Negroes were required to post only a £30 bond, but any Negro freed before he was twenty-one could be bound out to service (making him, in effect, an indentured servant or apprentice).[30] Even the mildest regulations discouraged manumissions, however. A Connecticut master could manumit his slaves without posting any bonds or paying an annual sum; still, he knew that he and his heirs could be held responsible for an indeterminate sum to provide for a Negro who might suffer an incapacitating illness or accident.

New York and New Jersey were the only northern colonies to bar Negroes from owning property. A New London Town Meeting asked the Connecticut Assembly for such a law, and although the lower house complied, it was never enacted into law. When New York revised its slave code in 1730, it elimi-

[29] *N.Y. Documents,* V, 460–61; *N.Y. Colonial Laws,* I, 922–23; Allinson, *N.J. Acts,* p. 316.
[30] *Conn. Colonial Records,* IV, 375; Greene, *Negro in New England,* p. 138; Du Bois, *Philadelphia Negro,* pp. 413–14.

nated the ban on free Negro landowning, but this ban remained in effect in New Jersey until after independence. Pennsylvania's slave code imposed other restrictions on free Negroes. They could be sold into slavery if they lived in marriage with whites. Freedmen trading with other Negroes without a license or concealing fugitive slaves were to be fined and if unable to pay the fine were to be reenslaved.[31]

In colonial New England Negroes occupied a unique legal position. The Puritans' aim of establishing a bible commonwealth led them to grant Negro slaves rights based on the Mosaic laws of bondage, which regarded slavery as a mark of personal misfortune and not as evidence of inherent inferiority. Consequently, New England slaves enjoyed rights that were regarded as incompatible with slavery in other colonies. Slaves could own property and serve as witnesses even against white men. The wife of a slave could not be compelled to testify against her husband. Slaves could sue in the regular courts. The right to institute civil suits proved to be an entering wedge for abolition—Negroes could sue their masters for their freedom if there was any doubt about the validity of the master's title. Furthermore, slaves had the same procedural rights in courts as freemen; they were indicted by grand juries and tried by ordinary juries, they were allowed to appeal the decisions of lower courts, and they could challenge jurors in the same manner as free defendants.[32]

The harsh slave codes of the middle colonies were the product of fear—a fear that was often reinforced by the discovery of Negro plots or rumors of Negro risings. In 1741 New Yorkers fled the city in the wake of rumors of another slave revolt. Carts to transport goods out of the city were at a premium and hysteria gripped the community. Several fires, mysterious in origin, had led to the plot rumors, and investigators, by forcing Negroes to "confess" and implicate other to save themselves, established a long but tenuous chain of evidence. Two Negroes, whose masters testified that they had

[31] William C. Fowler, "The Historical Status of the Negro in Connecticut," *Historical Magazine*, 3d ser., III (1874), 13; *N.Y. Colonial Laws*, II, 679–88; Du Bois, *Philadelphia Negro*, p. 414.

[32] Greene, *Negro in New England*, pp. 177–83.

both been home at the time of the fires, were nonetheless sentenced to be burned to death. A last minute reprieve failed to save them for, at the insistence of the crowd, they were burned anyway. A total of eleven Negroes were burned at the stake, eighteen were hung, and fifty deported to the West Indies. There is no evidence that there was any slave plot nor, for that matter, any connection between the fires and the hapless Negroes. Despite the fury with which the slaves were punished, at least one contemporary realized that he was witnessing an outbreak of mass hysteria. A New Englander compared events in New York to the Salem witchcraft trials. He predicted that "Negro & Spectre evidence will turn out alike," maintaining that the Salem tragedy had proved that extorted confessions were worthless, and he begged New Yorkers "not to go on to Massacre & destroy your own Estates by making Bonfires of the Negros." [33]

Although many rumored slave risings proved to be as groundless as those that precipitated the 1741 panic, white men had to investigate any suspicious movements among the slaves to avoid a repetition of the 1712 disaster. An alert white man was able to prevent a revolt of Somerset County, New Jersey, Negroes who supposedly planned to murder slaveowners, ravish their women, and burn their property. The plan was uncovered before any damage was done when a drunken plotter challenged a white man, telling him that "English-men were generally a pack of Villains, and kept the Negroes as Slaves, contrary to a positive Order from King George." When the white man called the Negro a rascal, the slave pointedly asserted that he was "as good a Man as himself, and that in a little Time he should be convinced of it." This threat, veiled as it was, led to a thorough examination. One slave escaped, one was hung, and one had his ears cut off. Numerous other Negroes were soundly whipped. One commentator wryly noted that the reason the slaveowners had executed only one slave was probably because "they could not well spare any more." There were other plots and many more ominous rumors, leaving slaveowners with the

[33] T. Wood Clarke, "The Negro Plot of 1741," *New York History,* XXV (1944), 167–81; *Letters and Papers of Cadwallader Colden* (9 vols; *Collections of the N.Y. Hist. Soc.,* 1917–23, 1934), VII, 270–72.

uneasy feeling that they might wake up one night with knives at their throats. During war time, many suspected that the slaves would rise and join the enemy, and a great rash of slave-plot rumors broke out in the first few years of the Revolution. Some men feared that their departure for military service would leave their wives and children at the mercy of the slaves.[34] Even when there was no danger of a slave rebellion, individual Negroes could revenge themselves on their masters by burning their property or poisoning the master and his family. Slave plots, both real and imagined, as well as individual acts of vengeance, contributed to the widespread fear of the Negro population and resulted in the severe laws enacted for their control.

The courts, which administered these laws, decreed harsh punishments. Before the penal reforms of the late eighteenth century, courts often inflicted cruel punishments, but slaves probably suffered more severe penalties than white men. A New York City court ordered a slave who had escaped from prison and stolen a boat to be tied to a cart and given ten lashes at every corner as he was dragged around the city. He was also branded on the forehead with the letter *R*, so that he could more easily be identified if he were to run away again. A New Jersey Negro sentenced to death in 1694 first had his right hand cut off and then was hung; later his body was burned. In the wake of the New York "Negro plot" of 1741, two New Jersey Negroes, convicted of barn-burning, were burned alive, and in 1750 two New Jersey Negroes, convicted of murder, were burned alive in front of all the other Negroes in the area. A Negro who had been forced to witness a similar execution near Poughkeepsie, New York, shortly before the Revolution, remembered it to the end of his days. A young slave had fired his master's barn, confessed, and was condemned to be burned to death: "He was fastened to the stake, and when the pile was fired, the dense crowd excluded the air, so that the flames kindled but slowly, and the dreadful screams of the victim were heard at a distance of three

[34] *New York Gazette*, March 25, 1734; *Archives of the State of New Jersey*, 1st ser., XI, 335–37; John Oldmixon, *The British Empire in America. . . .* (2d ed., London, 1741), I, 295; *Pennsylvania Archives*, 1st ser., IV, 792.

miles." It was a horrible sight and his master "who had been fond of him, wept aloud." He asked the sheriff to put the Negro out of his misery. The sheriff complied by drawing his sword, "but the master, still crying like a child, exclaimed 'Oh, don't run him through!'" The sheriff then parted the crowd, the flames shot up and he commanded the Negro to "swallow the blaze," which finally put him out of his misery.[35]

Northern masters did not usually punish their slaves as severely as slaveowners in the plantation colonies. Cadwallader Colden was forced to send a sullen and abusive Negro woman to the West Indies because "the Custome of the Country . . . will not allow us to use our Negroes as you doe in Barbados." He was convinced that the woman would "make as good a slave as any in the Island after a little of your Discipline." In their master's advertisements northern runaways were rarely identified by whip marks, but chronic runaways were sometimes punished by having to wear a heavy iron collar around their necks. As late as 1806 a visitor to Pennsylvania saw a twelve-year-old Negro boy wearing such a device, with an iron bow attached to each side of the iron collar, crossing the boy's head. A New Jersey runaway had "an iron Collar with two Hooks" around his neck and a pair of hand cuffs with a six-foot chain. Another New Jersey slave had been forced to wear an iron collar because he had plotted with another Negro "to rob his master and attempt for New-York." Runaway Joe was in very bad shape. He had "one leg a little shorter than the other, part of one of his great toes cut off, lost some foreteeth, and his back is much scarrified and in lumps by whipping." [36]

[35] *Collections of the N.Y. Hist. Soc.* (1912), 34–35; James C. Connolly, "Slavery in Colonial New Jersey and the Causes Operating Against its Extension," (*Proceedings of the New Jersey Historical Society*), new ser., XIV (1929), 199; *Boston Evening-Post,* July 6, 1741 in *N.J. Archives,* 1st ser., XII, 98–99; William A. Whitehead, *Contributions to the Early History of Perth Amboy* (New York, 1856), pp. 318–19; William J. Allinson, *Memoir of Quamino Buccau, A Pious Methodist* (Philadelphia, 1851), p. 5.

[36] Colden to Jordan, March 26, 1717, *Colden Papers,* I, 39; Robert Sutcliff, *Travels in Some Parts of North America, in the Years 1804–1806* (York, Eng., 1811), p. 184; *Pennsylvania Journal,* August 20,

Horrible as the punishments meted out to Negroes convicted of crimes may have been, they were exceeded by instances of cruelty committed by sadistic masters. In 1804 Carl A. Hoffmann of New York was convicted of seriously mistreating his slave. His twelve-year-old Negro had committed some fault; to punish him, Hoffmann tied his hands and legs, forced him to eat two teaspoonfuls of salt, and then hung him from the ceiling in a closed room where he was suspended for two days without food or water. After the boy was taken down, Hoffmann administered 139 lashes. He was not through. He finished off by rubbing salt and brandy into the boy's cut back.[37]

Another sadistic master was Amos Broad. He kicked a Negro child when it did not walk well. He stripped his female slave, whipped her, threw her into the snow, and then threw water on her. He forced her to take an unneeded purgative. His wife participated in horsewhipping the slave, and when his "wench" brought in a teapot with too much water in it, he poured some of the scalding liquid on her hands. The case was brought to trial by the New York Manumission Society, which persuaded Broad to free his slaves. In addition, Broad and his wife were fined $1,250.[38] At an earlier time, similar instances of unrefined cruelty may have taken place, but then there was no one to come to the defense of the abused slaves.

The conduct of these perverted masters was certainly exceptional and aroused widespread horror and indignation. Yet by allowing one man virtually unlimited control over another, the slave laws of the middle colonies provided ample opportunities for aberrant behavior and unrestrained cruelty.

The harsh slave codes of the middle colonies, devised at the beginning of the eighteenth century, were designed to control an alien population, regarded as heathen in origin and barbarous by nature. The laws denied the slave equal protection by refusing to accept his testimony against whites,

1761 in *N.J. Archives,* 1st ser., XX, 602–3; *New Jersey Gazette,* November 13, 1782; December 27, 1780.

[37] *True American* (Trenton, N.J.), December 24, 1804.

[38] *Trial of Amos Broad and his Wife. . . .* (New York, 1809), pp. 5 ff.

by providing special courts, and by inflicting different punishments. In the case of slaves, the laws assumed guilt, not innocence—any Negro found away from home without a pass was presumed to be a runaway, any slave engaged in trade was presumed to be a thief, and any slave having sexual intercourse with a white woman was presumed to be a rapist. The laws discouraged manumissions and severely limited the rights of free Negroes. Especially in New York and New Jersey, the object of the slave codes was to keep the Negroes terrified and to prevent them from inflicting their revenge upon the whites. Although the colonists' views of the Negro underwent a gradual transformation and the Negroes became more assimilated into the European-American culture, the laws took little notice of this change until after the nation's independence was established.

RELIGION, EDUCATION, AND ACCULTURATION

By the middle of the eighteenth century, through the persistence of representatives of the SPG and other dedicated ministers, many Negroes were brought into the church and some even became preachers. Although a few masters continued stubbornly to resist efforts to convert their slaves, others encouraged their bondsmen to go to church. New York masters were now reported to be "more desirous than they used to be" to have their Negroes instructed. In New England, although the SPG (representing the Church of England) was less welcome than in the middle colonies, Negroes were admitted to the Congregational churches, where they usually sat in segregated pews. In Connecticut slaves were admitted to membership but were excluded from voting on matters of church discipline. Following a policy of racial equality in religion could lead to an awkward situation, as Peter Mosimy, a slave in Weston, Massachusetts, could testify. Peter "owned the covenant" and became a church member in 1741 although his owner, Ebenezer Hunt, was not admitted to church membership until 1748.[39] How

[39] *New-York Journal*, October 13, 1774 in *N.J. Archives*, 1st ser., XXIX, 499; Klingberg, "The S.P.G. in N.Y.," pp. 332–33; C. F. Pascoe,

did Ebenezer treat Peter during the seven years when the slave was of the elect and the master was not?

Quakers, despite their leadership in the abolition movement and their early interest in bringing religion to the slaves, hesitated to admit them to full membership. In 1784 a British Quaker took American Friends to task for this. Their conduct was inconsistent with "your repeated declarations of their being your *fellow men* and the principles of our Society." Negroes are "as much qualified" to enter into a religious society as into a civil one and "your own avowed opinions of their intellects and capacity for salvation put the matter . . . out of dispute." He accused American Quakers of being "far behind the Papists [and] Moravians" in this respect. "It seems peculiar," he concluded, "to endeavour to obtain their liberty, inform their understandings, and instruct them in religious duties & after all this refuse them the benefits of religious community." The issue came to a head at the 1796 Yearly Meeting of New Jersey and Pennsylvania Quakers, after a Negro woman who had applied for admission to the society had been rejected solely on the basis of her color. The Yearly Meeting ruled that there was no reason why Negroes could not be admitted and opened membership to all qualified applicants "without distinction of nation or colour." A pious Quaker confided to his diary that "the spirit of prejudice which had been imbibed on account of colour" had delayed this ruling for twenty years.[40]

The Dutch Reformed church established a program of Negro catechism in 1747 and admitted qualified Negroes to church privileges. In the Dutch-American churches Negroes usually sat in the galleries and were not allowed to approach the communion table until after the whites had been served. The church debated slave membership in 1783 and ruled

---

Two Hundred Years of the S.P.G. (London, 1901), I, 46; Greene, *Negro in New England,* pp. 282–83; Mary H. Mitchell, "Slavery in Connecticut and Especially in New Haven" (*Papers of the New Haven Historical Society,* 1951) X, 300; Town of Weston, *Births, Deaths, and Marriages . . . Church Records . . .* (Boston, 1901), pp. 428, 438, 458.

[40] James Phelps to James Pemberton, July 15, 1784 (Pemberton MSS, Historical Society of Pennsylvania), XLI, 150; "John Hunt's Journal," *Friends' Miscellany,* X, 272–74.

that the Scriptures did not require that the permission of the master had to be obtained before a slave was admitted, but it resolved that care should be taken "for the promotion and establishment of peace in households." In 1792 the church ruled that "No difference exists between bond and free in the Church of Christ" and admitted slaves to all sacraments.[41]

The SPG took an early lead in the education of Negro slaves; Elias Neau was only the first of a series of catechists for New York Negroes. The slaves were eager to learn. An Albany, New York, minister told the SPG that the "poor negros are very fond of my instruction, and seem to be extremely thankful for my care and attention to their spiritual concerns." The work of the catechists was not easy. A Long Island cleric could teach the slaves only at night because they were "confined all day to their labour," and masters would only permit the slaves to attend classes in winter, "confining them close to labour" at other times. Nonetheless, he had "with great difficulty and pains, learned some to spell, some to read, and some to write."[42]

Education was valued highly in the Puritan colonies, and New Englanders were among the first to encourage the instruction of Negroes. As early as 1674 John Eliot urged masters to allow their slaves to be educated, and he offered to instruct them once a week. Cotton Mather was also an advocate of Negro education, and in 1717 he established a charity school for Negroes and Indians. In 1728, the *New-England Weekly Journal* announced the establishment of a school "for the Instruction of Negro's in reading, Catechizing, & Writing if required." Most of these early ventures were short-lived, but some masters continued to instruct their own Negroes.[43]

In 1758 the Associates of Dr. Bray, an English philanthropic society, established a Negro school in Philadelphia "to

[41] Charles Corwin, "The Church and Negroes in Colonial Days," *Tercentenary Studies; Reformed Church in America* (New York: Compiled by the Tercentenary Commission on Research and Publication, 1928), pp. 399–400.

[42] Klingberg, "S.P.G. in N.Y.," pp. 345, 360.

[43] Greene, *Negro in New England*, pp. 236–39; *New-England Weekly Journal*, April 8, 1728.

teach 30 Children, the Boys to read, and the Girls to Sow, Knit, read, & work." Ten years later, fifty-nine Negro children had been admitted, and in 1768 of the twenty-seven attending the school, nineteen were slaves. When Benjamin Franklin visited the school in 1763 the experience gave him "a higher opinion of the Natural Capacities of the black Race."

The benevolent Quaker schoolmaster, Anthony Benezet, established a night school for Negro slaves in Philadelphia in 1750. The Society of Friends had urged masters to instruct their slaves in religion as early as 1696, and in the latter part of the eighteenth century the Philadelphia Yearly Meeting periodically admonished masters to give their slaves "sufficient instruction and learning, in order to qualify them for the enjoyment of the liberty intended." [44]

When the slaves first arrived in the North, only those who had come from another English-speaking colony could speak the language. Most of them spoke an African tongue, and those who came from the West Indies often spoke French or Spanish. As the Negroes became more assimilated, the ability to speak English ceased to be an identifying feature in runaway slave advertisements. Many of the slaves who served New York and New Jersey masters learned to speak Dutch and some became multilingual. A New Jersey master advertised for the return of a slave who could speak "very good English and Low Dutch, also pretty good High Dutch." Moreover, he was "noted for his sense, and particularly for his activity at any thing he takes in hand." One runaway was a real linguist; he could speak English, Dutch, Spanish, and Danish.[45]

[44] Edgar L. Pennington, "The Work of the Bray Associates in Pennsylvania," *Pa. Mag. of Hist.*, LVIII (1934), 7, 10; Richard I. Shelling, "Benjamin Franklin and the Dr. Bray Associates," *Pa. Mag. of Hist.*, LXIII (1939), 288; George S. Brookes, *Friend Anthony Benezet* (Philadelphia, 1937), pp. 45–52; Society of Friends, *A Brief Statement of the Rise and Progress of the Testimony of the Religious Society of Friends, Against Slavery and the Slave Trade* (Philadelphia, 1843), pp. 8, 27.

[45] "Eighteenth Century Slaves as Advertised by their Masters," *Journal Negro Hist.*, I (1916), 164–94; *Pennsylvania Journal*, October 13, 1763 in *N.J. Archives*, 1st ser., XXIV, 252; *New York Gazette*, December 5, 1768 in *N.J. Archives*, 1st ser., 333.

Toward the end of the colonial period, an increasing number of slaves were literate. One New Jersey slave could "read the bible very well" and another could "speak good English, and writes a good hand." A slave's ability to write could cause trouble for his master. In 1768 two Negro slaves ran away, taking "Pen and Ink with them," and, since one of them could write, their master ruefully noted it was "not unlikely they will produce a Pass." [46] In the late colonial period, many masters suspected that their runaway slaves had forged their own passes.

By the end of the eighteenth century, when importations from Africa had virtually ceased, most northern slaves had been born in this country, spoke English and possibly a second language, and some of them could read and write. Despite the continued opposition of some masters, most Negroes had been exposed to religious influences. The Christianization of the slaves played an important part in making the African Negroes part of American society. The churches not only taught the slaves to read and write, but more important, through religion the Negroes adopted some of the values of their masters' society. One historian has compared baptism of slaves to "tribal adoption"—the ritual acceptance of an alien into a new culture. [47] The Christianization of the Negroes also had an important effect on their masters. By regarding the slaves as human beings, capable of baptism, marriage, and salvation, masters were gradually induced to question the need for a harsh slave code, and ultimately many of them came to doubt that slavery was in fact consistent with "true Christian liberty." By the time of the Revolution, most northerners had ceased to regard the Negroes as the treacherous, uncivilized creatures they had once seemed to be, and they slowly modified their treatment of the subject race.

Masters now often accorded their Negroes privileges that were unheard of in an earlier period. A New Yorker, who

[46] *Pennsylvania Chronicle,* October 8–15, 1770 in *N.J. Archives,* 1st ser., XXVII, 279; *Pennsylvania Gazette,* May 26, 1768 in *N.J. Archives,* 1st ser., XXVI, 172.
[47] Klingberg, "African Immigrant," p. 145.

had promised to send several slaves to the governor of Quebec in 1763, had to confess his inability to keep his promise since it was "an invariable indulgence here to permit Slaves of any kind of worth or Character who must change Masters, to choose those Masters," and "there is no persuading them to leave their Country (if I may call it so), their acquaintances & friends." Slaves were sometimes given passes to go and look for a new master. In this way, the lines between the Negro's status as a slave and a hired hand were blurred. A New Jersey man who wanted to purchase "a good farm negroe," assured his master that "a generous price will be given," and added that "the negroe, by good behavior, may be assured of the best of treatment." In the post-Revolutionary period New York Negroes were often advertised for sale "by their own desire." A Negro woman and her four-month-old son were offered for sale because her master was "about to remove into the country . . . where she is not willing to go." Henry Lloyd II, who had wanted to sell a Negro woman and her children to a South Carolina master, agreed to sell them for ten pounds less than the southerner had offered when she objected to being sent to the South.[48] Although slaves had no legal right to object to their sale, humane masters consulted their Negroes before disposing of them. In this way the purchaser could be assured of receiving a willing slave and the Negro had some protection against being sold to a cruel master. At the same time, the hold of property rights as opposed to human rights was gradually weakened.

Some masters were genuinely concerned about their slaves' welfare. Jeremiah Langhorne, a prominent Pennsylvania political figure and a large Bucks County landholder, had over thirty slaves. When he died, he freed them and gave each a house and a plot of land to cultivate. James Lloyd II, who had hired out his slave Cato, was pleased to hear that his

---

[48] *Letter Book of John Watts* (*Collections of the N.Y. Hist. Soc.,* 1928), p. 151; *N.J. Gazette,* December 27, 1780; *New York Daily Advertiser,* March 18, 1797; *New York Daily Advertiser,* supplement, March 18, 1799; *Papers of the Lloyd Family* (2 vols.; *Collections of the N.Y. Hist. Soc.,* 1926–27), II, 735, 746.

Negro was "Contented & behaves Well." He wanted him to be "as happy as possible and would not have him want for any thing that's for his Comfort & Suitable for him." Several years later, "At Cato's desire," he sent him "a shirt or two & a pair [of] old Breeches for Sundays." [49]

The "American Farmer," Crèvecoeur, describing life in rural Orange County, New York, noted that the Negroes had their own meetings and were "often indulged with their masters' sleighs and horses." A New Jersey man allowed his slave to use his horse and a two-wheeled gig and put some money in his pocket when the slave went to visit his wife. This master also allowed his Negroes to give a party every year between Christmas and New Year's to which the "respectable" Negroes of the neighborhood were invited. Mrs. Anne Grant recalled that while living in pre-Revolutionary Albany, she had "never seen people so happy in servitude as the domestics." Their children were baptized and "shared the same religious instruction with the children of the family." In their early years, the Negro children were treated almost the same as the children of the family; they wore similar clothes and ate the same food. When a Negro child became three, it was given to a member of the family, and slave children were never sold to anyone outside of the family without their mother's permission. When the slaves misbehaved and all efforts to "reform" them failed, "no severe punishments were inflicted at home. But the terrible sentence, which they dreaded worse than death, was passed—they were sold to Jamaica." Slaves destined for transportation had to be carefully watched to prevent them from committing suicide. [50]

In many New England communities, Negro slaves participated in mock elections and one of them was chosen as "governor." In Portsmouth, New Hampshire, a Negro was elected "king," and a court of minor officials was also elected. These officers apparently held trials and punished slaves for minor infractions. Election days were universal holidays for

---

[49] William J. Buck, "Jeremiah Langhorne," *Pa. Mag. of Hist.*, VII (1883), 82; *Lloyd Papers*, II, 721, 725.

[50] J. Hector St. John de Crèvecoeur, *Sketches of Eighteenth Century America*, ed. Henri L. Bourdin *et al.* (New Haven, 1925), p. 148;

the slaves, comparable to the Christmas holidays for southern slaves. The Negroes dressed in their finest clothes and fiddled and danced.[51]

An upstate New York master's contract with his slave whom he promised to free probably exemplified the currently accepted privileges and duties of slaves in that region at the beginning of the nineteenth century. The slave was to work for his master on all days except holidays—three days at Christmas, two days at New Year's, two days at Easter, and three days at the Dutch holiday of Pinkster. He was allowed to visit his wife once every three weeks, leaving Saturday night and returning by Monday morning. He was not to commit adultery or run away, and he was to leave his fiddle with his master and not go fiddling except on holidays or with his master's permission. He was required to attend church once every four weeks. If he did any damage through neglect, or otherwise violated these rules, he was not to go free but was to remain a slave for life. (In addition, he was to give his master an interest-free note for $90.) [52]

Slaves sometimes lived in the same house as the rest of the family. In New England slaves were often treated as part of the family—attending the same church and even sitting down at the same table as the whites. Negroes were sometimes quartered in the garret or cellar, but in other instances they slept on the same floor as their masters. Where slaveholdings were larger, the Negroes lived in separate huts. This was true in the Narragansett region of New England, in parts of Connecticut, and in the middle colonies. A visitor was told that in northern New Jersey, Negroes were confined to "low buildings of one storey" because their "pilfering disposition" made it impossible to allow them to sleep in the main house. Sojourner Truth, who served as a slave in Ulster County, New York, in the opening years of the nineteenth century,

Andrew D. Mellick, Jr., *The Story of an Old Farm* (Somerville, N.J., 1889), pp. 603, 606; Anne Grant, *Memoirs of an American Lady* (2 vols.; New York, 1903), I, 80–83.

[51] Greene, *Negro in New England,* pp. 249–52; Charles W. Brewster, *Rambles About Portsmouth,* 1st ser. (Portsmouth, N.H., 1859), p. 210.

[52] Percy M. Van Epps, "Slavery in Glenville, N.Y.," *Sixth Report of the Town Historian* (Glenville, N.Y., 1932), pp. 7–8.

recalled that her master forced all of his slaves to sleep in the cellar "on . . . damp boards, like the horse, with a little straw and a blanket." [53]

Almost all observers agreed that slavery in the North, especially in the late eighteenth century, was much milder than in the South. The Marquis de Barbé-Marbois reported that slaves in Pennsylvania and in the other northern states were "regarded as being part of the family." They were well cared for when sick and were devoted to their masters. The Dutch especially dealt with their slaves on terms of near equality. On a typical day, the marquis observed, the slave woke the master, they ate breakfast together, worked together, and then they dined together "like equals." They dressed in a similar fashion and the slave could be "recognized only by his color." These observations were confirmed by others. [54]

When the Duc de la Rochefoucauld-Liancourt visited a large plantation near Elizabeth, New Jersey, he learned that the owner supplied this estate with slaves from his other plantation in Jamaica. Slavery in New Jersey, La Rochefoucauld-Liancourt noted, was far less severe than in the islands, and the slaves on this farm were treated in all respects as well as any free men. But there were no laws to prevent a master from "beating or otherwise cruelly using, his negro slave"; despite the great contrast between New Jersey and Jamaica, "manners, not laws, produce the only difference." [55] Although most northern slaves may have been treated well and accorded many privileges, they had no rights. They were at the absolute disposal of a master who might be kind, but who could also be cruel or capricious. This was the real horror of slavery.

---

[53] Greene, *Negro in New England,* pp. 222–24; Henry Wansey, *Journal of an Excursion to the United States of North America in the Summer of 1794* (Salisbury, Eng., 1796), p. 100; [Olive Gilbert], *Narrative of Sojourner Truth* (Boston, 1850), pp. 14–15.

[54] Eugene P. Chase (ed.), *Our Revolutionary Forefathers* (New York, 1929), p. 156.

[55] François Alexandre Frederic duc de la Rochefoucauld-Liancourt, *Travels Through the United States of North America,* trans. H. Neuman (2 vols.; London, 1799), I, 543–44.

Although Negro slavery as defined in the colonial black codes was a system of race relations, it was first and foremost an economic system. Negroes were first imported and later commanded high prices because they were needed as a labor force in a land that for white men meant opportunity, a chance for economic independence. As Cadwallader Colden told a London merchant, despite "the great numbers which every year come into the Country," great difficulties resulted from a chronic labor shortage. Freemen emigrated because they wanted their own land; they were not content to remain as laborers. In 1647 the Dutch West India Company was advised to send slaves to America because the new colony could be more extensively cultivated by slave labor. White agricultural laborers, "conveyed thither at great expense," sooner or later became tradesmen and neglected agriculture. Slaves, on the other hand, "being brought and maintained . . . at a cheap rate," could raise abundant produce. By the end of the seventeenth century the labor market in New York had not improved. The Earl of Bellomont noted that there were not over a hundred laboring men to be had in the colony for the high wage of three shillings per day and that most of the work was done by Negroes. White men preferred earning more money in trade or keeping sloops.[1]

New England also suffered from a labor shortage. Emanuel Downing told Governor John Winthrop that he could not see "how wee can thrive vntill wee gett into a stock of slaves suffitient to doe all our buisines." White servants did not

[1] *Letters and Papers of Cadwallader Colden* (9 vols.; *Collections of the New-York Historical Society,* 1917–23, 1934), II, 32; Edmund B. O'Callaghan (ed.), *Documents Relative to the Colonial History of the State of New-York* (11 vols.; Albany, 1856–61), I, 246; Samuel McKee, Jr., *Labor in Colonial New York, 1664–1776* (New York, 1935), p. 11.

want to work for other men and would do so only for "verie great wages." Slaves, on the other hand, would also be cheaper since "wee maynteyne 20 Moores cheaper than one Englishe servant." Philadelphia merchants repeatedly opposed attempts to levy a high duty on imported Negroes on the grounds that this would aggravate the shortage of labor. And at times slaves were also in short supply. A Philadelphian told Cadwallader Colden in 1725 that despite continued efforts she had been unable to procure "a Negroe man that would Suit thy business." Henry Lloyd, prosperous lord of the manor of Lloyd's Neck, had the same problem in 1746, although he had "taken a great deal of pains to buy a good Slave." [2]

Some historians have questioned the value of slave labor within the diversified northern economy.[3] Taking the southern plantations as the norm, these writers assume that Negro labor could only be employed advantageously on large tracts, worked by the gang system. They believe that because Negroes were ignorant, unskilled, and irresponsible, they could work only at simple tasks under close supervision. Although it is true that Negroes had to be more highly skilled and better trained to work in the diversified economy of the North, it is also true that northern Negroes received this training and became skilled in virtually all aspects of northern agriculture, manufacturing, and crafts.

[2] Downing to Winthrop, August, 1645 [?], *Winthrop Papers* (5 vols.; Boston: Massachusetts Historical Society, 1929–47), V, 38; William E. B. Du Bois, *Suppression of the African Slave-Trade* (2d ed., New York, 1954), p. 23; *Colden Papers*, VIII, 180; *Papers of the Lloyd Family* (2 vols.; *Collections of the N.Y. Hist. Soc.*, 1926–27), I, 368.

[3] For discussions of the profitability of slavery in the North see: Lorenzo J. Greene, *The Negro in Colonial New England* (New York, 1942), pp. 101–3; Edward R. Turner, *The Negro In Pennsylvania* (Washington, D.C., 1911), pp. 14–16; Edward R. Turner, "The Abolition of Slavery in Pennsylvania," *Pennsylvania Magazine of History and Biography*, XXXVI (1912), 135–36; Richard R. Wright, Jr., *The Negro in Pennsylvania* (Philadelphia, 1908), pp. 18–23; William E. B. Du Bois, *The Philadelphia Negro* (Philadelphia, 1899), p. 16; Simeon Moss, "The Persistence of Slavery and Involuntary Servitude in a Free State (1695–1866)," *Journal of Negro History*, XXXV (1950), 300; Francis B. Lee, *New Jersey as a Colony and as a State* (New York, 1903), IV, 28; McKee, *Labor in N.Y.*, pp. 168–69.

SLAVE SKILLS

The colonial economy was predominantly agricultural, and most slaves in the North as well as in the South were farm laborers. Many Negroes advertised for sale were "fit for country business"—farming and related skills. A New Jersey farmer offered to rent his 470-acre property with "three very good Negroes, who understand all the Branches of Farming." Other farms were leased "with Negroes and Stock." Although most New England farmers who relied on slave labor employed only one or two Negroes on their small plots, the Narragansett planters of Rhode Island, some of whose farms extended over 1,000 acres, used slave labor extensively in the cultivation of food and forage crops and in raising the pacing horses for which the area was famous. Robert Hazard of South Kingstown converted part of his 12,000 acres into a dairy farm and employed twenty-four Negro women in the creamery alone.[4]

Slaves were trained to do many of the tasks essential to maintaining the near self-sufficiency of large colonial farms. The owner of a 2,000-acre plantation in Morris County, New Jersey, leased his property with twenty Negroes "bred to farming and Country Work." This group included "a good Blacksmith, a Mason, and a Shoemaker." Another New Jersey farm was advertised for sale with "sundry valuable men, women, and children slaves, one of them an excellent miller, and another a cooper." The rest were "house and farm slaves." On a third New Jersey plantation the slaves could perform a variety of tasks. One Negro was a miller, a carter, and a farmer.

A younger woman was "an excellent house-servant, and besides washing and ironing," she could "spin wool and flax, knit," and manage the dairy, making butter and cheese. In some instances, the slaves were capable of running the entire farm by themselves; a group of New Jersey slaves were "brought up from their Infancy to the farming Business" and

---

[4] *Pennsylvania Gazette,* January 11, 1759 in *Archives of the State of New Jersey,* 1st ser., XX, 316–17; *Pennsylvania Gazette,* January 19, 1758 in *N.J. Archives,* 1st ser., XX, 172; Greene, *Negro in New England,* pp. 103–8.

had "managed the Farm for some Years, without an Over-seer." On a large farm north of Albany, New York, Negroes served as cooks, domestics, woodcutters, threshers, seam-stresses, and laundresses. Besides the slaves engaged in house-hold work and in "cultivating to the highest advantage a most extensive farm," there was a slave who was "a thorough-bred carpenter and shoemaker." Another slave was "an universal genius who made canoes, nets, and paddles; shod horses," and mended farm tools. He also "managed the fishing . . . reared hemp and tobacco, and spun both; made cider, and tended wild horses . . . which it was his province to manage and break." On this well-run estate, there were slaves trained "For every branch of domestic economy." [5]

Wheat was an important crop in the middle colonies, and slaves not only helped to raise the grain but also processed it into flour. In 1745 a New Jersey man offered to sell his 300-acre plantation with "Things necessary for carrying on grinding, bolting and baking," including three Negroes, "one of them a good Miller" and two who could do the baking, bolting, and "Country Work." [6]

As the colonial economy became more diversified Negro labor early assumed an important role in the beginning of American manufacturing enterprises. Many iron forges in New Jersey and Pennsylvania relied heavily on the labor of Negro slaves. When the owners of Andover Furnace in Sussex County, New Jersey, offered to lease the works, they included six slaves "who are good Forgemen, and understand the making and drawing of Iron well." Charles Read, another New Jersey ironmaster, had two slaves for sale—one "a good finer, and the other a good hammer-man." Negroes were capable of filling responsible positions in the industry, and one manufacturer sought to buy or hire a Negro who "fully understands managing a Bloomery." Slaves were also

[5] *New-York Gazette,* March 21, 1768 in *N.J. Archives,* 1st ser., XXVI, 88–90; *New-York Gazette,* June 22, 1772 in *N.J. Archives,* 1st ser., XXVIII, 168–70; *Pennsylvania Packet,* March 13, 1780; *New York Journal,* April 6, 1769 in *N.J. Archives,* 1st ser., 408; Anne Grant, *Memoirs of an American Lady* (2 vols.; New York, 1903), I, 265–66.

[6] *New York Weekly Post Boy,* May 20, 1745 in *N.J. Archives,* 1st ser., XII, 257–58.

used to extract the ore; a New York newspaper carried notice of the sale of two Negro men who "understands Mining." [7]

Other manufacturing enterprises found Negro slaves equally useful. "A Very convenient and commodious Tan-Yard" in Gloucester, New Jersey, used three Negro men "who understand the Business well." A Bostonian's slave had been "brought up in a ship Carpenters Yard as a Sawyer & boarers of holes" and had also been "employ'd at the Smith's business." Another Boston Negro was "for many years used to the distilling business," and a Pennsylvania slave could produce a less potent beverage—he was skilled at "brewing and bottling spruce-beer." Colonial entrepreneurs could buy a business complete with a skilled labor force to run it. A tobacco-pipe manufacturer of Flushing, New York, offered to sell twenty acres of clay land, suitable for pipe making, "with two Negro slaves . . . and other conveniencies to carry on that business." [8]

Negro slaves also entered the ranks of colonial craftsmen. New York Negroes worked as carpenters, cabinetmakers, plasterers, locksmiths, and butchers. Some slaves were very highly skilled; a baker and a cooper were described as "Masters of their Trades." A Negro was even employed in the prestigious "goldsmith's business." Some valuable pieces of colonial furniture may have been produced by slave artisans; a Pennsylvanian employed two Negroes in the "Joiner's and Windsor Chair businesses." Runaway slaves advertised in the Pennsylvania press included a brick layer and plasterer, a barber, and a slave who could "bleed and draw Teeth, Pretending to be a great Doctor." A "good house

[7] Charles S. Boyer, *Early Forges and Furnaces in New Jersey* (Philadelphia, 1931), p. 7; Arthur C. Binning, *Pennsylvania Iron Manufacture in the Eighteenth Century* (Harrisburg, 1938), pp. 112, 114–15; *Pennsylvania Gazette*, October 4, 1770 in *N.J. Archives*, 1st ser., XXVII, 271–73; *New York Journal*, September 22, 1774 in *N.J. Archives*, 1st ser., XXIX, 482; *Pennsylvania Chronicle*, July 11, 1768; *New York Evening-Post*, August 25, 1746 in *N.J. Archives*, XII, 316.

[8] *Pennsylvania Gazette*, April 5, 1764 in *N.J. Archives*, 1st ser., XXIV, 346; *Lloyd Papers*, II, 560–61; Greene, *Negro in New England*, p. 114; *Pennsylvania Gazette*, June 23, 1773; *New-York Gazette*, March 24–31, 1735; Rita S. Gottesman (compiler), *The Arts and Crafts in New York, 1725–1776* (*Collections of the N.Y. Hist. Soc.*, 1936), p. 317.

carpenter and joyner" could be purchased in Boston in 1718. Another Boston Negro was a ropemaker, and a Negro slave served as pressman for the first newspaper published in New Hampshire. New Jersey masters were frequently forced to advertise for runaway craftsmen. Since labor was in short supply an employer did not often question the status of a skilled Negro who offered his services. "A Mulatto Fellow named Jack" was "a good taylor"; his master suspected that he was "probably . . . sulking in some part of the country, working at that trade." Another runaway could "handle a File, and understands the Brass Founder's Business." [9]

In the New England colonies, many vessels were manned in part by Negro slaves. The Massachusetts fishing and whaling fleets included Negro crew members, and runaway slaves were sometimes taken on board by the masters of undermanned ships. A Pennsylvania Negro, "fit for town or country," was used for "the management of Shallops and other small craft." Several New Jersey slaves were employed as ferry boat operators, and a mulatto runaway was "bred to . . . loading and unloading boats." Negro slaves even served at the difficult task of piloting ships through New York harbor. [10]

Negro women performed many chores on the farm and in the home. A New Yorker offered to sell his twenty-year-old slave woman who did "all sorts of House work"; she could "Brew, Bake, Boyle soaft Soap, Wash, Iron & Starch" and she was "a good Darey Woman." She could also "Card and Spin at the Great Wheel." An "excellent cook" was advertised for

[9] McKee, *Labor in N.Y.*, pp. 125–27; *Pennsylvania Packet*, November 11, 1780; *Pennsylvania Gazette*, January 29, 1739; "Eighteenth Century Slaves as Advertised by their Masters," *Journal Negro Hist.*, I (1916), 195; *Pennsylvania Packet*, November 7, 1774; *Pennsylvania Gazette*, September 11, 1740 in *N.J. Archives*, 1st ser., XII, 51; Greene, *Negro in New England*, pp. 113–14; *New Jersey Gazette*, May 30, 1781; *New-York Gazette*, June 25, 1776 in *N.J. Archives*, 2d ser., I, 134.

[10] Greene, *Negro in New England*, pp. 115–17; *Pennsylvania Packet*, February 10, 1781; *New-York Gazette*, February 28, 1774 in *N.J. Archives*, 1st ser., XXIX, 273; *Pennsylvania Journal*, October 13, 1763 in *N.J. Archives*, 1st ser., XXIV, 251–52; Edwin Olson, "Negro Slavery in New York, 1626–1827," (Ph.D. dissertation, New York University, 1938), p. 91.

sale in 1781. She was "honest, industrious, neat, and a very good oeconomist, spins very well, and is fond of children." Her master suggested that she would "particularly suit a genteel tavern or a family that entertains much." Another Negro woman was not only skilled in "country work," but she could also be used as a city servant, "being a good house servant and a good seamstress." Not all women were suitable for farm work; a Pennsylvania master offered to sell a strong and healthy Negro girl because she was not "capable of country work." She was, however, experienced in taking care of children.[11]

Many Negro women were children's maids. In 1721 Cadwallader Colden tried to buy a young thirteen-year-old Negro girl for his wife who wanted her "Cheifly to keep the children & to sow & theirfore would have her Likely & one that appears to be good natured." Shortly before the Revolution, a New York newspaper noted the sale of an unusually talented children's governess. She had been born in the West Indies, spoke French well, and was "very well calculated to wait upon young Ladies and children . . . Amongst children, where the French language is desired to be used, she is as proper a Person . . . as can be procured."[12]

Housework was also done by male slaves. One of these, "a likely Black Man," was "of a good size for a house servant, short and stout." He was a good cook and could wash, bake, scrub, and clean furniture. He could also do "all kinds of farming work." His master informed the public that "He is sold for no other fault, but that he does not know when he is well treated, and is dissatisfied with good living." Another Negro man was only "a tolerable cook," but he could "shave and dress a wig very well." He had been employed as a house servant for some time, and was sold for no fault "likely to affect a purchaser who needs not intrust a servant with liquor or the laying out of money." Young boys served as waiters and older men were valets. A New Jersey master advertised

---

[11] *New-York Weekly Journal,* April 15, 1734; McKee, *Labor in N.Y.,* p. 126; *New Jersey Gazette,* March 14, 1781; *ibid.,* July 9, 1783; *Pennsylvania Packet,* February 10, 1781.

[12] *Colden Papers,* I, 51; *Rivington's New-York Gazetteer,* February 16, 1775.

two slaves for sale in 1776, "one of them a valuable and compleat farmer in all its branches . . . The other a genteel footman and waiter who understands the care of horses well, the management of a carriage, drives either on the box or as postillion." He was "in every respect suitable for a genteel family, or a single Gentleman, and is fond of farming." "A Likely negro boy" could do housework, shave and dress, and was also "a very good gardener" and could do "farming work." [13] Many household servants participated in home manufacturing—making soap, spinning, and making candles —and even some "gentlemen's servants" were also farmers and gardeners.

Although some of the richest colonists could afford the luxury of a full staff of Negro attendants—butlers, waiters, maids, and footmen—most northern slaveowners employed their Negroes as laborers. Considerable time was needed to train new Negroes for the labor of the area, which required "skill & dexterity as well as strenth," but the Negroes received the requisite training and became valuable servants who could be sold for high prices.[14]

SLAVE PRICES

Slave prices varied greatly, depending upon the value of the currency as well as the age, skill, and deportment of the Negro and the demand for his services. The master of the West Indian Negro woman who could serve as a French-speaking governess sought £100 for her, a high price for an unusually talented slave. In 1720 when George Clarke, Secretary of the Province of New York, needed several slaves, he enlisted the aid of his private secretary Isaac Bobin. Bobin reported that a ship from Barbados had brought in several Negroes, but only one of them could be recommended as "a real good slave"—he could cook, wait on tables, and make himself useful "in all manner of Household Affairs." The price was £55 "ready money." Bobin was forced to reject him

[13] *True American* (Trenton, N.J.), January 7, 1805; *New Jersey Gazette*, August 12, 1778; *Pennsylvania Journal*, February 28, 1776 in *N.J. Archives*, 2d ser., I, 543; *New Jersey Gazette*, April 23, 1783.
[14] *Colden Papers*, II, 32.

because "as to matters belonging to the field he is a stranger"
and it turned out that Clarke needed a farm Negro. Bobin
turned down another slave because he thought that £50 was
too high a price (apparently, field Negroes were priced lower
than household servants). A few years later Bobin was
pressed into service again, this time to find a Negro girl for
Mrs. Clarke. "A garl that may be train'd up to any manner of
business" was priced at £45. Another Negro woman, six
months pregnant, who "understands every thing belonging
to Household affairs," was available at the same price, but
her master refused to allow her to go to Clarke on a trial
basis. A New York doctor was willing to let Mrs. Clarke try
out his Negro girl, "not doubting you will find her a good
slave." The price was £55. A few days later, Bobin sent her to
Clarke, explaining that the girl was "unwilling to be sold,
and her Mistress as unwilling to part with her, which makes
the Dr afraid she'll be stubborn and say she can do nothing
but [he] desires you'll not believe her for she can do everything belonging to a House, except milking a cow." [15]
Youthful slaves were more valuable than older ones. When
Joseph Lloyd, owner of a large tract on Long Island, died
in 1730, his estate included a fifty-year-old Negro woman
valued at £35 and an eighteen-year-old girl worth £45.
Young men skilled in a trade commanded very high prices.
An inventory of the estate of William Bird, a Pennsylvania iron manufacturer, revealed that in 1763 Bird owned
ten Negroes, three of them men between the ages of nineteen
and twenty-six worth £120 each.[16]

A New York Loyalist, whose estate had been confiscated
during the Revolution, told a British commission on Loyalist
claims that a "good slave" was worth £50 in 1776 and that
the average value of a slave in the pre-war period was £40.
The value of 150 slaves claimed by New York Loyalists aver-
aged at £53 each, adult males were worth an average of £65.
During the war prices fluctuated widely as faith in the conti-

[15] *Rivington's New-York Gazetteer,* February 16, 1775; *Letters of Isaac Bobin, Esq.* (Albany, 1872), pp. 33, 35–36, 39, 41, 109, 116, 128–29, 151–52, 157.

[16] *Lloyd Papers,* I, 311; Paul N. Schaefer, "Slavery in Berks County," *Historical Review of Berks County,* VI (1941), 110.

nental currency declined. A fifteen-year-old boy was offered for sale in New Jersey for £80 "in gold or silver," his master claiming that he was cheap at the price. Other masters, despairing of receiving hard currency for their Negroes, resorted to bartering. In Pennsylvania the master of a seven-year-old Negro boy sold him for fifty bushels of wheat and fifty bushels of rye. After the war, prices were higher. John Neilson paid £120 for a Negro woman and her two girls in 1787, and in 1794, he was offered a twenty-one-year-old Negro "boy" for £90. Neilson thought this was "a high price," but for a good slave he was "willing to pay a good price." [17]

A general picture of the value of Negro slaves can be obtained from a study of New Jersey estate inventories. In the decade 1750–60 the average price of thirty-two Negro men was £47.10 each. After the Revolution prices were substantially higher. Seventy-two men included in New Jersey estate inventories between 1794 and 1801 had an average value of £76.12; twenty-seven of them were worth £100 or more. The average price had increased more than fifty per cent over the 1750–60 level. [18]

New England currency fluctuated widely, making it almost impossible to determine the value of slaves at any particular time. In 1706, £40 to £50 was the "common price" for a Negro. In 1745, when a Negro girl sold for £30, a horse brought £6. By the middle of the eighteenth century inflation had made serious inroads into the New England economy. The estate of Peter Faneuil, who died in 1743, included five Negroes worth from £110 to £150 each. A leading merchant of Providence, Rhode Island, left five Negroes when he died

[17] Olson, "Slavery in N.Y.," pp. 76–77; *New Jersey Gazette,* July 18, 1781; Martha B. Clark, "Lancaster County's Relation to Slavery. . . ," (*Historical Papers and Addresses,* Lancaster County Historical Society, 1911), XV, 46; "Slaves Sales and Purchases," (James Neilson Papers, MSS in the Rutgers University Library, Rutgers, N.J.), fol. 45. For additional material on slave prices, see the Appendix, Tables 1, 2, and 3.

[18] Figures derived from *N.J. Archives,* 1st ser., XXXII, 6–258; New Jersey Wills, books and files, MSS in the Superior Court Clerk's Office, Trenton, N.J. See also the Appendix, Tables 4, 5, and 6.

in 1762. They were appraised at £1,000 or more each. In 1770, however, Dr. Joseph Warren, famous Revolutionary hero, paid only £30 for a Negro boy, and five years later a Boston man sold an eighteen- or nineteen-year-old boy for only 10 shillings. When Rhode Island decided to enlist slaves for her regiment in the Continental army, a maximum price of £120 was allowed as compensation to the masters of enlisted slaves.[19]

A large holding of slaves represented a considerable investment. In 1796 a Bergen County, New Jersey, estate included fourteen Negroes; three of the men were worth £100 each and two were worth £120 each. The total investment in slaves was £968—nearly one-quarter of the total estate of £4,285. Another New Jersey master left seven Negroes worth $1,012 in a total estate valued at $3,657.[20] For these masters slavery represented not only a labor system but a substantial cash investment.

Slaves were sometimes hired instead of sold. Hiring was so common in New York City that a special public market was established to accommodate the trade. A master could make a good profit by renting the services of his Negroes. A slave worth £25 in 1687 was hired out in 1695 at £5 per year; the rate was increased £1 per year in 1697 and again in 1698, ultimately bringing his master £50 for eight years' service. In 1726 a forty-six-year-old Negro woman (valued at £35 four years later) was hired at £9 per year. Hiring out slaves continued to be profitable after the Revolution. In 1806 a New Jersey man paid $150 for the services of a Negro for two

[19] Greene, *Negro in New England,* pp. 43–44; "Computation that the Importation of Negroes is not so profitable as that of White Servants," *Boston News-Letter,* June 10, 1706: reprinted in George H. Moore, *Notes on the History of Slavery in Massachusetts* (New York, 1866), pp. 106–8; William B. Weeden, *Economic and Social History of New England, 1620–1789* (2 vols.; Boston, 1890), II, 895, 909; William B. Weeden, *Early Rhode Island* (New York, 1910), p. 263; Greene, *Negro in New England,* p. 45; John R. Bartlett (ed.), *Records of the Colony of Rhode Island and Providence Plantations in New England* (10 vols.; Providence, 1856–62), VIII, 360.

[20] Bergen County Wills, 2644, Monmouth County Wills, 7239, Superior Court Office, Trenton, N.J.

years at a time when $300 was a good price for a prime slave.[21]

The comparative cost of free, indentured, and slave labor can only be estimated on the basis of very meager data. Shortly before the Revolution a large Hudson River estate used slaves, indentured servants, and free workers. Eight slaves were valued at £34 each, while four indentured servants cost £33 for three years service. The two free workers earned £12 per year. The full price of a slave, therefore, was equivalent to a little more than the price of three years' service of an indentured or free worker (all the workers were supplied with food, although the servants and free men probably supplied their own clothes). An Englishman who settled in western Pennsylvania in the years before independence paid £56 for two Negroes and £4 per year for each of his indentured German servants. The price of the Negroes was equal to seven years' service of an indentured German. For another Pennsylvania farmer who used both indentured servants and slaves, the cost of the Negroes was nearly the equivalent of eight years' service of an indentured white. Theophile Casenove, who traveled through New Jersey's Morris County in 1794, observed that "good dependable" Negro men cost £100 and that a white farm hand received £30 or £40 a year ("and you must treat him politely.") Farmers in the area must have preferred slaves for, according to Casenove, "There as everywhere in Jersey all the servants are black slaves." The Duc de la Rochefoucauld-Liancourt reported that in 1796 Negro men sold for $400 in upstate New York. Free laborers were scarce for "as soon as they have been able to amass a little money, they go to the new countries and become farmers themselves." When available, free men received $10 or $12 per month and as much as $2 per day during the harvest.[22] According to the figures reported by

[21] McKee, *Labor in N.Y.*, p. 129; *Lloyd Papers*, I, 110, 115, 147, 161, 271, 311; "Calvin Green's Diary," *Proceedings of the New Jersey Historical Society*, LXIX (1951), 125.

[22] *American Husbandry*, ed. Harry J. Carman (New York, 1939), pp. 80–81, 136–37, 141; *A Record of the Journey of Theophile Cazenove through New Jersey and Pennsylvania*, ed. Rayner W. Kelsey (Haverford, Pa.. 1922), p. 3; François Alexandre, duc de la Rochefoucauld-

both these visitors, the price of a Negro slave was about the equivalent of three years' wages for a free man.

Whether it was more profitable to hire free or indentured white laborers or to buy Negro slaves is difficult to determine; men faced with the choice at the time gave different answers. A man trying to choose the most economical form of labor would have to weigh such factors as the high initial investment required to buy a slave and the chance of suffering a total loss if the slave died, was incapacitated, or ran away, compared to the difficulty of getting free workers at harvest time. The Duc de la Rochefoucauld-Liancourt thought "the convenience of having them constantly at hand for any work" was the major advantage of slave labor, but that otherwise "the labour of white people is less expensive." [23] A colonial entrepreneur deciding what kind of labor to use would have to estimate the comparative efficiency of slave and free labor—the fact that slaves and indentured servants had to be clothed, fed, and maintained even when there was no work for them as well as the fact that he could ordinarily expect capital gains as his slaves reproduced. If he spent a great deal of effort training an indentured servant he would face the loss of a skilled worker when his indenture expired; but an expensive Negro slave might run away after he had learned a trade. The choice each employer made was a complex decision, based on a great number of variable factors.

Sometimes an employer had no choice. Aaron Malick, a tanner whose wife stoutly opposed slavery, refused to buy Negroes for years. Nonetheless, in 1786 he was so "sorely pressed for help" that he bought a Negro who was a "master-hand at tanning, currying and finishing leather." An Englishman could not hire enough laborers to run his farm on Long Island and was forced to buy Negroes. Since he opposed slavery, he applied the equivalent of the Negroes' wages to the purchase of their freedom. Those who refused to compromise their antislavery principles often made a real sacrifice. John Adams recalled that because of his abhorrence

Liancourt, *Travels Through the United States of North America,* trans. H. Neuman (2 vols.; London, 1799), II, 233–34.

[23] La Rochefoucauld-Liancourt, *Travels Through the U.S.,* I, 376.

of slavery he had never owned a Negro. This refusal to use slave labor cost him "thousands of dollars for the labor and subsistence of freemen," which he might have saved "by the purchase of negroes at times when they were very cheap" and when "the practice was not disgraceful." [24]

The decision to use slave labor depended on many factors: the availability of free or indentured servants and Negro slaves; the price of Negroes and the wages of freemen; the suitability of the available freemen and slaves for the task at hand. In view of the many varying factors it is not surprising that some farmers and craftsmen bought slaves while others relied on free labor. As under any other system, the slave-owner probably made a profit in some years and sustained a loss in others, praising his skill in the first instance and cursing his luck in the second. Obviously, when a man consistently paid high prices for Negro slaves he asserted his belief that slavery was a profitable investment and an economical labor system.[25]

RESTRICTIONS ON THE IMPORTATION OF NEGROES

Even though slavery was regarded as profitable by many individual slaveowners, it was questionable if slavery was beneficial to the interests of the community. White laborers often saw slavery as unwelcome competition. In 1707 several Philadelphians complained to the assembly of "the Want of Employment, and Lowness of Wages, occasioned by the Number of *Negroes,* . . . who being hired out to work by the Day, take away the Employment of the Petitioners." A Boston town meeting enjoined a man from employing a slave as a cooper in 1661 in accordance with a law that may have been enacted at the request of white artisans. (The law soon became a dead letter.) New York City was forced to prohibit

[24] Andrew D. Mellick, *The Story of an Old Farm* (Somerville, N.J., 1889), pp. 602–3; John Harriott, *Struggles Through Life* (2 vols.; London, 1807), II, 194; *The Works of John Adams,* ed. Charles Francis Adams (10 vols.; Boston, 1856), X, 380.

[25] Examples of conspicuous consumption (buying valuable Negroes to impress others) would clearly be exceptions; but most Negroes in the North were employed in economically useful occupations.

slaves from hiring themselves out as porters because of the disastrous effect of this practice on the licensed porters of the city. George Clarke (then lieutenant governor of New York) told the assembly in 1737 that "the artificers complain and with too much reason of the pernicious custom of breeding slaves to trades, whereby the honest and industrious tradesmen are reduced to poverty for want of employ." John Adams went so far as to suggest that the "real cause" of the abolition of slavery in Massachusetts was "the multiplication of labouring white people, who would no longer suffer the rich to employ these sable rivals so much to their injury." Adams, who had a keen fear of the mob, believed that if the slaves had not been freed, the white workers "would have put the negroes to death, and their masters too, perhaps." He thought that white workers had succeeded in making slavery unprofitable. "Their scoffs and insults, their continual insinuations, filled the negroes with discontent, made them lazy, idle, proud, vicious, and at length wholly useless to their masters." [26] Although we may doubt the efficacy of the measures attributed to them, it is clear that white workers resented slave competition.

The possibility of slave rebellions aroused opposition to the extension of slavery and prompted restrictive import duties. In the wake of the New York Negro plot of 1712, a large number of Pennsylvanians asked their assembly to discourage the importation of Negroes. The legislature responded with an act "to Prevent the Importation of Negroes and Indians," imposing a £20 duty on imported slaves. The law, which took note of the danger of "plots and insurrections," was disallowed by a royal government that would brook no interference with the profitable African trade. In 1715 a duty on Negroes was deleted from an impost bill because of the "Opposition likely to be made by the

[26] *Votes and Proceedings of the House of Representatives of the Province of Pennsylvania* (6 vols.; Philadelphia, 1752–76), I, part 2, 132; Greene, *Negro in New England*, p. 112; Olson, "Slavery in N.Y.," p. 90; Charles Z. Lincoln (ed.), *State of New York, Messages from the Governors* (3 vols.; Albany, 1909), I, 260; "Letters and Documents Relating to Slavery in Massachusetts," *Collections of the Mass. Hist. Soc.*, 5th ser., III, 402.

Merchants of this City, and by the African Company." A £5 duty, enacted over the opposition of the Philadelphia merchants as a separate measure, met the expected royal veto. The same duty was reestablished in 1718, but since the act was not submitted to the Privy Council, it was allowed to stand. Pennsylvania merchants continued to oppose the restrictive policy. In 1727 several iron manufacturers asked for permission to import Negroes without paying duty because of the "Difficulty of getting Labourers, and their excessive Wages." Two years later the assembly reduced the duty to £2, a figure so low that it was probably intended only for revenue, and slaves flooded into the Philadelphia market to be sold at semi-weekly public auctions.[27]

During the French and Indian War members of the assembly complained about the enlistment of indentured servants. They pointed out that if the tenure of indentured servants was made insecure, Pennsylvanians would be forced to buy slaves, which would be detrimental to the colony: an "Increase of White Inhabitants" would be prevented, the province would be weakened since "every Slave may be reckoned a domestick Enemy," and there would be fewer white recruits for the army. In 1761 the assembly, responding to antislavery sentiment based on these considerations as well as to a growing religious opposition to slavery, enacted a £10 duty bill. Philadelphia merchants strongly opposed the bill. They argued that they wanted to "extend the Trade of this Province," and because of the difficulties caused by a "want of Labourers" they had "encouraged the importation of Negroes." The assembly refused to heed these arguments and the high duty remained in effect for the rest of the colonial period. [8]

New York's duty laws were designed to prevent the impor-

[27] *Pa. Votes,* II, 110, 175; III, 31; William R. Riddell, "Pre-Revolutionary Pennsylvania and the Slave Trade," *Pa. Mag. of Hist.,* LII (1928), 8–12; Thomas E. Drake, *Quakers and Slavery in America* (New Haven, 1950), p. 39.

[28] *Minutes of the Provincial Council of Pennsylvania* (Harrisburg, 1851), pp. 37–38; Du Bois, *Suppression of Slave-Trade,* p. 23; Riddell, "Pa. and the Slave Trade," pp. 15–18.

tation of undesirable slaves. Beginning in 1709, the province placed a higher duty on slaves not imported directly from Africa. According to the assembly, this discrimination would "discourage an Importation from the Plantations, by whom we are supplied with the Refuse of their *Negroes*." The West Indian planters, the New Yorkers bitterly observed, sent them slaves who would have been executed for their crimes "had not the Avarice of their Owners, saved them from the publick justice by an early Transportation into these Parts, where they not often fail of repeating their Crimes." Although most New York duty bills were not designed to prevent the importation of African slaves, a law enacted after the Negro plot was vetoed by the governor on the grounds that it violated British policy by hampering the slave trade.[29]

On several occasions New York governors pointed to the dangers of a rapidly increasing Negro population. In 1734 Governor William Cosby told the assembly that he saw

with Concern that whilst the neighbouring provinces are filled with honest usefull & laborious white people, the truest riches and Surest Strength of a Country; this province seems regardless of the vast advantages which Such acquisitions might bring them and of the disadvantages that attend the too great Importation of Negroes and Convicts.

The assembly refused to heed his warning that the "greatest evill" might result from a continued reliance on Negroes rather than whites. Lieutenant Governor James De Lancey recommended to the 1757 assembly a tax on slaves, on the ground that it would "naturally tend to Introduce white Servants, which would augment the Strength of the Country." He also observed that "the Price of Labour is now become so high" that the slaveowners "reap such Advantage, that they cannot reasonably complain of a Tax on them." [30] In New York the governors, rather than the legislature, were

[29] *Colonial Laws of New York* . . . (4 vols.; Albany, 1894), I, 677; *Journal of the Legislative Council of the Colony of New-York* (2 vols.; Albany, 1861), I, 433–34; *N.Y. Governors Messages,* I, 171.

[30] *N.Y. Legislative Council,* I, 631, II, 1308.

concerned with the fact that slavery tended to discourage immigration and to weaken the community.

Following the New York slave revolt, New Jersey also imposed restrictions on the importation of Negroes. A £10 duty was levied on slaves not imported directly from Africa and, beginning in 1716, the same duty was applied for seven years to all slaves imported for sale in New Jersey. Governor Robert Hunter explained to the Board of Trade that the act was intended to "Encourage the Importation of white Servants for the better Peopeling" of the country. A similar law in Pennsylvania, he noted, had had that effect.

After the expiration of the 1713 law, no further move was made to tax the slave trade until 1739, when the council vetoed an assembly bill for that purpose. In 1744 another assembly bill was vetoed by the council during a general period of disagreement between the two houses. The upper chamber thought that the £10 duty on West Indian slaves and the £5 levy on African slaves "was plainly intended [as] an intire Prohibition of all Slaves being imported." If the bill passed, "the People of this Province in general (a few Labourers only excepted) and the Farmers in particular, would be great Sufferers by it." The councilors pointed out that many men were away on an expedition to the West Indies and others were engaged in privateering, and this had caused a labor shortage and high wages. Moreover, the development of the linen industry in Ireland and European wars had led to a decline in immigration. Therefore, "it would be more for the interests of the People of this Colony to encourage at this Time the Importation of Slaves." By 1761 it had become obvious that since New York and Pennsylvania had adopted import duties on slaves, New Jersey was in danger of becoming a way station for slave importers who wanted to avoid paying duties in the neighboring colonies. Governor Josiah Hardy told the home government that New Jersey was becoming overstocked with slaves, which hindered "in a great measure settling the Colony properly." Despite Hardy's plea, the crown disallowed a New Jersey duty law because it taxed importers, not the final purchasers. Finally, in 1769 the assembly passed a duty bill that met the crown's objections. The preamble clearly stated its aim: "the Introduction of sober, industrious Foreigners . . . and promoting a Spirit of Industry among the Inhabitants." The law imposed a £15 duty, severely limiting the importation of Negroes.[31]

In New England only Massachusetts and Rhode Island placed restrictions on the slave trade. In 1700 a Boston committee tried to obtain a 40s. duty on imported Negroes "to discourage the bringing of them," and a year later a Boston town meeting instructed its representatives to the General Court to ask for a law to encourage the importation of white servants and "to put a period to Negroes being Slaves." Apparently the legislature took no action on these requests, but in 1705 it passed a law "For the Better Preventing of a Spurious and Mixt Issue," levying a £4 duty on imported Negroes.[32]

A year later a writer in the *Boston News-Letter* summarized all the practical objections to slavery. "Negroes," he pointed out, "are generally Eye-Servants, great Thieves, much addicted to Stealing, Lying and Purloining." They could not serve as soldiers. The death of a slave cost his master thirty pounds whereas the loss of an indentured servant cost only ten pounds. Three years' interest on the price of a Negro would almost be enough to pay for a white servant, and the white man would be more useful to the community. These arguments probably had little effect and, in 1718, when a bill "for Encouraging the Importation of White Male Servants and the preventing of the Clandestine bringing in of Negroes" was proposed in the General Court, it could not muster enough support to obtain a third reading.[33]

Rhode Island placed a £3 duty on imported slaves in 1708. Four years later the legislature passed another duty bill,

---

[31] William Bradford (printer), *Laws and Acts of . . . New-Jersey* ([New York], 1717), p. 43; *N.J. Archives,* 1st ser., IV, 196; XV, 30, 31, 50, 343, 345, 384–85; IX, 345–46, 348, 382–83, 447; Josiah Hardy to the General Assembly, December 20, 1761 (MS in the New Jersey State Library) ; Samuel Allinson (compiler), *Acts of the General Assembly of the Province of New Jersey . . .* (Burlington, N.J., 1776), p. 315.

[32] Greene, *Negro in New England,* p. 50; "Diary of Samuel Sewall," (*Collections of the Mass. Hist. Soc.*) 5th ser., VI, 16; Samuel G. Drake, *The History and Antiquities of Boston* (Boston, 1856), p. 525.

[33] Moore, *Slavery in Mass.,* 107–8; Greene, *Negro in New England,* p. 51.

observing that "the bringing in of Negroes" discouraged "the importation of white servants" and would in time prove "prejudicial to the inhabitants of the colony." The Rhode Island law, however, allowed the importation of Negroes directly from Africa without duty, and both the Massachusetts and Rhode Island laws were frequently evaded. In 1732, at the command of the crown, Rhode Island repealed its duty act.[34]

THE PROFITABILITY OF SLAVERY

The restrictions placed on the importation of slaves by northern colonies was evidence that a number of colonists regarded slavery as an undesirable institution. It is not, however, as some historians have argued, an indication that slavery was not profitable in the North.[35] If slavery was unprofitable, it would not have been necessary to make it less profitable by levying a restrictive duty on imported Negroes. The distinction should be made between two separate questions: Was slavery profitable for slaveowners? Was slavery beneficial to the interests of the community?

Those who maintain that slavery was unprofitable or less profitable than white labor base their arguments on the mental incapacity or ignorance of Negroes and their inability to do the skilled work required in a diversified economy. It is clear, however, that northern Negroes received the requisite training and eventually became highly skilled in a great number of divers trades. Although it is true that newly imported Negroes suffered in their first northern winter, once they became acclimated, they could tolerate the rigors of a northern climate. A New Jersey slave dealer took account of the northern market when he advertised the sale of a group of "Gambia Slaves" as "much more robust and

[34] *R.I. Records,* IV, 34, 131–35, 471; Greene, *Negro in New England,* pp. 51–57.

[35] Irving S. Kull, "Slavery in New Jersey," *New Jersey, A History,* ed. Irving S. Kull (6 vols.; New York, 1930), II, 733; "The earliest argument against slavery was an economic one—the unprofitable or less profitable character of it . . . [This argument] first gained legal expression in New Jersey in 1714 when a statute was adopted putting a duty of £10 on every Negro imported for sale."

tractable, than any other Slaves from the Coast of Guinea, and more capable of undergoing the Severity of the Winter Seasons in the North-American Colonies." For this reason, he added, they were "vastly more esteemed and coveted in this Province and those to the Northward." [36] Many men considered slaves as a profitable investment, and Negroes continued to bring high prices until abolition.

Men held different opinions about whether slavery was desirable and suited to the best interests of the community. Merchants and farmers, faced with a labor shortage, thought that slavery provided an answer to the economic difficulties of the colonies. Other men, haunted by the fear of slave revolts, tried to limit the importation of Negroes. Those who supported restrictive duties argued that slavery discouraged white immigration and that white laborers were preferable because they would eventually become independent farmers, paying taxes, serving as soldiers, and settling on the frontier, thus protecting the established settlements from Indian raids. Massachusetts' first duty act was ostensibly prompted by a desire to avoid miscegenation. Other duty laws may have been prompted by white laborers who resented slave competition.

As more free labor became available, slavery in the North became less necessary, although it is doubtful that the increased European immigration made slavery unprofitable. At the same time that slavery became less essential, there was a more significant development. The Society of Friends, a powerful sect in Pennsylvania and West Jersey, became increasingly dedicated to eliminating slavery from among its own members and throughout American society, and the struggle with Great Britain brought a spirit of idealism and a belief in the Rights of Man that was incompatible with the continuance of human bondage.

[36] *Pennsylvania Journal,* May 27, 1762 in *N.J. Archives,* 1st ser., XXIV, 39–40.

The history of the early abolitionist movement is essentially the record of Quaker antislavery activities. Although a few non-Quakers firmly denounced slavery, the Society of Friends was the only group to advocate emancipation in the years before the American Revolution. Quakers did own slaves (they were deeply involved in all aspects of slavery), but in the period before the Declaration of Independence they gradually came to the conclusion that participation in the slave trade, the purchase or sale of Negroes, and finally owning slaves, were incompatible with the tenets of their religion.

QUAKERS AND SLAVERY

A small group of Dutch and German Friends who testified against the "traffick of mens-body" was the first to proclaim to an American Quaker meeting the inconsistency of slavery with the teachings of Jesus. The authors of the famous Germantown protest of 1688 pointed out that all men dreaded enslavement and that therefore slavery must be a violation of the Golden Rule. That the slaves were of a different race made no difference; the command of the Golden Rule was universal, "macking no difference of . . . Colour." Therefore, "tho' they are black," there is no more "liberty to have them as slaves as it is to have other white ones." Slavery reminded these Quakers of the conditions that had forced them to leave their homelands. In Europe "there are many oppressed for Conscience sacke," but "here there are those oppressed w[hi]ch are of a black Colour." Slavery involved other sins—receiving stolen goods (the slaves were stolen from Africa) and adultery (slaveowners separated husband and wife). "Oh! doe consider well this thing . . . if it is done according [to] Christianity."

Turning to a more practical consideration, they reminded their fellow colonists that "This mackes an ill report in . . . Europe" and would discourage the immigration essential for the success of the province. For Quakers, with their pacifist principles, there was an additional difficulty: if the slaves should "fight for their freedom . . . will these masters . . . warr against these poor slaves?" If it came to that, "have these negers not as much right to fight for their freedom, as you have to keep them slaves?" The Germantown Friends brought this protest before their monthly meeting, which referred it to the Philadelphia Quarterly Meeting. This group in turn forwarded it to the highest authority, the Yearly Meeting for Pennsylvania and New Jersey (the Philadelphia Yearly Meeting). The members of the Yearly Meeting found that the issue was extremely complex. They must have felt the truth of what the Germantown Friends said, but they also realized that they were judging a system involving property rights, race relations, and a method of dealing with an acute labor shortage. Furthermore, the Pennsylvania and New Jersey Quakers could not escape the fact that the interests of their brethren in Virginia and Barbados were vitally involved in this question. It would be impossible to obtain the near unanimity required for action by Quaker meetings. "It was adjudged not to be so proper for this meeting to give a positive judgment in the case, . . . and therefore at present they forbear it." The issue had been dropped, but only for "the present."[1]

Even before the Germantown protest the dynamic of the Quaker belief, the imperative to consult the inner light, had led the society's founder, George Fox, to remind the colonists that God had made all nations of one blood and that "Christ died for all . . . for the tawnies and for the blacks as well as for you that are called whites." He suggested that slaves be

---

[1] "The Germantown Protest," reprinted in *Pennsylvania Magazine of History and Biography,* IV (1880), 28–30; Thomas E. Drake, *Quakers and Slavery in America* (New Haven, 1950), pp. 11–13.

freed after a limited period of servitude and not be sent away "empty-handed." [2]

Only a few years after the Germantown protest the followers of George Keith (a schismatic group of Quakers) spoke out against slavery. They urged the colonists to consider that *"Negroes . . . are a real part of Mankind"* and that true followers of Christ must not "bring any part of Mankind into . . . Slavery or Misery." Faithful Friends should exhibit a Christlike compassion "and set them free of their hard Bondage, whereby it may be hoped, that many of them will be gained by their beholding these good Works . . . and prepared thereby . . . to imbrace the true Faith." The Keithites pointed out that slavery was in violation of the biblical command not to oppress strangers and servants: "But what greater Oppression can there be inflicted upon our Fellow Creatures, than is inflicted on the poor Negroes!" They are separated from their families, and many people "Do exceedingly afflict them," forcing them to work hard, giving them little food, and punishing them harshly. Quakers should not buy slaves (except to free them) and should manumit their Negroes after a reasonable period of moderate service (to pay their cost), meanwhile educating them and preparing them for emancipation. Slavery would bring God's judgment on the community, for slavery is a sin and God will punish sinners.[3]

Since the Keithites had separated from the Society of Friends, their views could be ignored; but eight years after the Philadelphia Yearly had postponed action on the Germantown protest, several members brought in new papers "relating to the keeping and bringing in of negroes." In response the 1696 Yearly Meeting advised Friends to "be careful not to encourage the bringing in of any more negroes" and to take care of the religious needs of those they owned.[4] This mild statement marked the acceptance by the

[2] Drake, *Quakers and Slavery*, pp. 5–8.

[3] *An Exhortation & Caution to Friends Concerning Buying or Keeping of Negroes* (New York, 1693), reprinted in *Pa. Mag. of Hist.*, XIII (1889), 265–70; Drake, *Quakers and Slavery*, pp. 14–15.

[4] Society of Friends, *A Brief Statement of the Rise and Progress of the*

Yearly Meeting of the position that at least one aspect of slavery, the cruel slave trade, was incompatible with the gentle tenets of their sect. Furthermore, the recommendation that Friends give their slaves religious training reflected the assumption that Negroes were capable of salvation, thereby preparing the way for the recognition of their humanity and ultimately their rights.

A PURITAN ABOLITIONIST: SAMUEL SEWALL

Although most of the early antislavery writers were members of the Society of Friends, a Puritan, Judge Samuel Sewall of Massachusetts, was increasingly "dissatisfied with the Trade of fetching Negroes." Several times, he confided in his diary, he had been inclined to write something on the subject but had put it aside. In 1700 a series of events brought the matter to his attention again: the General Court considered a petition for the emancipation of two unjustly enslaved Negroes; the court also debated a bill to discourage the slave trade; and Cotton Mather planned to publish a pamphlet urging masters to work for the conversion of their slaves. Sewall hoped that he was "call'd of God to Write this Apology for them," and five days later he published *The Selling of Joseph.*[5]

Sewall immediately placed slavery on the defensive: "Forasmuch as *Liberty* is in real value next unto *Life:* None ought to part with it themselves, or deprive others of it, but upon most mature Consideration." He noted that "The Numerousness of Slaves at this day in the Province, and the Uneasiness of them under their Slavery, hath put many upon thinking whether the Foundation of it be firmly and well laid." Questioning the expediency of Negro slavery, Sewall charged that "All things considered, it would conduce more to the Welfare of the Province, to have White Servants for a Term of Years." Negro slaves did not add to the defense of

---

Testimony of the Religious Society of Friends, Against Slavery and the Slave Trade (Philadelphia, 1843), p. 8.

[5] "Diary of Samuel Sewall," (*Collections of the Massachusetts Historical Society*), 5th ser., VI, 16.

the colony; their presence, instead of white servants, discouraged immigration from Europe and meant an absence of soldiers, husbands, and new settlers. The Negroes could never be made part of the body politic because they were too different in appearance. Furthermore, white servants would serve their masters better, for the slaves' "continual aspiring after their forbidden Liberty, renders them Unwilling Servants."

Slavery was not only inexpedient, it was incompatible with Christianity. God had made all nations of one blood and therefore all men had an "equal Right unto Liberty." Just as Joseph's brothers had no right to sell him into slavery, those who bought him (or those who bought Negro slaves) had no right to their "property," and "he that shall in this case plead *Alteration of Property,* seems to have forfeited a great part of his own claim to Humanity. There is no proportion between Twenty Pieces of Silver, and LIBERTY." To those who said that the slave trade was a justifiable means of converting the heathen, Sewall replied that evil may not be done for the good that may come out of it. He denounced the horrors of the slave trade and equated it with murder. It resulted in the separation of families and friends.

To the argument that the Negroes were legitimately enslaved as prisoners of war, Sewall made the observation that an unjust war could not make lawful captives. If it were argued that the Israelites were allowed to own slaves, he would answer that Christ had altered the old laws and that slavery was not permissible for Christians.[6]

Sewall's sharp attack on slavery inspired his colleague, Judge John Saffin, to issue a stinging rebuttal, denying that the story of the selling of Joseph had any bearing on the morality of purchasing heathen slaves. He went further and accused Sewall of an attempt "to invert the Order that God hath Set." Sewall had said that all men have a right to liberty, but according to Saffin, God had decreed that there be different orders of men—masters and slaves. Was Sewall accusing God of injustice for allowing inequality? Was he attempting to put men on a basis of "meer parity?" Saffin

[6] Samuel Sewall, *The Selling of Joseph* (Boston, 1700), reprinted in "Sewall Diary," note, pp. 16–20.

conceded that white servants were more useful than Negroes but, he asked, "doth it therefore follow, that it is altogether unlawful for Christians to buy and keep Negro Servants . . . [and] that those that have them ought in Conscience to set them free, and so lose all the money they cost?" For Saffin it was primarily a question of property rights. He suggested that if Sewall could persuade the General Court to pass an emancipation bill that provided compensation for those who chose to free their slaves and an absolute prohibition of further imports, " 'tis probable there would be more of his opinion." But even compensated abolition would not solve the problem because the freed Negroes would then have to be deported "or else the remedy would be worse than the Disease"; a population of idle and vicious free Negroes would be much more dangerous than the continuance of slavery.[7]

Sewall did not reply to Saffin's pamphlet, despite its personal attack on his integrity. For nearly twenty years, however, he sent copies of *The Selling of Joseph* to friends, members of the legislature, and even casual acquaintances. In 1705 Sewall resumed the attack, reprinting an English antislavery pamphlet that charged that slavery and the slave trade were "Unlawful, and especially contrary to the great law of CHRISTIANITY." His views were not popular, and he confided to a friend that his antislavery activities had brought him "Frowns and hard Words." [8]

Sewall may have written the anonymous antislavery article printed in the *Boston News-Letter* in 1706. This essay, designed to show that "the Importation of Negroes in not so profitable as that of White Servants," repeated many of the practical objections to slavery that Sewall had urged six years

[7] John Saffin, *A Brief and Candid Answer to . . . The Selling of Joseph* (Boston, 1701), reprinted in George H. Moore, *Notes on the History of Slavery in Massachusetts* (New York, 1866), pp. 251–56. See also: Lawrence W. Towner, "The Sewall-Saffin Dialogue on Slavery," *William and Mary Quarterly*, 3d ser., XXI (1964), 40–52; Ola Winslow, *Samuel Sewall of Boston* (New York, 1964), pp. 162–68.

[8] Mary S. Locke, *Anti-Slavery in America from the Introduction of African Slaves to the Prohibition of the Slave-Trade* (Boston, 1901), pp. 18–19; Towner, "Sewall-Saffin Dialogue," pp. 46, 50; "Letter-Book of Samuel Sewall," (*Collections of the Mass. Hist. Soc.*) 6th ser., I, 326.

earlier. Slavery entailed great potential loss to masters whose slaves died; and the rest of the community suffered because Negroes did not contribute to its defense.[9]

QUAKERS AND SLAVERY: THE LONELY CRITICS

The publication of this essay marked the end of a brief flurry of interest in abolition among the Puritans of Massachusetts. For most Puritans the mandate to establish a Bible commonwealth did not require the abolition of slavery, an institution sanctified by Old Testament precedent. The Puritan ethic did encourage masters to educate their slaves, to bring them to church, and to treat them well, but it did not require emancipation. For the Society of Friends slavery proved to be a much more difficult issue. Some of the more radical Quakers followed the doctrine of the inner light to its ultimate conclusion and fervently believed that their religion required them to free their Negroes and to persuade their brethren to follow suit. Other Quakers, however, believed in common with the Puritans that their duty to their Negroes extended no further than to bring them religion and to treat them well. Consequently, abolition proved to be an issue that could shatter the peace of the meeting house.

Friends from Chester Quarterly, the southernmost meeting belonging to the Philadelphia Yearly (which included parts of Virginia), reported to the 1711 annual meeting that they were increasingly "dissatisfied with Friends buying and encouraging the bringing in of negroes." But in view of the fact that "Friends in many other places are concerned in it as much as we are," the Yearly Meeting could only repeat its advice of 1696 and urge merchants to discourage their correspondents from sending any more. At the 1712 meeting antislavery Friends renewed their attack hoping to end not only the slave trade but slavery itself. Seeking guidance, Philadelphia Quakers wrote to the London Meeting. They told their English brethren that they had been concerned for many years with the morality of slavery. They mentioned their action of 1696 but explained that there were many

[9] Moore, *Slavery in Mass.,* pp. 106–8.

non-Quaker traders in the province who had "increased and multiplied negroes amongst us, to the grief of divers Friends." Last year the matter had been brought up again, but "Friends being more concerned with negroes in divers other provinces . . . we thought it rather too weighty to come to a full conclusion therein." They sought the advice of the London Meeting and suggested that English Quakers consult with Friends in other colonies.[10] They wanted London to solve the problem by establishing a uniform policy for all American meetings.

The decision to consult London was a compromise measure, strongly opposed by several antislavery Friends including William Southeby, who had first spoken against slavery at the 1696 Yearly Meeting. Now he contended that Philadelphia Quakers should do their duty and leave others to act for themselves. Seeing that the appeal to London was futile (if he could not convince Philadelphia Quakers, how could he hope to convince other meetings?), he decided to go beyond the Quaker meeting and appeal directly to the Pennsylvania Assembly to free the Negroes. This appeal also failed; the Quaker-dominated legislature ruled that it was "neither just nor convenient to set them at Liberty." [11]

When the reply from London was read at the next Yearly Meeting, Southeby realized the accuracy of his prediction. English Friends were as anxious to avoid the issue as their Philadelphia brethren. They suggested that the Philadelphia Meeting should have consulted other meetings—which is precisely what the Pennsylvanians had suggested to the London Meeting. They did observe, however, that the slave trade was not "a commendable nor allowed practice" for Friends. Philadelphia Quakers replied that they agreed, but they pointed out that a recent law laying a heavy duty on imported Negroes had been disallowed by the queen and

[10] *Brief Statement,* pp. 9–10; Allan C. Thomas, "The Attitude of the Society of Friends Toward Slavery in the Seventeenth and Eighteenth Century," (*Papers of the American Society of Church History*), VII (1897), 269–70; "William Southeby," *The Friend* (Philadelphia), XXIX (1855), 301.

[11] "William Southeby," p. 301; *Votes and Proceedings of the House of Representatives of the Province of Pennsylvania* (6 vols.; Philadelphia, 1752–76), II, 110.

they hoped that the English group would use their influence to prevent the veto of any new legislation to restrict the slave trade. They testily reminded their correspondents "that our request unto you was, that you would . . . consult . . . with Friends in other plantations . . . because they hold a correspondence with you but not with us, and your meeting may better prevail with them." London's reply to this epistle was no more satisfactory than the last.[12]

Many conservative Quakers were tired of the issue. Isaac Norris, a wealthy Philadelphia merchant, thought the 1715 Yearly Meeting would have been a good one "if it were not for the warm pushing by some Friends, of Chester chiefly, in the business of negroes." The abolitionists had tried again to persuade the meeting to discourage the purchase of Negroes. According to Norris, the opposition thought the proposal was "of dangerous consequences to the peace of the church." The meeting warned members not to import slaves and urged Friends to treat their Negroes with humanity, but on the issue of holding slaves it pointedly advised "that all do forbear judging or reflecting on one another, either in public or private." Abolition was not a proper subject for discussion. In 1716 Friends from Chester returned to the fight. They asked the meeting to agree that buying freshly imported Negroes was hardly different from importing them. But most Friends considered this proposal to be the same as the one they had rejected the year before and they repeated their earlier statement with one addition however: "in condescension to such Friends as are straitened in their minds against holding them, it is desired that Friends . . . avoid buying such negroes as shall hereafter be brought in, rather than offend any Friends who are against it." Yet, they added, "this is only caution and not censure." [13]

This small victory failed to satisfy the abolitionists. William Southeby, seeing that the meeting rejected his

---

[12] Thomas, "Friends and Slavery," pp. 270–71; Sydney V. James, *A People Among Peoples* (Cambridge, Mass., 1963), pp. 118–19.

[13] John F. Watson, *Annals of Philadelphia and Pennsylvania in Olden Times* (2 vols.; Philadelphia, 1857), II, 263; *Brief Statement,* p. 12; Ezra Michener, *A Retrospect of Early Quakerism* (Philadelphia, 1860), p. 340.

plea—that the position of the Quaker colony was unique and that "More and better fruits may be reasonably expected from us"—defied the meeting. He published several antislavery papers without approval (a breach of Quaker discipline). When he was admonished, he apparently withdrew his pamphlets but later issued another missive on the subject. In 1718 he was threatened with disownment. Whether this sentence was actually carried out is not known, but in 1722, the year of his death, he sent another "application . . . about *Negroes*" to the legislature. This petition was quietly tabled.[14] The first advocate of legislative emancipation died knowing that Friends both in the meeting house and in the assembly had rejected his plea on behalf of the slave.

At the same time that Southeby was attempting to convince Philadelphia Quakers to take a resolute antislavery stand, New York Friends began to examine the morality of the institution. At the New York Quarterly Meeting of 1717 Horsman Mullenix expressed his concern about "byeing Negroes for slaves." The question was referred to the Yearly Meeting, where the matter was "tenderly spoken two," but was postponed. A year later, several Friends declared that they were "fully sattisfied" that slavery "was not Rite." Like the Philadelphia Quakers, the New Yorkers decided to consult London, observing that although slavery "greatly toucheth peoples intrust & manner of living in this part of the world yett a contiencious Scruple rests upon ye spirits of several friends." The members of the New York Meeting would gladly follow God's will, if only they could know what He demanded. Slavery was discussed again at the 1719 Yearly Meeting, and a year later the answer from London was read and approved. It probably was little different from the advice the English Friends had given to the Philadelphia Meeting—which dealt largely with the evils of the slave trade—and there the matter rested.[15]

The Quakers' concern about whether slavery was consist-

---

[14] "William Southeby," pp. 301–2; Drake, *Quakers and Slavery*, p. 29.

[15] John Cox, Jr., *Quakerism in the City of New York, 1657–1930* (New York, 1930), pp. 55–57. Since the copy of the reply from London and the records of the New York meeting are missing, the tenor of the letter from London can only be conjectured.

ent with Christianity was widespread. At the same time that Philadelphia and New York Friends questioned the morality of slavery, the Dartmouth (Massachusetts) Monthly Meeting asked the Rhode Island Quarterly "whether it be agreeable to Truth, for Friends to purchase slaves, and keep them [for] term of life." The Quarterly referred the question back to the monthly meetings. Nantucket and Dartmouth agreed that slavery was "inconsistent with Truth," but the other meetings only deprecated the slave trade. In response to a request for advice from the Quarterly Meeting, the New England Yearly merely noted the "weighty concern" resting "on the minds of Friends on account of importing and keeping slaves," but it took no action to implement these feelings.[16]

The conservatives of the Philadelphia Yearly Meeting who hoped that with the death of William Southeby the slavery issue would be forgotten soon realized that they had won only a brief respite. In 1729 Friends from Chester issued a new plea for a ban on the purchase of imported Negroes. The issue was referred to the quarterly and monthly meetings. The Chesterfield (New Jersey) Monthly Meeting thought that since "Friends both here and elsewhere have been in the practice" of buying slaves and in view of the fact that many members held differing opinions on the issue, "restricting Friends at this time . . . will not be convenient lest it create contention." Members who disagreed should confine their opposition to efforts to persuade their brethren. But this view no longer represented the opinion of a majority of Pennsylvania and New Jersey Quakers, and the 1730 Yearly decided "that Friends ought to be very cautious of making any such purchases for the future, it being disagreeable to the sense of this meeting." The Yearly urged subordinate meetings to admonish members who purchased slaves and to caution them "how they offend therein." [17] The Pennsylvania and New Jersey Friends had moved from discouraging the importation of slaves to cautioning members not to buy them.

[16] *Brief Statement*, p. 43.

[17] *Ibid.*, pp. 13–14; Thomas Woody, *Quaker Education in the Colony and State of New Jersey* (Philadelphia, 1923), p. 276.

Although the official Quaker position on slavery changed only very slowly (Quaker meetings required near unanimity for most important decisions, making radical action unlikely), individual members occasionally urged a forthright abolitionist view. The early Quaker abolitionists did not view slavery as a well-entrenched evil, for the system had been only recently defined and differentiated from indentured servitude. The Quaker abolitionists of the first decades of the eighteenth century were not so much concerned with the concept of enforced servitude (indentured or apprenticed whites were also not free) as with the idea that in the case of Negroes servitude was for life and was passed on to succeeding generations. These abolitionists attacked a relatively new labor system, and they made a great and noble effort to reverse the trend. That they were unable to convince their brethren of the evils of slavery was not because they did not try. They were at once too early and too late—too early to take advantage of the wave of humanitarianism that marked the latter part of the eighteenth century and too late to prevent the beginnings of a new labor system before self-interest was involved. Their failure meant that the second generation of American Quakers was to be more deeply involved in all aspects of slavery than any before or since.[18] Nonetheless, there were always a few conscientious Quakers to remind the Society of Friends that human slavery was not compatible with Christianity.

Several of these lonely dissidents, like William Southeby, attempted to persuade non-Quakers to give up slavery and submitted their views to the public in the form of pamphlets. John Hepburn of New Jersey, who had heard of a neighbor's slave whose despair had driven him to suicide, published an *American Defence of the Christian Golden Rule* in 1715. He denounced slavery as a "vile . . . contradiction to the Gospel of the blessed Messiah" and told his brethren that they risked damnation by continuing in this "Anti-christian" practice. Fifteen years later a Nantucket Quaker, Elihu Coleman, published *A Testimony Against that Anti-christian Practice of Making Slaves of Men*. Although self-interest had

---

[18] Drake, *Quakers and Slavery*, p. 34.

closed the eyes of most men to the evils of slavery, Coleman felt it his duty to print the truth on the question—slavery is a sin.[19]

In Philadelphia a prosperous Quaker merchant took up the cause. Ralph Sandiford had seen the evils of slavery in the West Indies, and when he arrived in Philadelphia in 1729 he was shocked by the public slave auctions that disgraced the Quaker capitol. Although he was threatened by the chief justice of the province, Sandiford wrote and circulated an antislavery tract, *A Brief Examination of the Practice of the Times.* Observing that God had granted so much to Americans, he asked "shall we go to Africa for Bread, and lay the burden . . . [of] our Bodily Support on their Shoulders? Is this Living by the Gospel?" Slavery was an "Eternal stinking Iniquity" that hindered the progress of the Gospel among the heathens. Like Southeby, Sandiford argued that Friends at least should have served as an example and "been a burning and shining light to these poor Heathen, and a Precedent to the Nations." Instead, "both Elders and Ministers . . . were cloathed" with the sin of slavery. He asked those who protested that their slaves were well-treated how they knew "what Barbarous Hands" these slaves might later fall into. To those who said they could not live without their slaves' labor, he said "it were better to lose that Life, that we may find a Life in Righteousness." He closed his essay by observing with pleasure the steps taken by the Pennsylvania Assembly to limit the slave trade, but he was saddened by the thought that he could not publish his treatise with official Quaker approval. The Philadelphia Friends were far from ready to endorse his radical views.[20]

The most colorful of these lonely abolitionists was Benjamin Lay. His physical appearance alone was startling—he was

[19] John Hepburn, *The American Defence of the Christian Golden Rule, or an Essay to Prove the Unlawfulness of Making Slaves of Men* (n.p., 1715), reprinted in American Antiquarian Society, *Proceedings,* LIX (1949), 114; Drake, *Quakers and Slavery,* pp. 37–38.

[20] Roberts Vaux, *Memoirs of the Lives of Benjamin Lay and Ralph Sandiford* (Philadelphia, 1815), pp. 60–64; Ralph Sandiford, *A Brief Examination of the Practice of the Times . . .* ([Philadelphia], 1729), dedication, pp. 4–5, 7–9, 26–27, 64, 68, 71–72.

a dwarf and a hunchback. He exaggerated his natural liabilities by constantly standing in a twisted position, and he rarely trimmed his unruly white beard. Lay's way of life was odd, too. He retreated to a cave where with his diminutive wife he followed a strict vegetarian regimen and wore only homespun. Beyond his appearance, there was much to shock the well-fed, conservative Quakers of Philadelphia in the 1730's. Although not a Quaker (he had been one in England), he believed it his special mission to convert the Society of Friends from slaveholding. He constantly argued with all who would listen, telling them that slavery was a sin and should be renounced. When more and more people refused to hear him out, he adopted techniques for dramatizing the evils of slavery that were not to be equaled until the days of P. T. Barnum. Once he appeared at the Yearly Meeting and harangued the gathered Friends, telling them that they knew that slavery was a sin and a direct contradiction of the Golden Rule. They continued to go against reason and humanity by keeping their Negroes in bondage; they might as well throw off the cloak as he did. Dropping his plain Quaker coat, he revealed his deformed body, draped in full military regalia, complete with sword. After thus vividly demonstrating that the gentle, pacific Quaker doctrines were mere cloaks for warlike actions, he told his startled audience that it would be as justifiable in the eyes of God to plunge a sword through the hearts of their Negroes. With that, he ran his sword through his Bible, puncturing a concealed bladder filled with a red liquid, and generously splattering those nearest him with the symbolic blood of their slaves.[21] On another occasion he stood in the snow outside a Quaker meeting with his right leg and foot naked. As Friends passed him to enter the meeting, they warned him that he was risking his health. This gave him his opening: "Ah, you pretend compassion for me, but you do not feel for the poor slaves in your fields, who go all winter half clad." Another time Lay kidnapped a neighbor's son, so that at the height of the farmer's frantic search Lay could tell him that his son was safe, but now perhaps he could understand the sorrow the

---

[21] Vaux, *Lay and Sandiford*, pp. 13–26.

farmer had brought upon the parents of the Negro girl he held as a slave.[22]

In 1737 Lay gathered all his antislavery notes, took them to Benjamin Franklin, and asked him to print them. Franklin agreed but said that he did not know how to arrange this mass of material. Lay told him to start and stop where he liked. The result was a book with a formidable title: *All Slave-Keepers That Keep the Innocent in Bondage, Apostates Pretending to Lay Claim to the Pure & Holy Christian Religion.* . . . In it Lay told the Quakers that he could see no worse stumbling blocks erected by the devil "than our ministers and elders keeping slaves," and that they, "by straining and perverting the Holy Scriptures, preach more to hell than ever they will bring to heaven by their feigned humility and hypocrisy." Was it not intolerable, he asked, "that three or four men that has the mark of the beast, . . . slavekeepers, upon them . . . should have the whole rule of discipline, and govern contrary to all justice and equity?" To the horror of the respectable Quakers, these words followed a preface in which Lay claimed: "These things following are so far from offending my true and tender Friends, called *Quakers*, who love truth more than all, that it is by their request and desire made publick; for . . . I love them . . . and covet their sweet Unity." Far from granting "sweet Unity," the Yearly Meeting publicly denounced Lay and his book.[23]

Lay was not to be silenced. He attended various churches and exhorted non-Quakers as well as Friends. He entered one church in sack cloth and interrupted the service to address the congregation: "I do not approve of all the minister has said, but I did not come here to find fault with the preaching; I came to cry aloud against your practice of slaveholding." Often, he was forcibly ejected, yet he persisted in his personal crusade against slavery.[24]

While Lay continued his lonely fight, an ally appeared on

[22] *Ibid.*, pp. 27–29.

[23] Drake, *Quakers and Slavery*, pp. 43–44, 46; Benjamin Lay, *All Slave Keepers That Keep the Innocent in Bondage, Apostates . . .* (Philadelphia, 1737), preface; *American Weekly Mercury*, October, 19–26, 1738 in *Archives of the State of New Jersey*, 1st ser., XI, 550–51.

[24] Vaux, *Lay and Sandiford*, p. 34.

the scene, a man as saintly as Lay was irascible. In 1743 John Woolman, a twenty-three-year-old Quaker of Mount Holly, New Jersey, was asked by his employer to write a bill of sale for a Negro slave, a routine matter in a slave society. John Woolman, however, was no routine Quaker. The transaction made him "uneasie," but because his master directed it, and since the purchaser was a good Quaker, Woolman wrote the document. Yet, he later recalled, "at the Executing it I was so Afflicted in my mind, that I said before my Master and the friend, that I believed Slavekeeping to be a practice inconsistent with the Christian Religion." Although this declaration abated his anxieties, he concluded that he should have refused to draw up the instrument for the sale of a human being and the next time he was asked to perform this service, he refused.[25]

Three years later Woolman made a trip to the South and became further convinced of the evils of slavery. He tried to show slaveowners the inconsistency of the practice that appeared to him "as a dark gloominess hanging over the Land," with future consequences that "will be grievous to posterity." His impressions of the horrors of slavery induced him to use for the cause of freedom that pen he had denied to slaveholders. Woolman did not submit his *Considerations on the Keeping of Negroes* to the Quaker meeting for approval until eight years after he wrote it, but in 1754 the Society of Friends not only approved the work, but published it and gave it a wide distribution through the network of Quaker meetings.[26]

"When we remember that all Nations are of one Blood," Woolman wrote, "it seems to raise an Idea of a general Brotherhood." On the other hand, if we think only of differences and distinctions, we are "apt to be filled with Fond Notions of Superiority," and this leads to erroneous conduct. "To consider Mankind otherwise than Brethren, to think Favours are peculiar to one Nation . . . plainly supposes a Darkness in the Understanding: For . . . God's love is universal." Furthermore, "to conclude a People . . . worse

[25] Amelia M. Gummere (ed.), *The Journals and Essays of John Woolman* (Philadelphia, 1922), pp. 161–62.

[26] *Ibid.*, pp. 167, 173; Drake, *Quakers and Slavery*, p. 56.

by Nature than others . . . will excite a Behaviour toward them unbecoming the Excellence of true Religion." By denying the importance of the distinctions between white and black and emphasizing the common denominator—humanity—Woolman struck squarely at the root of slavery. Although Negroes were obviously not at the same educational and cultural level as their masters, Woolman cogently argued that this was the result of slavery, not of any innate inferiority in the darker race. God has treated us well, he pointedly reminded the colonists, but

> If we do not consider these Things aright . . . [and] through a stupid Indolence, conceive Views of Interest, separate from the general Good of the great Brotherhood, and . . . treat our Inferiors with Rigour, to increase our Wealth . . . what then shall we do when God riseth up, . . . what shall we Answer him? [27]

In the period between the writing and the publication of his tract, Woolman continued to urge individual Quakers to give up slavery. He was consistent in his refusal to write bills of sale or wills involving slave property, which was a real sacrifice for a man who earned his living by drafting legal documents. His efforts resulted in several manumissions; after hearing Woolman explain why he could not write a will that treated men as property, masters sometimes manumitted their Negroes. Yet the majority of Quakers remained unconvinced that slavery was wrong, and Woolman's refusal "to do writings relative to keeping slaves" was "a means of sundry small tryals" to him.[28]

THE CRISIS OF THE 1750's

At the same time that Woolman was preaching his message of universal brotherhood, the Society of Friends was being shaken by a severe crisis. Like other religious groups, the Quakers were sensitive to currents generated by the Great Awakening and were demanding a return to the purity of their faith, to the simplicity of speech, clothes, and way of

[27] John Woolman, *Some Considerations on the Keeping of Negroes* (Philadelphia, 1754) , pp. 2–3, 6–8, 19–20.
[28] Gummere, *Woolman Journals*, pp. 174–75, 179–80.

living of the early Quakers. Political events exacerbated the crisis. Ever since the beginning of William Penn's holy experiment, Quakers had governed Pennsylvania. But with the beginning of the French and Indian War and a series of Indian raids on frontier settlements, the Quaker leadership faced a serious challenge. In view of their pacifist principles, the Friends in the assembly could not vote the funds necessary to protect the frontiersmen, and the crown joined the non-Quaker settlers of the frontier in applying pressure on the Quaker-dominated legislature, putting the governing group of Friends in an impossible situation. After much soul-searching and on the advice of English Quakers, the Friends decided they should abandon their role in government. This crisis, which marked the end of the holy experiment of a Quaker colony, forced the Society of Friends to undertake a rigorous self-examination. Why had God brought this terrible warfare to the peace-loving Quakers? Where had they erred? John Woolman and his friend, Anthony Benezet, had a ready answer: the sin of slavery. The Philadelphia Quakers, freed from the responsibilities of government and abandoning the political world of compromise and concession, turned from the realm of the possible to the realm of the ideal. They renewed their dedication to following the dictates of the inner light and turned their energies to reform. Again Woolman and Benezet pointed the direction: abolition.[29]

After the 1730 Yearly Meeting, when the purchase of imported slaves was forbidden for Quakers, the Yearly had done little but repeat this advice periodically. Despite the pleadings of Sandiford and the antics of Lay, it was not until the crisis brought on by the outbreak of war in the 1750's that the antislavery cause was again to make significant progress among the Quakers of New Jersey and Pennsylvania. Now, however, Woolman was successful where others had failed. In 1753 the Yearly Meeting took up the subject of slavery in an epistle to Friends in Virginia. The next year, the Philadelphia Yearly sent a strong statement (written by

[29] James, *A People Among Peoples*, p. 137; Drake, *Quakers and Slavery*, p. 55–56. For a penetrating analysis of the effects of the crisis of the 1750's on the Quakers, see James, *A People Among Peoples, passim.*

Woolman) attacking slavery to its own subordinate meetings.[30]

The 1754 epistle noted with sorrow that although the Yearly had frequently opposed the importation of Negroes and had urged Quakers to avoid "promoting the bondage of such unhappy people," still the number of slaves "is of late increased among us." Therefore, "we have thought proper to make our advice and judgment more publick, that none may plead ignorance of our principles." The epistle argued, as had virtually all of the early abolitionists, that slavery was inconsistent with religion: "To live in ease and plenty by the toil of those whom violence and cruelty have put in our power, is neither consistent with Christianity nor common justice, and we have good reason to believe draws down the displeasure of Heaven." Those who owned slaves should treat them well and "train them up, [so] that if you should come to behold their unhappy situation in the same light with . . . many of your brethren . . . and should think it your duty to set them free, they may be more capable of making a proper use of their liberty." The Yearly Meeting asked its slaveholding members "seriously to weigh the cause of detaining them in bondage." If they kept their Negroes in slavery for "private gain, or any other motive than their good, it is much to be feared that the love of God . . . is not the prevailing principle in you." [31] Here at last was a forthright condemnation of the principle of slavery. Slavery should be judged in the light of the slave's interest, not the master's, and if a slave was not prepared to make good use of his freedom, it was the master's duty to prepare him for liberty.

The slow evolution of Quaker thought on the justice of slavery aroused widespread opposition among slaveholding Friends. At the 1758 meeting of the Yearly the issue came to a head. During the previous summer several Philadelphia Quakers had purchased slaves in contravention of the new policy. Now they sought to persuade the meeting to reverse

[30] Drake, *Quakers and Slavery*, pp. 42, 56; *Brief Statement*, p. 15.
[31] *An Epistle of Caution and Advice, Concerning the Buying and Keeping of Slaves* (Philadelphia, 1754), reprinted in George S. Brookes, *Friend Anthony Benezet* (Philadelphia, 1937), pp. 475–77.

EARLY ABOLITIONISTS

74

its stand on slavery and justify their conduct. Antislavery
Quakers not only succeeded in defeating this move, they took
the offensive and tried to strengthen the antislavery position
of the society. A spirited debate ensued. Although no one
openly justified slavery, several members urged a cautious
policy; the times were not ripe for further action and if the
meeting waited, perhaps the Lord would show a way out of a
difficult situation that involved the interests of so many
members. Woolman's reply demolished this argument. He
reminded his opponents that Quakers should follow "the
Mind of Truth," regardless of material interests. The cries of
the oppressed slaves had been heard by God and "he hath
opened our understandings." If, despite this holy mandate,
Quakers still hesitated because of the outward interests of
some members, waiting for "some extraordinary means to
bring about their freedom, it may be that *by Terrible things
in Righteousness* God . . . [will] answer us in this matter." [32]

Woolman's arguments, firmly backed by the benevolent
Anthony Benezet, won over the meeting. In the background,
a series of events aided the abolitionists. English Quakers had
just issued a stinging indictment of the slave trade, and the
Pennsylvania Quakers' withdrawal from politics was now
nearly complete. [33] In addition, the depredations of war
deeply impressed the Friends with the terror of God's wrath.
Under these circumstances, the many hours spent by Woolman in quietly convincing individual Quakers of the sin of
slavery finally bore fruit.

The new policy statement that Woolman and Benezet
convinced the 1758 Yearly to adopt after "prolonged discussion" marked an unprecedented victory for the abolitionists.
It reported "an unanimous concern . . . to put a stop to the
increase of the practice of importing, buying, selling, or keeping slaves for term of life." Quakers now condemned not only
the foreign and domestic slave trade, but slavery itself; they
had finally struck at the very heart of the system. The report
issued by the meeting reflected the situation faced by the
colonies "which, by the permission of Divine Providence,
have been visited with the desolating calamities of war and

[32] Gummere, *Woolman Journals*, pp. 215–17.
[33] Drake, *Quakers and Slavery*, p. 60.

bloodshed, so that many of our fellow-subjects are now suffering in captivity." To a people who believed that God manifested his displeasure by bringing war and disaster, current events presented a powerful argument for reform. The Yearly Meeting urged its members to "steadily observe the injunction of our Lord . . . 'To do unto others, as we would they should do unto us'; which it now appears to this meeting, would induce such Friends who have any slaves, to set them at liberty." The majority of New Jersey and Pennsylvania Friends had finally accepted the arguments of the Germantown Quakers that slavery was incompatible with the Golden Rule. The meeting warned that if any members ignored "the sense and judgment of this meeting, now given against every branch of this practice" and continued "to vindicate it, and be concerned in importing, selling or purchasing slaves," then they would be excluded from all positions of responsibility within the Society of Friends. Quakers had at last accepted the view of Benjamin Lay; no longer would pro-slavery Friends be able to control the policy of the society. Lay was on his deathbed when he heard that the 1758 meeting had finally taken the bold action against slavery that he had so long advocated: "I can now die in peace." [34]

Although the 1758 statement claimed unanimity, it would have been too much to expect complete agreement on this radical departure. Woolman was more candid in his *Journal*. He recalled that "many Friends said that they believed liberty was the Negroes right, to which at length no opposition was made *publickly*." Men who had owned slaves for years would not readily admit that they had committed a sin. The task that now confronted antislavery Quakers was the long process of convincing these individual slaveholding Quakers of the righteousness of the new policy. Joshua Evans, a pious New Jersey Quaker, was one of those who spread the antislavery philosophy. He visited slaveowners in his neighborhood but noted that "this labour at that time, went hard with some who held slaves, and who thought it would cause uneasiness between them and their black

[34] The text of the 1758 statement on slavery is printed in *Brief Statement*, pp. 21–23; Vaux, *Lay and Sandiford*, p. 51.

servants; and so would scarcely permit us to perform the visit." To avoid the charge that his visit might lead to a slave rebellion, Evans decided "first to sit down in silence with the whole family, and not to let our communication give the blacks any knowledge of our business." Later, he would speak to the master alone and try to persuade him to emancipate his slaves. Evans recalled that he "had never felt a greater reward than in pleading the cause of these poor, injured, captive people." [35]

Those who persisted in violating the rules by purchasing Negroes were now subjected to discipline. In 1759 a member of the Buckingham (Pennsylvania) Monthly Meeting purchased several slaves. Following the usual Quaker procedure, the meeting appointed a committee to talk with him. Evidently it was a difficult case; a report was not made until 1762. After the report was read, the offender was brought before the meeting and "after much weighty advice," it was "left for him . . . to consider whether he cannot find freedom to bring up such negroes as are young in useful learning . . . and at a proper age, if they desire it, to set them free." If he refused, he could not "have the unity of Friends." [36]

The ban on the sale of slaves was sometimes difficult to adhere to since it denied the Quaker master the usual means of ridding himself of a recalcitrant slave. In 1770 the Gwynedd (Pennsylvania) Meeting reported that "Jonathan Robeson acknowledges selling a negro woman, who was very troublesome in his family. . . . He never intends to do the like again." [37] Apparently the Welsh Quakers of Gwynedd were willing to let a promise of future rectitude wipe out a past sin.

Pennsylvania and New Jersey Quaker abolitionists, having won a major victory at the 1758 Yearly Meeting, worked

[35] Gummere, *Woolman Journals,* p. 217 (my italics); "Joshua Evans's Journal," *Friends' Miscellany,* X (1837), 17–18.

[36] Thomas Woody, *Early Quaker Education in Pennsylvania* (New York, 1927), pp. 238–39.

[37] Howard M. Jenkins, *Historical Collections Relating to Gwynedd . . . .* (2d ed.; Philadelphia, 1897), p. 394.

patiently to gain compliance with the new rule—a difficult task since there were so many obstacles to manumission. Slaveowning among Quakers was widespread; Isaac Jackson, a member of a committee to visit slaveholders, reported that in one year he had visited the masters of over 1,100 slaves, all members of a quarterly meeting near Philadelphia. Furthermore, the law still required masters to post a large bond to secure the community in case the freed Negroes should become paupers. At the 1764 Yearly Meeting the committee on slavery expressed its concern that despite the 1758 statement many slaveowners continued to hold positions of leadership in the society. Woolman, who had fought so hard for the new policy, nonetheless "felt a Tenderness" for the offenders. He realized that the requirement that masters post bonds imposed a great hardship on many by obliging well-intentioned members not only to surrender their investment in slaves, but to accept a financial responsibility that made it "Impracticable for them to set their slaves free without changing their own way of life." [38]

Within the individual monthly meetings committees continued to "labor with" slaveowning Friends. Especially difficult cases were referred to the Yearly and were carefully followed by the abolitionists. Samuel Allinson, a New Jersey Quaker, asked a Friend what had been done about "the two negro cases which came before the last Y[early] M[eeting] & seemed so much to divide you." He offered to come and help solve the problem if "it would not be thought officious in a young man to urge his elder brethren to works of justice, peace & love." [39] The abolitionists realized that they could expect no further antislavery action by the Yearly until more members accepted the 1758 statement that slavery was inconsistent with Christianity. They devoted a great deal of time and effort to the slow process of persuading others to give up their property in slaves and to renounce a labor system that, until recently, few had criticized.

[38] Thomas, "Friends and Slavery," p. 275; Gummere, *Woolman Journals,* p. 268.

[39] Samuel Allinson to Richard Hartshorne, December 26, 1772 (Allinson Letters, MS copies in the Rutgers University Library, Rutgers, N.J.).

QUAKERS FREE THEIR SLAVES

New Jersey and Pennsylvania Quakers were not alone in their increasing concern with the sin of slavery. In 1758 English Friends had denounced the slave trade and in 1760 New England Quakers adopted this indictment as part of their discipline. They also queried their subordinate meetings: "Are Friends clear of importing negroes, or buying them when imported; and do they use those well, where they are possessed?" Nine years later members of Rhode Island Quarterly were troubled by the query's tacit approval of slaveowning. They asked the Yearly if the phrase " 'and use them well' . . . ought not to be either amended, or obliterated." The question was referred to a special committee that favored the proposal but suggested that before any alterations were made, a large committee should visit members who owned slaves to persuade them voluntarily to manumit their Negroes. The meeting adopted this plan.[40]

At the next session, the Yearly revised the query. In addition to inquiring if members adhered to the ban on the slave trade, the New England Meeting now asked monthly meetings whether their members treated well those Negroes who were not "in circumstances . . . to be set at liberty" and whether they had freed all those "that are of age, capacity, and ability suitable for freedom." [41]

The members appointed in 1769 to "labour with" slaveholders reported in 1771 that "Some Friends manifested a disposition to set such at liberty as were suitable;" others were unwilling to free their slaves, but promised to consider the matter; and "a few others manifested a disposition to keep them in continued bondage." By the following year, a few New England Quakers had freed their slaves but others were "so reluctant . . . that they *have been disowned* for not complying with the advice of this meeting." In 1773 the New England Quakers took the final step; they agreed that members should free all their Negroes, regardless of age or capacity, so that the society could boast "we do no more claim

[40] *Brief Statement*, pp. 43–45; Thomas, "Friends and Slavery," p. 279.
[41] *Brief Statement*, pp. 45–46.

property in the human race." New England Friends had given their unqualified support to emancipation; and nine years later, after expending a great deal of effort persuading members of the justice of the policy and disowning those who refused to comply, the Yearly could report that "we know not but all the members of this meeting are clear . . . of holding or dealing with mankind as slaves." In 1783 New England Quakers went even further and initiated a policy of compensating their former slaves for their past services.[42]

In Pennsylvania and New Jersey the patient efforts of the abolitionists succeeded, despite the formidable difficulties, in persuading many Quakers to free their slaves, and in 1774, a year after the New England Meeting had adopted a policy of complete emancipation, antislavery Friends were ready to ask the Philadelphia Yearly Meeting to revise its restrictions on slavery. The Yearly responded by appointing a large committee to hear all members who wished to speak on the subject, and then it issued a new policy statement. The meeting hesitated to take the ultimate step and expel all slaveowners, realizing that many Quakers still owned slaves and being "apprehensive that a Christian duty has not been so fully discharged to them as their various circumstances appear to require." Therefore the subordinate meetings were directed to engage "in a speedy and close labour with such members; and where it shall appear that any, from views of temporal gain, cannot be prevailed with to release from captivity such slaves as shall be found suitable for liberty," their cases were to be brought before the next session of the Yearly. Friends "honestly and religiously concerned for their own relief, and the essential benefit of the negro" were to receive the help of their monthly meetings. Finally, the Yearly told its members to instruct their young Negroes to prepare them for freedom.[43] Slaveholding members, who had been told in 1758 that they could no longer serve in responsible positions in the society, were now warned that they were jeopardizing their membership by refusing to free their Negroes.

The 1775 Yearly Meeting was pleased to hear reports that

[42] *Ibid.*, pp. 46–47.
[43] *Ibid.*, pp. 24–27.

"a considerable number" of Negroes had been emancipated, but results of efforts to persuade slaveowners to surrender their Negroes differed widely. Salem (New Jersey) Quarterly reported in 1775 that the task of securing manumissions was nearly completed and urged that the committees on slavery now devote their efforts to Negro education. On the other hand, Chesterfield (New Jersey) Monthly Meeting reported that several members were "disposed to set their Negroes free, but most . . . are discouraged from the apprehension of incumbrance which it might occasion to their outward estates and some few refuse at present." [44]

In the fall of the year of the Declaration of Independence, the Philadelphia Yearly Meeting took the final step. A committee appointed to review the reports from the quarterly meetings reported that many slaves had been manumitted in the preceding year. Yet, the committee noted with sorrow, many members, "notwithstanding the labour bestowed," still continued to hold their Negroes in slavery. "Under the calming influence of pure love," the meeting decided "with great unanimity" that the subordinate meetings should make one more effort to convert slaveholding members, but if "any members continue to reject the advice of their brethren" and refused to free all their slaves, the monthly meetings were directed to "testify their disunion with them." [45] Slaveowners were to be expelled.

New York Quakers moved much more slowly than their brethren in Philadelphia. Although by 1759 the New York Yearly Meeting had accepted the position that Friends should not participate in the slave trade, as late as 1760 a member confessed to having been active in the importation of Negroes. Not until 1762 did the New Yorkers adopt a policy of discouraging the purchase as well as the importation of slaves, a policy accepted by the Philadelphia Meeting thirty years earlier. Another violation of the rules barring Quaker participation in the slave trade was brought before

[44] *Ibid.*, p. 28; Marion M. T. Wright, *The Education of Negroes in New Jersey* (New York, 1941), p. 21; Woody, *Quaker Education in N.J.*, p. 276.

[45] *Brief Statement*, pp. 29–30.

the New York Meeting in 1767, when Thomas Burling admitted to having sent a Negro boy to the West Indies to pay a debt. The meeting accepted his apology that he "did condemn the practice of trading in Negroes, and was sorry for the breach of unity made thereby," but this case illustrated the pitfalls of partial action against slavery. It was almost impossible to hold Negroes in a slave society and not treat them as negotiable assets; even if the master treated them as human beings, his creditors viewed them as property. Although Dutchess County Quakers questioned the consistency of the policy on slavery in 1767, noting "the inconsiderable difference between buying slaves or keeping those in slavery we are already possessed of," the Yearly Meeting took no further action on the subject.[46]

By 1771, however, abolitionism was making progress among New York Friends. In that year the Yearly Meeting decided that members should not sell any of their slaves, and formed a committee to persuade slaveholding members to free "suitable" Negroes. Three years later the Yearly put teeth into its earlier pronouncements, ruling that Friends who bought or sold Negroes should be "treated with as disorderly persons." If the offenders refused to repent and set newly purchased slaves free, the monthly meetings were directed to "testify against them." In 1775 committees were appointed to visit slaveholders, and a year later those who refused to free their slaves were denied positions of trust within the society. The New York Yearly Meeting took the final step in 1777, asking the committees to visit recalcitrant slaveholders once more. If they still refused to free all their slaves, they were "to be testified against."[47] In a sudden wave of antislavery feeling, which coincided with the difficulties faced by the pacifist Quakers in the Revolutionary War, the New York Friends telescoped thirty years progress in a few years. They adopted a policy of disowning slaveholders only one year after the similar action of the Philadelphia Yearly Meeting.

[46] *Ibid.,* pp. 47–48; Cox, *Quakerism in N.Y.,* p. 58.
[47] *Brief Statement,* pp. 48–49, 50; Thomas, "Friends and Slavery," pp. 282–83.

COMPLETING THE TASK

For the Quaker abolitionists of New Jersey and Pennsylvania, the 1776 statement, like the radical departure of 1758, marked a goal rather than an accomplishment. It meant a redoubling of the efforts to persuade slaveholders to manumit their Negroes. The reports of the monthly meetings revealed a steady progress in this task. The Burlington (New Jersey) Meeting, which had reported early in 1776 "that a considerable number have manumitted their Negroes," noted only a year later that most of the slaves had been freed. In 1782 the monthly meeting's slavery committee reported that it had completed its work; "there is now none remaining amongst us in bondage." The Philadelphia Monthly Meeting was forced to disown seven recalcitrant members in 1778, but by 1783 none of its members owned slaves. Another Pennsylvania meeting also experienced difficulties. Bucks County Quarterly reported in 1777 that there were still some members who "persist in holding . . . slaves, notwithstanding the repeated care and labour of Friends." The Bucks County Quakers were unable to declare themselves free of slaveholding until 1799.[48]

Progress in some New Jersey meetings was exceedingly slow. As late at 1784 the Upper Springfield Monthly Meeting reported some recent violations of the rules on slavery. Ten years later the meeting reported that there was still one minor held in slavery by a member. In 1803 the Rahway and Plainfield Monthly Meeting confessed that one of its members still owned a slave and that another had sold a Negro for a limited period of service.[49]

Emancipation proceeded at varying paces in different areas. In New York and New Jersey, where there were more slaves and slavery was more intimately woven into the texture of daily life, progress was slower than in New England and Pennsylvania. In Pennsylvania Quakers were a

[48] Woody, *Quaker Education in N.J.,* pp. 274–75; *Brief Statement,* pp. 31, 32–33, 34.

[49] Woody, *Quaker Education in Pa.,* pp. 251–52; Woody, *Quaker Education in N.J.,* pp. 277, 281.

large and powerful sect and could more readily influence the attitude of the whole colony toward slavery, but in New York and New Jersey, members of the society were part of a larger community that accepted the legitimacy of slavery. Within meetings belonging to the same Yearly, the progress of emancipation also varied. In some monthly meetings the presence of one or two ardently abolitionist members undoubtedly did much to speed abolition, whereas other meetings, submitting only to the pressure of the distant Yearly, moved more slowly. Even within the lagging meetings, however, usually only one or two stubborn cases prevented the completion of the task.

Despite the few continued violations of the slavery rules in New Jersey, virtually all members of the Philadelphia Yearly had freed their slaves by 1783 and, furthermore, had agreed to give their former slaves a just compensation for their years of involuntary servitude. When New York Friends announced in 1787 that they had no more slaveholding members, northern Quakers had achieved the unique position of being the only major group that refused on grounds of conscience to hold slaves. They had achieved this goal as the result of a long struggle on the part of the abolitionists within the society. The Quaker abolitionists, having won their cause within the society, did not rest on their laurels. They now sought to make abolition universal. In 1779 the Philadelphia Yearly Meeting noted that "a tender Christian sympathy [for the slaves] appears to be awakening in the minds of many who are not in religious profession with us." [50] This feeling was cultivated and fostered to a great degree by members of the Society of Friends.

[50] Drake, *Quakers and Slavery,* pp. 79–80; *Brief Statement,* p. 38.

opposition to slavery on the eve of the Revolution

Quaker antislavery leaders realized at an early date that convincing members of the Society of Friends to renounce slavery was not enough; to wage effective war against this terrible sin they would have to win the support of thousands of non-Quakers. Accordingly, while abolitionists were arguing in their yearly meetings for action against slave-holding members, they also carried their views to the world outside the meeting house. They tried to convince all slave-holders to free their Negroes and urged colonial legislatures to take steps to discourage slavery. Foremost in this attempt to make abolition universal was the Philadelphia Quaker school master, Anthony Benezet.

BENEZET'S CAMPAIGN TO END THE SLAVE TRADE

Benezet, a leader in the struggle to convert Philadelphia Quakers to abolition, became the greatest propagandist of the early antislavery movement. Beginning in 1759 he published a series of pamphlets dramatically exposing the evils of the slave trade. Benezet claimed that nothing could be more inconsistent with Christianity nor "stained with Deeper Dye of Injustice, Cruelty, and Oppression" than the slave trade. Striking a chord that was to become increasingly popular in antislavery polemics, he pointed out that the participation of a Christian nation in that cruel trade might be the cause of the calamities that had befallen the American colonies. "Evils do not arise out of dust, nor does the Almighty willingly afflict the children of men." The slave trade was not only a violation of the great principles of religion and humanity, it was dangerous since it brought potential enemies into the colonies. Slavery corrupted society and led to idleness and vice among the whites.[1]

Benezet's most significant contributions to the growing body of antislavery literature were his detailed descriptions of the unparalleled horrors of the slave trade. Buttressing his arguments with extensive quotations from travelers and participants in the trade, Benezet destroyed all the remaining illusions of the benevolent nature of the African trade. The slave trader did not rescue his human merchandise from a life of poverty in Africa; Africa was a fertile continent with civilized natives who wanted only to be left in peace in their homeland. The victims of the slave trade were not, as some pro-slavery writers had argued, prisoners of war who would have been executed by their captors if they had not been rescued by the slave traders. On the contrary, the captains of slave ships working in collaboration with a few depraved chiefs instigated African wars. The survivors of these wars were put on board the hellish slave ships, where they were subjected to inhuman treatment. Many Negroes died on the long voyage to America, and those who survived suffered additional cruelties and hard labor in the plantation colonies.[2]

Condemning the slave trade was not enough. Benezet knew that men who readily agreed that the slave trade was evil and who would never participate in it nonetheless continued to hold slaves "for the Sake of the Profit arising from their Labour." This was highly inconsistent; title to the services of any Negro was ultimately no better than a certificate that the slave (or his ancestors) had been stolen from Africa. The slaveowner shared the guilt of the slave trader. Therefore, masters should free their Negroes, not only as an

[1] [Anthony Benezet], *Observations on the Inslaving, Importing and Purchasing of Negroes* (Germantown, Pa., 1759), pp. 2, 3, 7.

[2] [Anthony Benezet], *A Short Account of that Part of Africa, Inhabited by the Negroes* (Philadelphia, 1762), *passim;* Anthony Benezet, *Some Historical Account of Guinea* (Philadelphia, 1771), *passim.*

act of justice to individual slaves but to repay "a Debt due to them, . . . or their Ancestors," and as the best means "to avert the Judgments of GOD" for having "defiled themselves with this iniquitous Traffick." [3]

Benezet realized that emancipation would create difficulties, but he did not think that they were insuperable. As a first step to abolition the supply of slaves would have to be cut off by ending the slave trade. Those Negroes who were held as slaves should be freed when their labor had paid for their purchase price. The courts could determine how long individual Negroes should be required to serve, extending the servitude of any Negro who demonstrably neglected his duties. Benezet could understand the fears of the opponents of abolition—fears that freed Negroes would not work but would become a vice-ridden element in the population and a threat to the whites. To overcome these dangers, he suggested that newly freed Negroes be closely supervised for a number of years and that their children be educated to prepare them to become useful members of the community. Anticipating the economic and social problems of emancipation, Benezet proposed that wherever land was available, small tracts should be set aside for the freedmen and that they should be required to cultivate and live on these lands unless they were hired out to whites. "Thus both Planters and Tradesmen would be plentifully supplied with chearful and willing-minded Labourers; much vacant Land would be cultivated; [and] the Produce of the Country greatly encreased." Abolition would benefit white workers, who were often reduced to poverty by the competition of slave labor, and would encourage white immigration.[4] Benezet's plan for abolition was remarkably perspicacious in dealing with both the immediate and long-range problems of the Negro.

Benezet concentrated on getting the first part of his abolition plan adopted, for without ending the slave trade little progress could be made. To further this aim, Benezet not only published his antislavery pamphlets, but he was a tireless correspondent, constantly seeking recruits for a vigorous campaign against the slave trade. He asked the Society for the

[3] Benezet, *Short Account,* pp. 27–28.
[4] Benezet, *Short Account,* 2d ed. (Philadelphia, 1762), 70–71.

Propagation of the Gospel to condemn the trade as "the greatest impediment to the promulgation of the Gospel of Jesus Christ." Although the society sympathized with Benezet's concern for the Negroes, it refused to condemn slavery as unlawful, "finding the contrary very plainly implied in the precepts given by the Apostles." Spreading the doctrine that slavery was unlawful would be inexpedient and dangerous, and the society urged Benezet "not to go further in publishing your Notions, but rather to retract them." [5]

Despite this rebuff, Benezet was not discouraged. Convinced that an effective campaign against the slave trade required English support, he bombarded English Quakers with copies of his pamphlets and urged other prominent Englishmen who might be sympathetic to his aims to join his efforts to wipe out the iniquitous traffic. He told the Friends that if they were convinced of the evils of the slave trade they should take immediate action. "Can we be innocent and yet [be] silent spectators of this mighty infringement of every humane and sacred right?" Antislavery men would have to do everything possible to bring the question before king and Parliament. "Will any thing short of this excuse us to God, . . . more especially as this evil is maintained under the sanction of laws made by our representatives in Parliament?" If Friends would take the lead in an effort to end the slave trade they would be joined by many non-Quakers. "Who knoweth if we are not intended for such a service as this? And what judgements may fall on us . . . when deliverance ariseth another way?" [6]

By 1772, as the revolutionary crisis deepened and the Rights of Man became the subject of increased study, Benezet noted a gradual change in the colonists' attitude towards slavery. His correspondents had told him that Massachusetts was considering a bill to end the slave trade. John Hunt, a prominent New Jersey Quaker who had recently toured the

[5] Benezet to the Society for the Propagation of the Gospel, April 26, 1767 in George S. Brookes, *Friend Anthony Benezet* (Philadelphia, 1937), p. 272; Society for the Propagation of the Gospel to Benezet, February 3, 1768, MS, New-York Historical Society.

[6] Benezet to John and Henry Gurney, January 10, 1772 in Brookes, *Benezet*, pp. 283–87.

southern colonies, reported that the people of Virginia and Maryland were "so convinced of the unexpediency, if not all, of the iniquity" of the slave trade, that ten or twenty thousand were willing to sign a petition for a prohibition of further importation of Negroes. Benezet reported this to Granville Sharp, leader of the English antislavery forces, and told the Englishman of his efforts to persuade English Quakers to petition Parliament. Sharp, who had just succeeded in obtaining a decision in the case of the slave Somerset, in which the court ruled that slavery was not legal in England, was enthusiastic about Benezet's plans to petition Parliament. He thought that a petition from the southern colonies would not only show that they were not "destitute of Christian and social principles," but "would probably lay the foundation for a total prohibition" of the slave trade. It would deprive the pro-slavery forces of one of their principal arguments—that the colonies could not survive without slave labor. Sharp, however, was conscious of the debates on colonial rights and the argument that Parliament had no right to legislate for the colonies. *"With respect to the toleration of slavery in the colonies,* I apprehend the British Parliament has no right to interfere."* Therefore he thought that the petitions to Parliament should deal with the slave trade in general and that petitions to the king should ask for a total prohibition of slavery and for approval of colonial laws prohibiting the importation of slaves. Aside from this tactical advice, Sharp was enthusiastic about Benezet's petition plans.[7]

Benezet's reply was considerably less enthusiastic. The Philadelphia Quaker conceded that the colonial assemblies could initiate their own laws to prevent the importation of Negroes, but he pointed out that these would undoubtedly be disallowed in England. As for getting southerners to sign petitions against the slave trade, Benezet thought that most of those who would sign would do it "principally, if not wholly, from motives of self-interest;" few could honestly sign a petition such as Sharp had suggested, complaining of

[7] Benezet to Sharp, May 14, 1772, "Copies of Letters to Granville Sharp, 1768–1773 . . . ," MSS, N.Y. Hist. Soc.; Sharp to Benezet, August 21, 1772 in Brookes, *Benezet,* 418–22.

"the iniquity of the *Slave Trade in general.*" Benezet reported that he had sent copies of Sharp's letter to southern Quakers and that he was planning to send them copies of two petitions, one to go to the king and the other to Parliament. "Nevertheless I am afraid to give thee too much expectation . . . from any place where *Slave keeping* has taken deep root." [8]

In the meantime Benezet was busy in Philadelphia. He persuaded two local newspapers to publish antislavery materials, and at his request Benjamin Rush, the prominent Philadelphia physician, published an attack on slavery. Furthermore, he brought a petition to the Pennsylvania Assembly, asking it to urge the king to prohibit the slave trade. The petition "was, freely, agreed to by all the Clergy, of every denomination, and other weighty members in Society." It encountered very little opposition and if there had been enough time, Benezet thought he could have gotten as many as ten thousand to sign. The assembly gave the petition a cordial reception but did not think it expedient to comply. Instead, the legislature increased the duty on slaves from ten to twenty pounds and made the new duty perpetual. Although this amounted to a tacit prohibition of the importation of slaves, Benezet was unimpressed. Few Negroes were brought into Pennsylvania; but what was needed was a strongly worded petition to Parliament that would end the importation of Negroes in all the colonies. Nonetheless, Benezet secured a promise that if the new duty was disallowed, the assembly would reconsider petitioning for a total end to the slave trade. [9]

In an effort to persuade other assemblies to petition for an end to the slave trade, Benezet sent copies of Sharp's letter, Rush's pamphlet, and antislave trade petitions to Quakers in New York and New Jersey. The New York Quakers

[8] Benezet to Sharp, November, 1772 in "Sharp Letters."

[9] Benezet to Sharp, February 18, 1773 in "Sharp Letters"; Benjamin Rush to Benjamin Franklin, May 1, 1773, in Lyman H. Butterfield (ed.), *Letters of Benjamin Rush* (Princeton, 1951), I, 79; *Votes and Proceedings of the House of Representatives of the Province of Pennsylvania* (6 vols.; Philadelphia, 1752–76), VI, 428, 429, 439, 441–47, 453.

approved the idea but pointed out that their assembly's session was nearly over. In 1773, however, the New York Assembly approved a £20 duty bill, but the governor and council refused to concur; the reason (according to Benezet) was the "pretence" that it would prove a hardship to West Indian planters who wanted to bring their slaves with them on visits to New York. Benezet predicted, however, that the discussions evoked by the vetoed bill, as well as news of recent slave insurrections in the West Indies, would "open the Eyes of the people to see the iniquity and dangers of any farther import of Slaves." [10]

In New Jersey the 1773–74 session of the legislature was deluged with petitions, mostly from the Quaker counties of West Jersey, "setting forth the Mischiefs arising from personal Slavery" and asking for changes in the slave code. Some of these petitions asked for a revision of manumission procedures. (The requirement that masters who wished to manumit their Negroes had to post high bonds was creating difficulties for Quakers who wanted to follow the advice of the Yearly Meeting.) Other petitions asked for restrictions on the importation of slaves. Faced with this unprecedented flood of petitions, the assembly was forced to suspend its rule requiring all petitions to be entered on its minutes. Two separate bills were brought before the house, one to increase the import duty on slaves and another "for the more equitable Manumission of Slaves." By the time the assembly finished amending the latter bill, however, it could no longer inspire enthusiasm among the friends of the Negro. What the bill granted with one hand, it took away with the other. It allowed masters to free healthy, twenty-one-year-old slaves, certified as being capable of self-support, but it required masters to pay a fee or post a bond before manumitting older slaves. The bill severely limited the rights of manumitted Negroes; they would be required to pay taxes and fulfill all

[10] Benezet to Sharp, February 18, March 29, 1773, in "Sharp Letters"; *Journal of the Votes and Proceedings of the General Assembly of the Colony of New-York* . . . , (Albany, 1820), 1773, 22, 23, 87–88; *Journal of the Legislative Council of the Colony of New-York* (2 vols.; Albany, 1861), II, 1891, 1892, 1910, 1912.

other duties of citizens, but they were specifically denied the right to vote. They could not serve as witnesses except against each other, and marriage with whites was forbidden. Free Negroes who ran into debt or who were sentenced to prison could be bound out as indentured servants. Despite these elaborate precautions to insure the community against the supposed dangers of free Negroes, two petitions from East Jersey begged the assembly to reject the bill. Unable to decide, the assembly merely referred both bills to the next session.[11]

Although antislavery men presented new petitions when the assembly reconvened, the opposition had had time to organize and was able to present an increasing number of petitions against the manumission bill. Once more the assembly postponed action, meanwhile quietly dropping the bill to increase the duty on imported slaves. When the assembly met in the fall of 1775, the Quakers renewed their efforts. A petition from the Quaker settlement of Chesterfield asked the assembly to free all of the Negroes in the colony. This petition was tabled. When the manumission bill was brought forward once more, antislavery men found that they were unable to muster even enough support to refer the bill to a committee. Representatives from East Jersey led the opposition while assemblymen from the Quaker counties of West Jersey supported the bill. The assembly then put the bill back on its seemingly endless road from session to session. But the colonial assembly never met again; following the recommendations of Congress, New Jersey established an independent government. Although the manumission bill was dutifully carried over to the first session of the new state

[11] *N.J. 22 Colonial Assembly 2*, pp. 19–20, 23–26, 29, 59, 60, 65, 68–70, 73, 79, 114, 123–25, 132, 155, 161–62, 201. The manumission bill is printed on pp. 211–15. (Whenever sessional journals or laws of a state or colonial legislature are cited the following abbreviated form has been used: *N.J. 17 Assembly 2,* or *N.J. 17 Laws 2,* to indicate the journals or laws of the seventeenth New Jersey Assembly, second session. When no session number is provided, the citation refers to the first session. Whenever reprinted or compiled editions have been used, a full citation has been supplied.)

legislature, it was soon lost in the turmoil of transition politics.[12]

In Pennsylvania several petitions for revision of that colony's manumission laws, presented in the spring of 1776, were also lost in the Revolutionary crisis. Furthermore, the high duty enacted by the 1773 assembly was disallowed by the Lords of Trade.[13] Benezet's plan to persuade the legislatures of the middle colonies to enlist in the campaign against the slave trade had come to naught. The antislavery agitation in the middle colonies had failed to induce a single colony to alter its laws on slavery, and the only effective limitation placed on the slave trade had been vetoed by the British.

ANTISLAVERY FEELING IN PENNSYLVANIA

Although there were few concrete results from the antislavery campaign, Quaker abolitionists could see a gradual awakening of public opinion to the evils of slavery. The times were propitious for reformers. Philadelphia, by now the second largest city in the British Empire, was a center of Enlightenment thought, and the intellectual currents of the age spread widely in the American colonies in the period after 1763. A reasoned inquiry into social problems and a firm belief in the possibility of human progress through the critical examination of well-established institutions led men to concern themselves with a host of reform movements aimed at helping the pauper, the prisoner, and the slave. The Enlightenment impetus for social reform was reinforced by the new humanitarianism that had been stimulated by the Great Awakening. In this heady atmosphere of reform and change Anthony Benezet could find a receptive audience.[14]

[12] *N.J. 22 Colonial Assembly 3*, pp. 8, 14, 22, 26, 30, 40, 46; *N.J. 22 Colonial Assembly 4* (2d sitting), pp. 7, 8, 13, 14, 26, 27; *N.J. 1 Assembly*, p. 16.

[13] *Pa. Votes*, VI, 696, 705, 724; William R. Riddell, "Pre-Revolutionary Pennsylvania and the Slave Trade," *Pennsylvania Magazine of History and Biography*, LII (1928), 18–19.

[14] Carl and Jessica Bridenbaugh, *Rebels and Gentlemen: Philadelphia in the Age of Franklin* (New York, 1962), pp. 225–62.

The 1768 commencement at the College of Philadelphia featured a "forensic Dispute" on the legality of slavery, and antislavery articles appeared in the public press with increasing frequency. "Anti-Slavetrader" noted the inconsistency of slavery with the new concern for the Rights of Man. He taunted slaveowners: "you who spurn at the thoughts, of paying the poor pittance of a glass, a paper, and paint tax, and cry aloud on *freedom and virtue,* how can you lift up your heads in the noble contest for Liberty, and be at home the greatest tyrants on earth!" A New Jersey Quaker, David Cooper, pointed out that keeping slaves was the equivalent of keeping stolen goods and that to deny Negro children their liberty at the age it was customarily granted to others was a violation of natural law. Cooper's anonymous pamphlet proved popular and a second edition was soon in print. "A Friend to the Oppressed" used the columns of a Philadelphia newspaper in 1772 to attack the argument that the probable abuse of their freedom by the Negroes militated against emancipation. The misbehavior of some Negroes he attributed not to their race but to their lack of education. Therefore, masters should teach their Negroes to read and write to prepare them for business and to allow them to read the Bible and history. Then, "they would devote their Leisure Hours in Search of useful Knowledge . . . [instead of conduct] destructive to their Morals." Educated young Negroes could safely be set free at twenty-one or twenty-five, and the legislature could provide for the maintenance of the few who, through accidents of life, would be unable to maintain themselves.[15]

A powerful voice was added to the antislavery ranks when the respected Benjamin Rush, heeding the suggestion of Anthony Benezet, wrote *An Address to the Inhabitants of the British Settlements in America, Upon Slave-Keeping.* Published in Philadelphia in 1773 at the height of the petition campaign in Pennsylvania, it was republished in New York and Boston that same year. Rush argued with those who

[15] *Pennsylvania Chronicle,* November 21, November 28, 1768; [David Cooper], *A Mite Cast into the Treasury* (Philadelphia, 1772) , pp. 9, 11, 13; [William J. Allinson], "Notices of David Cooper," *Friends' Review,* XV (1861–62) , 722; *Pennsylvania Gazette,* January 30, 1772.

believed that the Negro was innately inferior and therefore could legitimately be held as a slave. He maintained that the vices exhibited by the Negroes were not proof of their inferiority but, rather, of their unsuitability for slavery. To those who defended slavery as a method for Christianizing the Negroes, Rush replied that Christianity would never be spread by methods other than those used by Christ and his Apostles. "Slavery is an engine as little fitted for that purpose as Fire or the Sword." Rush recommended that young Negroes be educated and emancipated but he conceded that older Negroes, who had acquired the vices of slavery, would probably have to remain in slavery.[16]

Replying to Rush, Richard Nisbet suggested that it would be far better if antislavery writers confined their efforts to making improvements in the institution, rather than calling for total abolition. "Till self-interest ceases to have influence over the actions of men, proposals that strike at the very root of their temporal concerns will never be pursued." Having dealt with the practical aspects, Nisbet proceeded to prove the thesis of his title: *Slavery Not Forbidden by Scripture.*[17]

Rush's second edition of the *Address* refuted Nisbet's reading of the Bible as well as his belief that Negroes were inferior. Rush argued that even if Negroes were inferior, however, this gave no man a right to enslave them, just as no man had a right to defraud a less intelligent neighbor. Ultimately, the question involved the Rights of Man: "If domestic Slavery is agreeable to the Will and Laws of God, political Slavery is much more so." If the colonists wanted to take a stand against political slavery, they should also oppose the slavery of the Negroes.[18]

Increasingly, the antislavery writers relied on arguments based on an analogy between the rights of the colonists and the rights of the Negroes. Another New Jersey Quaker,

[16] [Benjamin Rush], *An Address to the Inhabitants of the British Settlements in America Upon Slave-Keeping* (Philadelphia, 1773), pp. 2–3, 15–17, 20–22.

[17] [Richard Nisbet], *Slavery Not Forbidden by Scripture* (Philadelphia, 1773), pp. 1–2.

[18] [Benjamin Rush], *A Vindication of the Address* . . . (Philadelphia, 1773), pp. 32–33, 49.

William Dillwyn, entered the discussion in 1773, arguing that although custom had justified the slave trade, this did not make it right. Just as some Englishmen might formerly have maintained that Parliament had a right to tax the colonies, this did not mean that the right existed in fact. Now, more than ever, it was important to take a correct position on the legitimacy of slavery. "In the present contest between Great Britain and her colonies, it seems particularly necessary on our parts to convince her, that our opposition to her claims is not merely from selfish motives . . . but from a disinterested generous love of liberty, founded on principle." If the colonists needed divine aid in their struggle, Dillwyn asked, how could they expect to receive it when they ignored God's Golden Rule? If the colonists argued that they needed slaves, so could the British argue that they needed American taxes. Therefore, "while we persist in this practice of enslaving the Africans our mouths ought to be entirely shut, as to any duties and taxes Great-Britain may see cause to lay upon us." [19]

Thomas Paine, whose writings became important weapons in the struggle for independence, applied to the institution of slavery the same telling arguments derived from the natural rights philosophy that he was to use later to destroy the bond between Great Britain and her colonies. Paine maintained that slavery was "contrary to the light of nature, to every principle of Justice and Humanity, and even good policy." Since the Negroes had done nothing to forfeit their liberty, they had "a natural, perfect right" to freedom and the government "should, in justice set them free, and punish those who hold them in slavery." Paine urged that after achieving independence Americans should express their gratitude by passing laws to stop the importation of Negroes, "soften the hard fate of those already here, and in time procure their freedom." [20]

Although antislavery writers were turning to arguments

[19] [William Dillwyn], *Brief Considerations on Slavery and the Expediency of its Abolition* (Burlington, N.J., 1773), pp. 6–9. The last sentence is quoted by Dillwyn from another pamphlet.

[20] *Pennsylvania Journal,* March 8, October 18, 1775, in Moncure D. Conway (ed.), *The Writings of Thomas Paine* (4 vols.; New York, 1894–99), I, 4, 7, 66.

drawn from the Revolutionary struggle, "Amintor" based his abolitionism on the Bible. He confessed that he did not know why God allowed the colonists to "lord it over the Negroes," but he was convinced that it was not because He was displeased with the darker race. After all, God's chosen people had been enslaved in Egypt and "From this state of slavery, the almighty delivered them in a marvelous manner; which consideration ought to soften our hearts to those, who are in bondage to us." Although American slavery might be milder than that endured by the Jews in Egypt, it allowed the worst of men to practice great cruelties with impunity under laws sanctioned by men who would never mistreat a slave.[21]

An anonymous Tory (probably Richard Wells) turned the arguments of the patriots against them. After quoting numerous Revolutionary resolutions, he asked Americans whether they could "reconcile the *exercise of* SLAVERY with our *professions of freedom*." Could the colonists expect the English to believe the sincerity of their love of liberty when the whole world knew that there were slaves in every colony? "In vain shall we contend for *liberty* . . . 'till this barbarous inhuman custom is driven from our borders." He challenged those who claimed "an exemption from the controul of Parliamentary power" to show by what right they held their slaves. If, as the patriots maintained, the colonists had all the rights of Englishmen, then, since a Negro was held to be free the instant he landed on English soil (this was an interpretation of the decision in Somerset's case), all slaves could claim they were free when they landed on American soil. "I contend, that by the laws of the English constitution, and by our *own declarations,* the instant a Negro sets his foot in America, he is as free as if he had landed in England." He challenged the Whigs: "Were the colonies as earnest for the preservation of liberty, upon its *true* and *genuine* principles, as they are opposed to the supremacy of an English Parliament, they would enter into a virtuous and *perpetual* resolve, neither to import, nor to purchase any slaves introduced amongst them after the meeting of the Congress." [22]

The First Continental Congress, meeting in Philadelphia

[21] *Pennsylvania Packet,* January 31, 1774.
[22] *Ibid.,* January 8, 1774.

in the fall of 1774, took up this challenge. The Continental Association adopted by the delegates required the cessation of all slave imports and authorized a boycott of merchants who refused to cooperate. Anthony Benezet, seeing a magnificent opportunity to strike a blow for liberty, had worked tirelessly to secure the adoption of this policy, relentlessly pursuing individual delegates to argue in support of the plan. Congressional approval of a ban on the slave trade clearly tied the fight against Negro slavery to the struggle against British tyranny in the manner that many antislavery writers had long been urging. In 1776, when Congress lifted the ban on most imports, it retained the antislave trade provisions of the association, emphasizing that the trade in Negroes should be discontinued for reasons that went beyond expediency.[23]

OPPOSITION TO SLAVERY IN MASSACHUSETTS

The Revolutionary crisis came to a head in Massachusetts several years before it reached its peak in the middle colonies. Accordingly, the remarkable applicability of the anguished cries against British tyranny to the case of the Negro slaves occupied the attention of New England writers at an early date. When James Otis eloquently defended the rights of the colonists, he spoke for Negroes as well as whites: "the colonists, black and white, born here, are free born British subjects, and entitled to all the essential civil rights of such." [24]

Nathaniel Appleton's *Considerations on Slavery* included many of the religious arguments used by the Quakers, but his most telling points were based on the Revolutionary struggle. "Oh! ye sons of liberty," he asked, "is your conduct consistent? Can you review our late struggles for liberty, and think of the slave-trade at the same time, and not blush?" What could the patriots have answered if Great Britain had "thrown this inconsistency in our faces?" The successful fight

[23] Arthur M. Schlesinger, *The Colonial Merchants and the American Revolution, 1763–1776* (New York, 1957), pp. 426, 428, 580, 608–9; Anthony Benezet to Samuel Allinson, October 23, 1774 (Allinson Letters, MS copies in the Rutgers University Library, Rutgers, N.J.).

[24] James Otis, *The Rights of the British Colonies Asserted and Proved* (Boston, 1765), p. 37.

against the Stamp Act would "ever be memorable for the glorious stand which America has made for her liberty," but how much more noble it would be if America, at the same time freed her slaves. This would "show all the world, that we are true sons of liberty" and would "for ever prevent any bad ministry harbouring a thought of making the least infringements upon our privileges; for the people that will forego so lucrative a trade, on such principles, must be noble, must be an unconquerable people." [25]

As in Pennsylvania, the deepening Revolutionary crisis brought an increasing number of pamphlets declaiming against the inconsistency of holding slaves while invoking the Rights of Man in the ideological struggle with England. John Allen, who published an attack on the infamous Boston Port Bill, conceded that the colonists deserved punishment (at the hands of God, not men) for their practice of slaveholding. Although Allen strongly condemned the British, he saved his scorn for American Whigs: "Blush ye pretended votaries for Freedom! ye trifling patriots! who are making a vain parade of being advocates of the liberties of mankind." At the same time that these "patriots" were "fasting, praying, non-importing, non-exporting, remonstrating, resolving, and pleading for a restoration of . . . charter rights," they continued to enslave their fellowmen. He asked the patriots to consider "what is a trifling three penny duty on tea in comparison to the inestimable blessing of liberty to one captive?" [26]

A leading antislavery writer, Deacon Benjamin Colman of Newbury, echoed Allen's sentiments. In the spirit of Puritan Jeremiads, he asked the colonists to search among themselves for the cause of their calamities. To Colman, the cause of God's anger was clearly slavery—a "God-provoking and wrath-procuring sin." [27]

James Swan's *Disuasion to Great Britain and the Colonies*

[25] Nathaniel Appleton, *Considerations on Slavery* (Boston, 1767), pp. 19–20.

[26] [John Allen], *The Watchman's Alarm to Lord N --- H* . . . (Salem, Mass., 1774), pp. 25, 27, 28.

[27] *Essex Journal*, July 20, 1774, in Joshua Coffin, *A Sketch of the History of Newbury, Newburyport, and West Newbury, from 1635 to 1845* (Boston, 1845), pp. 339–40.

From the Slave Trade was designed to appeal to the Bay colonists' veneration for their charter. He maintained that the charter guaranteed liberty to all inhabitants, "Black as well as White," and therefore that slavery was unconstitutional. Swan issued a second edition of his pamphlet at the request of a group of Boston Negroes who proposed to send a copy to each town. Swan hoped that this would persuade the towns to instruct their representatives in the General Court to abolish the slave trade.[28]

At an early date, several towns had begun to take action against the slave trade. In 1755 Salem told its deputy to ask the General Court to prohibit the importation of slaves. In 1766 and again in 1767 Boston instructed its representative to advocate the total abolition of slavery. Worcester followed suit in 1767, requiring its deputy to "use his influence to obtain a law to put an end to that unchristian and impolitic practice of making slaves of the human species." At the height of the antislave trade agitation in the North in 1773, Medford, Salem, Sandwich, and Leicester all instructed their delegates to take action against the slave trade; furthermore the latter two towns also proposed a bill to emancipate all Negro children when they became twenty-one.[29]

Reflecting the increasing opposition to slavery and responding to instructions from constituents, the General Court made several attempts to end slavery and the slave trade. In 1767 the lower house debated a bill "to prevent the *unwarrantable and unusual* Practice . . . of inslaving Mankind in this Province, and the importation of slaves." The bill's title reflected the argument of Massachusetts abolitionists that slavery had never been legal, and that what was

[28] James Swan, *A Disuasion to Great-Britain and the Colonies, from the Slave-Trade to Africa* (Boston, [1772]), pp. 18, 43; *ibid.* (revised ed.; Boston, 1773), p. ix.

[29] Joseph B. Felt, *Annals of Salem* (2d ed., 2 vols.; Salem, Mass., 1845, 1849), II, 416–17; Samuel G. Drake, *The History and Antiquities of Boston* . . . (Boston, 1856), pp. 728–29; William Z. Lincoln, *History of Worcester* . . . (Worcester, 1862), pp. 167–68; *Massachusetts Gazette*, June 4, 1767; George H. Moore, *Notes on the History of Slavery in Massachusetts* (New York, 1866), pp. 133–35; Frederick Freeman, *The History of Cape Cod* . . . (2 vols., Boston, 1858, 1862), II, 416–17; Emory Washburn, *Historical Sketches of the Town of Leicester* . . . (Boston, 1860), pp. 472–73.

needed was a law to prohibit an institution that had the status of accepted custom but had no legal sanction. The majority was unwilling to take this radical step and abolish slavery at once, and the bill could not muster sufficient support for a third reading. Instead, a substitute measure laying a duty on imported Negroes passed the house, only to be lost when the lower chamber refused to concur in the council's amendments. The legislature took no further action until 1771 when the court approved a bill to "prevent the Importation of Slaves from Africa." This time the bill failed because Governor Thomas Hutchinson refused his assent, claiming that the measure was contrary to his instructions and was unnecessary, in view of the mild nature of slavery in Massachusetts.[30]

In 1773, at the same time that the Quaker-inspired campaign against the slave trade reached its peak in the middle colonies, Massachusetts abolitionists made a new attempt to end slavery. Since Massachusetts Negroes possessed some civil rights, and since they were the aggrieved party, they themselves petitioned the General Court. Boston Negroes circulated a petition, calling upon the legislature to consider how their lives were "embittered with this most intolerable reflection, that, let their behavior be what it will, neither they nor their children . . . shall ever be able to do or enjoy anything—no, not even *life itself*." In another petition the Negroes tied their struggle for liberty to that of the colony against British tyranny. They pointed out that they expected "great things from men who have made such a noble stand against the designs of their *fellow-men* to enslave them."[31]

"A Lover of True Liberty" who supported the petition of the Negroes asked "those mighty sticklers for *Slavery*" whether the Negroes were not freeborn British subjects, "justly entitled . . . by the laws of God and Man, to inherit and possess every Privilege which we enjoy?" The Negro petition to the General Court should please "every Friend of Mankind," and "Great Success is expected from this Petition,

[30] Moore, *Slavery in Mass.*, pp. 126–28, 130–32.

[31] William C. Nell, *The Colored Patriots of the American Revolution* . . . (Boston, 1855), pp. 40–41; Massachusetts Negro Petition, April, 1773, Plimpton Collection, Columbia University.

since THOSE, who are Guardians of our Rights, are led and influenced by the true principles of Liberty." It would be disappointing indeed if the slaveholders in the legislature should subordinate their love of freedom to mercenary motives. Another abolitionist asked the legislators to remember "the Ideas you entertain of *Liberty,* and Protestations you daily make against Slavery; and then, . . . you must give your Voice to *freeing*" the slaves. Any other action would be base hypocrisy.[32] Massachusetts antislavery writers made it clear that the vote on slavery should be considered a touchstone to determine the General Court's sincerity in its pronouncements on liberty and the Rights of Man.

In June several Negroes petitioned for a land grant as well as for their liberty, but this request was postponed until the next session of the General Court. Meanwhile the Negroes actively lobbied in support of their proposal. When the house met again in January, 1774, the Negroes presented a new memorial, stressing how slavery made it impossible for them to live a religious life. Their masters had made marriage a mockery by separating husband and wife. "We cannot searve our God as we ought whilst in this situation[.] Nither can we reap an equal benefet from the laws of the Land which doth not justifi but condemns Slavery." They asked the court to grant them their "Natural right" to freedom and to emancipate their children at twenty-one. This petition, as well as the one carried over from the last session, was referred to a committee that merely reported another bill to prohibit the importation of slaves. Rapidly approved by both houses of the legislature, the bill failed to obtain the governor's signature. Essentially the same bill was repassed in June, but General Thomas Gage, who had just been appointed to deal with the rebellious colonists, was no more willing than his predecessor to give in to the General Court on this point.[33] As a result, the refusal of the British to

[32] *The Appendix: Or, Some Observations on the Expediency of the Petition of the Africans . . .* (Boston, 1773), pp. 4–6; *Massachusetts Spy,* January 28, 1773, in *ibid.*, pp. 13–15.

[33] Moore, *Slavery in Mass.,* pp. 135–39, 142–43; "Letters and Documents Relating to Slavery in Massachusetts," (*Collections of the Massachusetts Historical Society*), 5th ser., III, 433.

sanction restrictions on the slave trade became another grievance in the Revolutionary struggle.

At the same time that Massachusetts Negroes sought to end slavery by appealing to the legislature, they were using a more novel method for attaining their liberty—they were suing for their freedom in the courts of the colony. Since the Massachusetts courts were open to slaves, the Negroes were able to institute suits in which their masters, as defendants, were obliged to show by what right they held title to their slaves. As early as 1701, the slave of John Saffin (the author of the reply to Samuel Sewall's antislavery tract) sued for his freedom on the grounds that Saffin had promised to manumit him. The slave won his case in the lower courts but the decision was reversed on appeal. In the decades before the Revolution, there was a marked increase in freedom suits. John Adams in 1766 attended the trial of an action for trespass brought by a mulatto woman who claimed that she had been illegally kept in slavery. Adams noted that it was the first case of this type that he had attended, but he had heard that there had been many others. Two years later Adams himself argued in a freedom case and secured a judgment in favor of his client, the slaveowner.[34]

Although it is clear that a number of Massachusetts slaves won their liberty by suing their masters, the implications of these cases are not clear. Some authorities have argued that the courts established the illegality of slavery in the colony, but the records do not indicate the basis for the courts' decisions. In some cases, undoubtedly, the points at issue were the validity of the masters' titles, involving such questions as whether the Negro had had a free or slave mother or had been previously manumitted. It is possible, however, that the courts sometimes went beyond the immediate points at issue and decided that under no circumstances was slavery legal in Massachusetts. According to Jeremy Belknap, who discussed the abolition of slavery in Massachusetts in 1795, the lawyers for the Negroes who sued for their freedom had

[34] Lorenzo J. Greene, *The Negro in Colonial New England* (New York, 1942), pp. 296–97; Lyman H. Butterfield *et al.* (eds.), *Diary and Autobiography of John Adams* (4 vols.; New York, 1964), I, 321; III, note, 289.

argued that the Massachusetts charter, which declared all men free, prohibited slavery. Furthermore, they had maintained that no man could be deprived of liberty without a jury trial; that although some provincial laws recognized slavery, they did not authorize it; and, in some cases, that although the slavery of the parents might be conceded, it was argued that this did not affect the rights of the children. John Adams recalled that the arguments in the freedom cases "were much the same as have been urged since in pamphlets and newspapers, . . . arising from the rights of mankind." It is possible that both Adams and Belknap, writing many years after these cases had been decided, were mistaken, but at least one contemporary account supports their thesis. John Allen, author of a pre-Revolutionary pamphlet on liberty, congratulated the referees in a freedom case for having decided that there was "no law of the province to hold a man to serve for life." [35] Although it may be true that the Massachusetts courts decided many of these cases on purely technical issues, the advocates for the Negroes were able to use the freedom cases as a means of spreading the doctrine that slavery itself was illegal in the province. Furthermore, the fact that Negroes could make use of imperfections in their masters' titles to obtain their freedom made slave property less secure in Massachusetts than elsewhere in the northern colonies.[36]

[35] Emory Washburn, "Extinction of Slavery in Massachusetts" (*Proceedings of the Mass. Hist. Soc., 1855–1858*), [III], 190–91. The Parish Collection of MS copies of documents relating to slavery, box XVI, New-York Historical Society, contains records of numerous cases in which Massachusetts Negroes sued for their freedom. The Negroes in these cases based their claims to freedom in part at least on alleged imperfections in their masters' titles. In no case is the basis for the court's decision given. "Queries Respecting the Slavery and Emancipation of Negroes in Massachusetts, Proposed by the Hon. Judge Tucker of Virginia, and Answered by the Rev. Dr. Belknap" (*Collections of the Mass. Hist. Soc.*) 1st ser., IV, 202–3; "Letters and Documents," p. 401; Allen, *Watchman's Alarm*, note, p. 28.

[36] See L. Kinvin Wroth and Hiller B. Zobel (eds.), *Legal Papers of John Adams* (3 vols.; Cambridge, Mass., 1965), II, 48–67 for the records of freedom cases found in the Adams papers. The editors conclude that "counsel for the slaves argued as much from precedent as from Enlightenment."

The availability of the courts for the emancipation of Negroes could serve as an incentive to legislative abolition. As one abolitionist pointed out, if the Negroes' petition for freedom was not granted by the General Court, they would increasingly resort to freedom suits that would be more inimical to the slaveowners' interests than an abolition bill since, if they lost, masters would be required to pay court costs as well as compensation to their Negroes. The antislavery forces were careful to see that no new legislation interfered with the progress of the freedom cases. An early version of an antislave trade bill, in 1774, contained a clause specifically stating that nothing in the bill should be construed as legislative recognition of the legality of slavery, and that the Negroes should have the same rights as they would have had if the bill were not enacted.[37] The supporters of the measure were evidently prepared for the possibility that the pro-slavery interests might allow the bill to pass and then argue in the courts that the legislature, by restricting the slave trade, had recognized the legality of slavery in Massachusetts.

The tenuous legal position of slavery in Massachusetts, as well as the widespread enthusiasm for the philosophy of the Rights of Man, offered antislavery men a great opportunity. They could effectively appeal to the charter (which was becoming increasingly honored as it was threatened by the British), to the general enthusiasm for natural rights, and even to the acts of the British (looked upon as signs of God's displeasure). Although the royal governors had refused to sanction the General Court's attack on the slave trade, the rapid dissolution of all royal control would give the abolitionists a chance to test the sincerity of the General Court's proclamations for liberty.

RHODE ISLAND AND CONNECTICUT END THE SLAVE TRADE

Both Connecticut and Rhode Island were peculiarly free of royal control. Therefore, their restriction of the slave trade was allowed to stand. In these two colonies alone, however,

[37] *The Appendix*, p. 6; Moore, *Slavery in Mass.*, pp. 138–39.

did the extensive agitation against the slave trade achieve its goal.

In Rhode Island, John Woolman took part in an early effort to end the slave trade. When he visited Newport in 1760, Woolman planned to attend the assembly to plead the cause of the enslaved Negroes, but since the chamber was about to adjourn, he asked the Quaker meeting to prepare a petition to be presented at the next session. Unable to obtain much support, Woolman had to be content with a memorial signed by individual Quakers without committing the organization. Fourteen years later, however, abolitionism had made great strides among Rhode Island Quakers, and at the same time that the New England Yearly was expelling slaveholders, the meeting appointed a committee to ask the assembly for an abolition law. By this time, antislavery feeling had become more general throughout the community. In 1774 Providence Town Meeting, in determining the disposition of several slaves who had become town property, decided that "it is unbecoming the character of freemen to enslave the said negroes." In addition, the meeting instructed its representatives in the General Assembly to obtain an act to prohibit the importation of slaves and to free all Negroes born in the colony after they reached maturity. The assembly agreed to end the importation of slaves, observing that "those who are desirous of enjoying all the advantages of liberty themselves, should be willing to extend personal liberty to others." Pressure from Newport slave traders, however, prevented the act from living up to the promise of its preamble to provide for gradual abolition, and the statute, much to the disgust of its supporters, contained important loopholes.[38]

Newport, much of whose wealth depended on the slave trade, was not sympathetic to the new antislavery spirit. The

---

[38] Amelia M. Gummere (ed.), *The Journals and Essays of John Woolman* (Philadelphia, 1922), pp. 234–37; Allan C. Thomas, "The Attitude of the Society of Friends Towards Slavery in the Seventeenth and Eighteenth Century" (*Papers of the American Society of Church History*), VII (1897), 278–79; John R. Bartlett (ed.), *Records of the Colony of Rhode Island and Providence Plantations in New England* (10 vols.; Providence, 1856–62), VII, 280–81, 251–53; Mack Thompson, *Moses Brown* (Chapel Hill, N.C., 1962), pp. 96–98.

Reverend Samuel Hopkins, one of the great leaders of the abolition movement in its early days, reported that the congressional resolve to end the slave trade "falls heaviest on this Town" and that it was very unpopular since it was considered to be detrimental to the interests of its citizens.[39]

Despite the opposition of the Newport slave interests, antislavery men brought an abolition bill before the 1775 session of the assembly. After some debate, the deputies decided to print the bill in the newspapers to test public opinion and to consider the measure again at a future session. In August, Moses Brown, a recent Quaker convert who had already made a name for himself as a bitter opponent of slavery, brought the abolition bill before the Providence Town Meeting, urging the freemen to instruct their delegates to support the measure. The town now drew back from its previous forthright endorsement of abolition. Instead, the meeting noted that the proposed bill contained matters of great importance that would "materially affect the property of individuals," and it resolved to reconsider the bill at a future meeting after due warning had been given to all the freemen of the town. But the beginnings of the Revolutionary War allowed attention to be diverted from the problem of abolition, and no further action on the bill was taken, either in the assembly or in the Providence Town Meeting.[40]

In the neighboring colony of Connecticut, several members of the clergy took the lead in the attack on slavery. Ebenezer Baldwin and Jonathan Edwards, Jr., son of the famous New England divine and pastor of the New Haven Church, wrote a series of antislavery articles for the *Connecticut Journal* in 1773–74. The Reverend Levi Hart preached a sermon in the fall of 1774, claiming that slavery was subversive of the democratic constitution of Connecticut and a violation of natural law and the social compact. Citing Rhode Island's law prohibiting further importation of slaves,

---

[39] Hopkins to Dr. Erskine, December 28, 1774 (MS copy in the Gratz Collection, Colonial Clergy, Historical Society of Pennsylvania).

[40] Jeffrey R. Brackett, "The Status of the Slave, 1775–1789" *Essays in the Constitutional History of the United States*, ed. J. Franklin Jameson (Boston, 1889), p. 293; Peter Force (ed.), *American Archives*, 4th ser. (6 vols.; Washington, D.C., 1833–46), III, 453.

he asked: "Can this Colony want motives from reason, justice, religion, or public spirit, to follow the example?" Only if Americans ended slavery, he concluded, could they consistently fight for their own liberties.[41]

A few weeks after Hart's sermon, the Connecticut Assembly cut off slave importation, but the legislature failed to take the high ground adopted by Rhode Island. The Connecticut lawmakers were content to condemn the slave trade as "injurious to the poor and inconvenient," leaving the morality of the practice to be debated by the clergy. Danbury Town Meeting was gratified with the new law, but suggested to the assembly that "something further might be done for the relief of such as are now in a state of slavery in the Colonies."[42] The problems of war, however, in Connecticut as elsewhere, delayed further antislavery legislation.

When the Revolutionary War began, slavery was no longer an institution that was accepted without question. The legitimacy of slavery had been seriously questioned in all the northern colonies, and the Continental Congress had taken a firm stand against the importation of Negroes. In Pennsylvania, West Jersey, and Rhode Island, the Quakers were in large part responsible for the changing attitude toward slavery, and in Massachusetts and Connecticut the growing Revolutionary sentiment contributed to the growth of antislavery feeling. In New York, where the Quakers were weak and the Tories claimed the loyalty of a great number of citizens, antislavery sentiment was slow to develop. Although the first result of the outbreak of hostilities between the newly united states and Great Britain served to push the Negroes' cause into the background, independence brought with it new efforts for the abolition of slavery.

[41] Mary H. Mitchell, "Slavery in Connecticut and Especially in New Haven" (*Papers of the New Haven Colony Historical Society,* 1951) , X, 302; Levi Hart, *Liberty Described and Recommended* . . . (Hartford, 1775) , pp. v, 16, 20.

[42] *Public Records of the Colony of Connecticut* (15 vols.; Hartford, Conn., 1850–90) , XIV, 329; Force, *American Archives,* 4th ser., I, 1038–39.

abolition during   5
the American
Revolution

Although war usually brings a halt to humanitarian reform movements, the issues involved in the American Revolution were closely allied to the antislavery argument. Men who opposed the continued slavery of the Negroes could argue convincingly that American liberty and the freedom of Negro slaves were not only compatible, but were inseparable goals.

ABOLITION IN NEW ENGLAND

The War of Independence brought with it a direct challenge to the patriot party on the slavery issue. All the talk of liberty and the Rights of Man, designed to bring a hesitant population to join in the fight against Great Britain, could be applied with equal force to the plight of the slaves. Especially in Massachusetts, the Whigs could argue that they had tried to aid the Negroes by attempting to end the importation of slaves, only to have these attempts frustrated by the royal governor's veto. When the General Court was suspended in 1774 and the patriots established an independent Provincial Congress, however, they could act without fear of a veto. But soon after the opening of its first session, the Provincial Congress rejected a demand that it consider "the propriety, that while we are attempting to . . . preserve ourselves from slavery, that we also take into consideration the state and circumstances of the negro slaves in this province." [1]

[1] *The Journals of Each Provincial Congress of Massachusetts . . .* (Boston, 1838) , p. 29.

Massachusetts Negroes continued their antislavery activities. The slaves of Bristol and Worcester petitioned the Worcester Committee of Correspondence to aid them in obtaining their freedom. Accordingly, the County Convention resolved "That we abhor the enslaving of any part of the human race," and the delegates promised to use all their influence to procure the emancipation of the Negroes.[2]

Abolitionists appealed to the patriots not to neglect the Negroes when they took up the cause of liberty. Shortly after the opening of hostilities, Benjamin Colman urged the General Court to liberate the slaves because slavery was incompatible with the goals of the Revolutionary struggle. The colonists had united in a resolve to risk their lives in the defense of liberty but refused to grant freedom to the poor, oppressed Negroes. "[I]f oppression and slavery be right, why do you fight against it? but, if it be wrong why do you allow of it?" The Reverend William Gordon of Roxbury reminded citizens of Massachusetts of the words of the Declaration of Independence. "If these . . . are our genuine sentiments, and we are not provoking the Deity, by acting hypocritically . . . , let us apply earnestly and heartily to the extirpation of slavery from among ourselves." A "Son of Liberty" recalled God's warning to the embattled Israelites: they would never defeat their enemies until they removed "the accursed thing" from their midst—Americans would not achieve independence until they abolished slavery.[3]

In the spring of 1777 Massachusetts Negroes pled their own case once more. Structuring their argument to parallel the claims of the patriots, the Negroes pointed out that they had followed the example of the oppressed colonists and presented numerous petitions for redress of their grievances, only to meet with a similar galling failure. Yet, "every principle from which America has acted in the course of her difficulties with Great-Britain, pleads stronger than a thou-

[2] William Z. Lincoln, *History of Worcester* . . . (Worcester, Mass., 1862) , p. 99.
[3] *Essex Journal*, March 8, 1776, in Joshua Coffin, *A Sketch of the History of Newbury, Newburyport, and West Newbury, from 1635 to 1845* (Boston, 1845) , pp. 340–42; *Independent Chronicle*, October 3, November 28, 1776.

sand arguments for your Petitioners." If Americans would liberate their slaves, they could no longer be "chargeable with the inconsistency of acting . . . the part which they condemn & oppose in others," and would succeed "in their present glorious struggles for Liberty." [4]

In the fall of 1776, the house appointed a committee to consider the condition of the Negroes, but took no further action. In the spring, however, a house member prepared the draft of a bill to prevent the "wicked & unnatural Practice of holding Persons in slavery." Condemning slavery as being contrary to natural law and unchristian, the bill would have freed all Negro children born in the future and prohibited the sale of any Negro without his consent. After debating another abolition bill, which would have freed all Negroes over twenty-one, the house decided to consult Congress before moving to a final vote. In their letter to Congress, the representatives claimed that they were "convinced of the justice" of abolition, but that they hesitated to pass the bill

from an apprehension that our brethren in the Other Colonies [*sic*] should conceive there was an impropriety in our determining on a question which may . . . be of extensive influence, without previously consulting your Honors.[5]

Congress, fully occupied with the problems of fighting a war and having neither the authority nor the inclination to make a pronouncement on the potentially divisive issue of slavery, made no reply. The decision to consult Congress enabled the house to approve the Negroes' petition without, however, enacting abolition.

[4] Parish Collection of MS copies of documents relating to slavery, box XVI, New-York Historical Society. For another version of the petition see: "Letters and Documents Relating to Slavery in Massachusetts" (*Collections of the Massachusetts Historical Society*), 5th ser., III, 436–37.

[5] George H. Moore, *Notes on the History of Slavery in Massachusetts* (New York, 1866), pp. 181–85; *Proceedings of the Mass. Hist. Soc.*, 1867–69, pp. 332–34. John Adams and James Warren opposed the abolition bill because of its possible divisive effect; see Warren to Adams, June 22, 1777 and Adams to Warren, July 7, 1777, in *Warren-Adams Letters* (*Collections of the Mass. Hist. Soc.*), LXXII, 335, 339.

But Massachusetts public opinion was becoming increasingly hostile to slavery. Several of the country towns resolved that they would not allow slavery in their midst and that they would allow masters to emancipate their slaves without posting the bonds normally required. The Reverend William Gordon suggested to the printers of the *Independent Chronicle* that if they were "Sons of Liberty from principle, and not merely from interest," they should refuse to print advertisements for the sale of Negroes. "Such advertisements in the present season are peculiarly shocking." [6]

While the war for liberty made slavery more incongruous than ever, it also brought fears of Negro insurrections. Abigail Adams reported to her husband in 1774 that Boston Negroes had been conspiring for their freedom. They had told the governor that they would fight for him in the struggle with the colonists if he would promise them their liberty. The authorities had quietly suppressed this conspiracy, but Mrs. Adams wished that "there was not a Slave in the province. It allways appeard a most iniquitous Scheme to me—to fight ourselfs for what we are daily robbing and plundering from those who have as good a right to freedom as we have." [7]

Despite growing antislavery sentiment, when the General Court drafted a constitution for the new state it took no steps to end slavery. On the contrary, the 1778 constitution (which was rejected by the electorate) recognized slavery and denied Negroes the right to vote. Before the 1780 constitutional convention, however, the western town of Pittsfield instructed its delegate to support the adoption of a bill of rights that would specifically state that "no man can be deprived of liberty, and subjected to perpetual bondage and servitude." The new charter that was finally adopted did include a bill of rights that, in language similar to that of the Declaration of Independence and the Virginia Bill of Rights, declared all men to be free and equal by birth. But the new constitution did not mention slavery, and there is no

[6] "Letters and Documents," p. 393; *Independent Chronicle,* May 15, 1777, in Moore, *Slavery in Mass.,* p. 179.

[7] Abigail Adams to John Adams, September 22, 1774, in Lyman H. Butterfield, *et al.* (eds.), *Adams Family Correspondence* (Cambridge, Mass., 1963), I, 162.

evidence that the convention considered its abolition.[8] Nonetheless, the 1780 constitution became the means for eliminating slavery in Massachusetts. In a new series of freedom cases, the abolitionists succeeded in persuading the courts to interpret the constitution in a way that was probably never intended by its framers.

In September, 1781, the Supreme Court of Judicature was asked to rule whether slavery was constitutional in Massachusetts. The case in which the issue came before the court was one of a series between a Negro, Quok Walker, his putative master, Nathaniel Jennison, and the Negro's employers, John and Seth Caldwell, who were accused by Jennison of enticing away his slave. The technical point at issue was the question of whether a previous master's promise to manumit Walker gave him a right to freedom. Walker's attorney, Levi Lincoln, based his arguments on other grounds, however. He argued that slavery was contrary to natural law and that in the absence of a positive law establishing the institution, slavery was illegal. Furthermore, Lincoln argued, slavery was contrary to the Bible and the declaration of rights in the Massachusetts constitution. Although the court ruled that Walker was a freeman, it did not record the basis for its decision.[9]

In June, 1782, Nathaniel Jennison presented a petition to the General Court, stating that he had been deprived of the services of ten slaves on the basis of a court decision that the equality clause of the constitution had ended slavery in Massachusetts. Jennison argued that this decision was based

[8] Article V of the rejected constitution limited the suffrage to free inhabitants: *Journal of the Convention for Framing a Constitution . . .* (Boston, 1832), p. 257; J. E. A. Smith, *The History of Pittsfield . . . From the Year 1734 to the Year 1800* (Boston, 1869), p. 366; Emma L. Thornbrough, "Negro Slavery in the North: Its Legal and Constitutional Aspects," (Ph.D. dissertation, University of Michigan, 1946), pp. 103–6; Moore, *Slavery in Mass.*, pp. 203–5.

[9] William O'Brien, S.J., "Did the Jennison Case Outlaw Slavery in Massachusetts?" *William and Mary Quarterly,* 3d ser., XVIII (1960), 223–33; John D. Cushing, "The Cushing Court and the Abolition of Slavery in Massachusetts: More Notes on the 'Quock Walker Case,'" *American Journal of Legal History,* V (1961), 118–26; "Letters and Documents," pp. 438–42.

on a misinterpretation of the constitution and asked the legislature either to reject this interpretation, or to free him from the obligation of maintaining these Negroes. Accordingly, a bill was brought into the House of Representatives to repeal the law requiring masters to post a bond before manumitting their Negroes. This bill was referred to the next session. In February, the house decided to go further, and it appointed a committee to bring in a bill declaring that slavery had never been legal in Massachusetts, indemnifying masters who had in fact owned slaves, and providing means for supporting destitute Negroes. A bill for these purposes was passed by the house, but the senate took no action on the measure.[10]

In the meantime, in April, 1783, Nathaniel Jennison was brought to trial for assaulting Quok Walker in his attempts to secure the return of the runaway Negro. Chief Justice William Cushing, in his charge to the jury in this case, rejected Jennison's plea that his actions merely constituted legitimate correction of a runaway slave. Cushing held that Walker was a freeman because of the promised manumission. He went further. The chief justice held that although slavery had been tolerated in Massachusetts, it was incompatible with the new spirit "favorable to the natural rights of mankind." The new constitution declared all men to be free and equal and guaranteed their liberty and their right to life and property. Therefore, "without resorting to implication in constructing the constitution, slavery is . . . as effectively abolished as it can be by the granting of rights and privileges wholly incompatible and repugnant to its existence."[11]

The Walker-Jennison cases were similar in almost every respect to the pre-Revolutionary freedom cases. As in these other cases, the plea for the Negro was based in part on technical questions, but the lawyers for the Negro went beyond this in arguing that slavery was never legal in Massachusetts. Cushing's charge to the jury, as well as Jennison's petition to the General Court, indicate that in this case the

[10] Cushing, "Cushing Court," pp. 126–27; Moore, *Slavery in Mass.,* pp. 218–21.

[11] Cushing, "Cushing Court," pp. 130–33.

courts accepted the doctrine that slavery was no longer legal in Massachusetts.

Despite the decision in the Jennison cases, there is no evidence that the constitutional convention intended to abolish slavery in Massachusetts. Although most of the judges in these cases had served in the convention, it may well be that they sought to accomplish by judicial decision what they had failed to obtain in the convention hall.

The direct effect of the Jennison cases is difficult to determine, but they did not lead to an immediate abolition of slavery; and slaves continued to be sold in Massachusetts.[12] Far from being hailed as revolutionary decisions, affecting the property rights of thousands of slaveowners, they went unnoticed in contemporary newspapers. The reason for the ambiguous results of the Walker-Jennison cases is that they were, in all probability, only several of a series of cases testing the constitutionality of slavery. At the same time that Levi Lincoln was arguing that slavery was incompatible with the declaration of rights for the benefit of Quok Walker in Worcester, Theodore Sedgwick was making a similar plea for Elizabeth Freeman in Berkshire County—and with similar results. These freedom cases ultimately had the desired effect. Some Negroes were encouraged to sue for their freedom; others, convinced that the courts would not return them to slavery, simply left their masters. As a result, when the first federal census was taken in 1790, Massachusetts reported that it had no more slaves.[13]

Although Massachusetts slaveholders acquiesced in the abolition of slavery, they did so reluctantly. "Mentor" urged voters to oppose all candidates for the House of Representatives who had supported the "execrable retrospective bill,"

[12] *Continental Journal,* March 1, 1781, advertised the sale of a seventeen-year-old Negro woman who had *"no notion of Freedom,"* in Moore, *Slavery in Mass.,* p. 209. A bill of sale for a slave, dated November 15, 1784, is reproduced in Richard B. Sheridan, "Slavery and Antislavery Literature," *Books and Libraries at the University of Kansas,* II, 4 (May, 1963), 13.

[13] O'Brien, "Jennison Case," pp. 240–41; Cushing, "Cushing Court," pp. 134–39; Henry W. Taft, "Judicial History of Berkshire" (*Collections of the Berkshire Historical Society,* 1892), I, 105; "Letters and Documents," p. 386.

which declared that slavery had never been legal. Designed to deprive men of their property, the measure was reminiscent of British tyranny and would have let loose upon the public a horde of Negro vagabonds. Although he conceded that the constitution declared that all men were free, "Mentor" maintained that this was a mistaken assertion. As late as 1795, when James Winthrop, chief justice of the court of common pleas, was asked several questions about the abolition of slavery in Massachusetts, he replied that "by a misconstruction of our State Constitution, which declares all men by nature free and equal, a number of citizens have been deprived of property formerly acquired under the protection of law." [14]

Whereas it required extensive judicial interpretation to abolish slavery in Massachusetts, the Vermont Constitution of 1777 explicitly outlawed slavery. The bill of rights, modeled closely on that of Pennsylvania, included an additional clause prohibiting slavery or compulsory service for those who were of age. Although the wording was somewhat vague (the constitution could be interpreted to retain Negroes in slavery until they reached the end of their minority), it seems clear that the intention of the framers was expressly to forbid all forms of slavery without making apprenticeships illegal. The legislature supported this interpretation when it noted in 1786 that "by the constitution of this state . . . the idea of slavery is expressly and totally exploded from our free government." [15]

New Hampshire Negroes adopted the same course as their fellow slaves in Massachusetts. Nineteen slaves petitioned the New Hampshire legislature in 1779, arguing that they had a natural right to freedom which they had never surrendered. They complained that they had been taken from their native land "where (though ignorance and unchristianity prevailed) they were born free," to a land "where (though knowledge, Christianity and Freedom are their boast) they are compelled . . . to drag on their lives in miserable servi-

---

[14] *Boston Evening-Post,* May 3, 1783; "Letters and Documents," pp. 389–90.

[15] John H. Watson, "In Re Vermont Constitution of 1777 . . ." (*Proceedings of the Vermont Historical Society,* 1919–20), pp. 244, **247**, 248, 256.

tude." Since slavery was unjustifiable in the light of natural law, reason, and religion, they asked the assembly to emancipate them so "that the name of slave may not more be heard in a land gloriously contending for the sweets of freedom." The Negro petition was read in the assembly in April, 1780. It was taken up once more in June, but the assembly resolved "that at this time the House is not ripe for a determination in this matter." Apparently, no convenient time was discovered and the Negro petition was not considered further.[16]

The final abolition of slavery in New Hampshire is surrounded with even more obscurity and ambiguity than abolition in Massachusetts. It is possible that the bill of rights of the 1783 constitution was interpreted in the same manner as the similar clauses of the Massachusetts Constitution. In 1788 Jeremy Belknap maintained that "the negroes in Massachusetts and New Hampshire are all *free,* by the first article in the Declaration of Rights. This has been pleaded in law, and admitted." No judicial records confirming this view have survived. An editor of the *New Hampshire State Papers* asserted that the bill of rights was intended to abolish slavery, and that although slaves were still taxed as property under a 1784 revenue act, this clause was deliberately expunged from a revenue bill passed in 1789. After the passage of this act, he maintained, "slaves ceased to be known and held as property in New Hampshire." In 1792, however, there were still nearly 150 slaves in the state. Three years later, Jeremy Belknap gave a different view of abolition in New Hampshire. He now maintained that the bill of rights had operated only to free those born after the adoption of the constitution. An act of July 26, 1857, finally clarified the situation by specifically banning slavery and declaring all Negroes to be full citizens of the state.[17]

As the Revolutionary War progressed, some New England

---

[16] Isaac W. Hammond, "Slavery in New Hampshire," *Magazine of American History,* XXI (1889) , 63–65.

[17] Belknap to Ebenezer Hazard, January 25, 1788, *Belknap Papers, (Collections of the Mass. Hist. Soc.)* , 5th ser., III, 11; Nathaniel Bouton (ed.) , *Documents and Records Relating to Towns in New Hampshire,* IX (Concord, N.H., 1875) , note, 896–98; Hammond, "Slavery in N.H.," p. 65; "Queries Respecting the Slavery and Emancipation of Negroes in

slaveowners became increasingly aware of the ideological inconsistency of keeping slaves while fighting for liberty. Captain William Whipple, who had been assigned to guard New Hampshire's northwestern frontier, noted that his slave was extremely dejected. When asked why he was so miserable, the Negro replied: *"You* are going to fight for your *liberty,* but I have none to fight for." Whipple could not deny the justice of this complaint and immediately freed the Negro. Thomas Hart Hooker of Farmington, Connecticut joined the army shortly after the battle of Lexington, but before leaving for war he manumitted his slave. "I will not fight for liberty and leave a slave at home." A Connecticut women freed her Negro slave in 1778, "because I believe that all Mankind ought to be free." [18]

Samuel Hopkins, minister of the Newport, Rhode Island church was pleased to see that "the conviction of the unjustifiableness of [slavery] . . . has been increasing" and that many slaveowners had become convinced that they should free their Negroes. "May this conviction soon reach every owner of slaves in *North-America!"* Hopkins urged the Continental Congress to complete the action begun by prohibiting the slave trade and to use its influence to bring about a total abolition of slavery in America. He took issue with those who argued that although abolition might ultimately be wise, action should be deferred until after the war. The war was evidence of God's displeasure with Americans for enslaving the Negroes, and they could not expect victory until they had reformed. Even if freeing the Negroes involved great expense, this should not justify a failure to end "a sin of crimson die, which is most particularly pointed out by the public calamities which have come upon us." Furthermore, slavery was increasingly dangerous because of the possibility

Massachusetts, Proposed by the Hon. Judge Tucker of Virginia, and Answered by the Rev. Dr. Belknap," (*Collections of the Mass. Hist. Soc.*), 1st ser., IV, 204.

[18] Charles W. Brewster, *Rambles About Portsmouth,* 1st ser. (Portsmouth, N.H., 1859), pp. 152–53; George F. Tuttle, *The Descendants of William and Elizabeth Tuttle* . . . (Rutland, Vt., 1883), p. 88; Mary H. Mitchell, "Slavery in Connecticut and Especially in New Haven," (*Papers of the New Haven Colony Historical Society,* 1951), X, 302.

that the Negroes would join the British and fight for their freedom. The only way to prevent this would be for the Americans to take the initiative and set the slaves free. Hopkins quoted the preamble to Rhode Island's act prohibiting the importation of slaves. "How becoming, honorable, and happy would it have been" if Rhode Island had followed through on the premises of that declaration and had taken the lead in abolishing slavery.[19]

The exigencies of war led Rhode Island to take the first hesitant step toward emancipation. In February, 1778, faced with a critical shortage of troops and the need to raise two battalions for the continental army, the legislature permitted slaves to enlist. In return for enlisting, the Negroes were unconditionally manumitted and entitled to the benefits normally granted soldiers. Slaveowners were compensated for the loss of their Negroes according to their value and up to a maximum of £120. The assembly was sharply divided on the wisdom of this move, and six members issued a protest against the plan. The dissenters pointed out that the enlistment of Negroes "would suggest . . . that the state had purchased a band of slaves to be employed in the defence of the rights and liberties of our country." This was not only "inconsistent with those principles of liberty . . . for which we are so ardently contending," but it would subject Rhode Island to the contempt of the other states and the rest of the world. Those who opposed slave enlistments also maintained that masters would not be satisfied with the compensation provided. Three months later, one of the first acts of the newly elected assembly was to reverse the previous policy and end slave enlistments. In the four months that the law was in effect, only 88 or 89 Negroes were actually emancipated at a cost to the state of over £10,000. The Negro soldiers who enlisted were not only deprived of the usual bounties granted to white soldiers but were never given the allowance paid to their white comrades to compensate them for the depreciation of the currency.[20]

[19] [Samuel Hopkins], *A Dialogue Concerning the Slavery of the Africans* . . . (Norwich, Conn., 1776), pp. iii, 29–31, 49n, 56, 57n.

[20] *Records of the State of Rhode Island and Providence Plantations in New England* (10 vols.; Providence, 1856–65), VIII, 358–61; Sidney

The termination of the plan to allow Negroes to win their freedom by enlisting in the Revolutionary armies did not spell the end of all plans for abolition in Rhode Island. In the fall of 1779 the assembly, to alleviate some of the evils of slavery "until some favourable Occasion may offer for its total abolition," banned the sale of any Rhode Island slave outside of the state without his consent.[21] The ban on slave exports would not only prevent one of the greatest evils of slavery—the separation of families—but it would forestall avaricious masters who, anticipating the passage of an abolition act, might protect their property by selling their Negroes in areas where slave property was more secure.

Even before the signing of the peace treaty in 1783, Rhode Island Quakers began a concentrated campaign to persuade the legislature to redeem its pledge to end slavery. Moses Brown quickly emerged as a resourceful leader of the abolitionists. He feverishly produced antislavery articles for the *Providence Gazette* and distributed countless pamphlets against slavery and the slave trade. In October, 1783, with several other Friends he prepared a petition, but after studying a list of the members of the legislature and their probable stand on slavery, decided to wait until after the forthcoming election and did not present the memorial until December. The assembly now seemed favorably disposed; a committee reported a bill, drafted with the aid of the Quakers, that granted every important demand—providing for abolition and for heavy penalties for participation in the slave trade. After some debate, the house referred the measure to the February session to allow the deputies to consult their constituents.[22]

Brown now stepped up his campaign in an effort to create a ground swell of public opinion. He submitted articles for

S. Rider, "An Historical Inquiry Concerning the Attempts to Raise a Regiment of Slaves in Rhode Island," *Rhode Island Historical Tracts*, X (Providence, 1880), v, 20, 35–36, 53–58. For a general discussion of the role of Negro troops in the war, see Benjamin Quarles, *The Negro in the American Revolution* (Chapel Hill, N.C., 1961), *passim*.

[21] *R.I. Assembly, October, 1779*, 5–7.

[22] Mack Thompson, *Moses Brown* (Chapel Hill, N.C., 1962), pp. 177–79; *R.I. Records*, IX, 738.

almost every issue of the *Gazette* and also supplied antislavery material for the *United States Chronicle*. He asked the religious leaders of Providence to preach the antislavery gospel to their congregations. As a result of these efforts, the Providence Town Meeting instructed its delegates to support the bill.[23]

When the legislature met in February, it rejected the bill by a two to one vote. But it accepted a substitute providing for a gradual abolition of slavery without effectively limiting the slave trade. Observing that slavery was incompatible with the Rights of Man, the bill freed all Negro children born after March 1, 1784. The law made elaborate provision for the protection of the property rights of slaveowners. Although freeborn Negro children would remain with the master who owned their mother for at least one year, the towns would assume the expense of raising and educating them. Furthermore, masters would now be allowed to free any healthy slave, twenty-one to forty years old, without assuming any financial responsibility.[24]

Rhode Island's abolition plan minimized the loss to slaveowners. No slaves living at the time the act was passed were emancipated. Although masters could no longer own the children born to their slaves, they were also freed from the expense of raising them. Nonetheless, pro-slavery men vigorously objected to the new law. Samuel Hopkins reported in April that at the recent elections Newport had chosen a new slate of representatives, hostile to all efforts to discourage slavery and the slave trade. He suspected that they had been elected for this reason. The principal objection to the law was the provision requiring towns to support free Negro children. Hopkins expected "a strong motion" to have the abolition law "altered or repealed at the next General Assembly," and he feared that "by the cunning and influence of a number, the latter will be effected." Although Hopkins' pessimism was undoubtedly influenced by the pro-slavery sentiments of his neighbors, the October session of the legislature did alter the abolition law. Noting that "subjecting towns to the support and education" of the Negro children

---

[23] Thompson, *Moses Brown*, pp. 179–80.
[24] *Ibid.*, pp. 181–82; *R.I. Records*, X, 7–8.

was proving to be "extremely burthensome, and . . . incompatible with the principles upon which the . . . act was passed," the assembly repealed this provision, leaving slave-owners responsible for the maintenance of their slaves' children.[25] Although this deprived the masters of a possibly lucrative source of income (the previous plan was wide open to fraud) they probably suffered little loss, since they were entitled to the services of the Negro children until they reached the end of their minority and this probably more than paid for the cost of their early maintenance.

In Connecticut the connection between the Revolutionary struggle and abolition was made at an early date. In the spring of 1776 a Connecticut man urged the assembly to abolish slavery. He pointed out that the citizens of Connecticut had pledged their wealth and blood in the defense of freedom, had sought God's aid by observing days of fasting, but had neglected to "keep that fast which the Lord himself has chosen; we have not undone the heavy burdens, nor have we let the oppressed go free!" His proposed plan for abolition was similar to that ultimately adopted by Rhode Island. Unfortunately, the member of the assembly who had promised to present the plan to the legislature was unable to do so. In 1777, however, in response to several petitions for abolition, the assembly appointed a committee to investigate the condition of the Negroes in the state and to consider what might be done to secure their emancipation. The committee reported a plan that would allow slaves to enlist in the army, provided that they could procure (by bounty, hire, or any other way) a sum equal to their value. These Negroes would then be unconditionally free and their masters freed from any responsibility for maintaining them in case they later became incapable of self-support. Although the assembly never enacted this plan, a bill passed in the fall of 1777, making it easier to manumit slaves, accomplished a similar purpose. The manumission bill allowed masters to free their slaves without having to assume any financial responsibility for their future maintenance, provided that the slaves were

[25] Hopkins to Moses Brown, April 29, 1784 in Edwards A. Park (ed.), *The Works of Samuel Hopkins* . . . (3 vols.; Boston, 1852), I, 120; *R.I. Records*, X, 132–33.

certified as healthy and that the town selectmen determined that manumission was for the slaves' best interests. This meant that masters could free their slaves and then allow them to serve as substitutes for themselves or their sons in the armed services. Under this system, the Negro received his freedom and the master fulfilled his military obligations without having to assume any financial responsibility for his freed Negroes. Accordingly, several hundred Connecticut Negroes enlisted in the Revolutionary armies. The Connecticut courts ruled that any slave who had enlisted with his master's permission was thereby manumitted and could no longer be claimed as a slave by his master.[26]

A bill for the gradual abolition of slavery in Connecticut was unsuccessfully brought before the legislature in 1779. The next year a bill emancipating all Negro children over seven years of age (but requiring them to serve until they were twenty-eight) passed the upper house, was continued to the next session, and then put aside.[27]

The legislature's refusal to enact any of the proposed gradual abolition plans may have induced the state's antislavery forces to try to achieve their goal by indirection. The legislature, perhaps unwittingly, took the first step in abolishing slavery when it assigned Roger Sherman and Richard Law to revise the laws. Among the revised laws submitted to the legislature in January, 1784, was one statute combining all previous laws on slavery. Appended to this was a section proclaiming that "sound Policy requires that the Abolition of Slavery should be effected as soon as may be" and declaring that all children born after March 1 would become free when they were twenty-five. On January 8, when the legisla-

[26] *Independent Chronicle* (Boston), November 14, 1776; William C. Fowler, "The Historical Status of the Negro in Connecticut," *Historical Magazine*, 3d ser., VIII (1874), 84; George Livermore, *An Historical Research* (3d ed.; Boston, 1863), pp. 113–15; *Public Records of the State of Connecticut* (9 vols.; Hartford, 1894–1953), I, 415–16; Bernard C. Steiner, "History of Slavery in Connecticut," *Johns Hopkins University Studies in Historical and Political Science*, XI (1893), 407.

[27] Frances M. Caulkins, *History of Norwich, Connecticut* (n.p., 1866), p. 520; Jeffrey R. Brackett, "The Status of the Slave, 1775–1789," *Essays in the Constitutional History of the United States*, ed. J. Franklin Jameson (Boston, 1889), p. 296.

ture approved the revised laws, it automatically adopted the gradual abolition of slavery.[28]

As in Massachusetts and New Hampshire, the abolition of slavery in Connecticut presents something of a mystery. Did the members of the legislature who agreed to assign Sherman and Law the task of revising the laws intend to abolish slavery? Was the abolition section of the law inserted by Sherman and Law or was it added by the legislature? Is it possible that some of the members of the legislature did not realize that by adopting the revised code they had enacted an abolition law? At any rate, the method followed by Connecticut in abolishing slavery was effective in preventing the development of any substantial opposition.

The action of Connecticut and Rhode Island meant that within a year of the conclusion of the Revolutionary War provision had been made for the abolition of slavery in all the New England states. As a result, the 1790 federal census reported only 3,763 slaves in New England, out of a total of 16,882 Negroes. Ten years later, there were only 1,339 slaves in New England, and by 1810 the total was reduced to 418—108 in Rhode Island and 310 in Connecticut.[29]

PENNSYLVANIA'S GRADUAL ABOLITION LAW

Slavery, much more firmly entrenched in the middle colonies, was correspondingly more difficult to eradicate. Only in Pennsylvania, with its long tradition of Quaker opposition to bondage, were the abolitionists successful during the Revolution. The political situation in Revolutionary Pennsylvania was, however, in many ways the reverse of that in New England. In Massachusetts and the other New England states, the Revolution had brought many of the sympathizers of abolition into positions of power, whereas in Pennsylvania the Quakers, hitherto the mainstay of the abolition move-

[28] Roger S. Boardman, *Roger Sherman* (Philadelphia, 1938), pp. 200–201; *Conn. Records*, V, 281–82; VIII, xviii; *Acts and Laws of the State of Connecticut in America* (New London, 1784), pp. 233–35.

[29] U.S. Bureau of the Census, *Negro Population, 1790–1915* (Washington, D.C., 1918), p. 57.

ment, were not only deprived of power but, because of their pacifist principles, were everywhere proscribed as Tories and British sympathizers. Although the Friends had retired from the government in the crisis of the 1750's, they had continued to control provincial politics through the Quaker party. But in the early days of the Revolution, a new coalition, composed of Philadelphia radicals and their Scotch-Irish backcountry allies, assumed the reins of power under the new and radical constitution of 1776. The Quakers, chagrined at seeing power struck from their hands and placed in the grip of their historic political enemies, expected only the worst from this radical transformation of the century-old pattern of Pennsylvania politics. They had little faith that the backcountry politicians (who had already demonstrated their implacable hostility to the Indians) would do anything to ease the bondage of the Negroes.

Furthermore, the Quakers were disorganized by the coming of the war and were forced to reduce their activities on behalf of the Negroes. War brought so many problems for the Society of Friends—compulsory military service, confiscations, and even deportation—that members of the society were forced to devote themselves to self-preservation. Anthony Benezet, who had been instrumental in the formation of the first society dedicated to promoting the interests of Negroes—the Society for the Relief of Free Negroes—saw this primarily Quaker organization disintegrate in the fall of 1775 after only four meetings.[30] Unexpectedly, however, the Pennsylvania abolitionists found a strong ally within the opposition party. George Bryan, the first vice-president under the new constitution, became the indefatigable champion of the Negro, and he was to succeed where the Quakers had hitherto failed.

Even before independence, there had been some evidence that the Whigs were willing to apply the philosophy of the Rights of Man to the cause of the Negro. The Pennsylvania Provincial Convention resolved in January, 1775, to urge the General Assembly to prohibit the importation of slaves, and

[30] Edward Needles, *An Historical Memoir of the Pennsylvania Society for Promoting the Abolition of Slavery* . . . (Philadelphia, 1848), pp. 14–16, 16 n.

in March, the Chester County Committee of Correspondence appointed a committee to draft a petition for the gradual abolition of slavery.[31]

In August, 1778, only a few months after the death of President Thomas Wharton, Jr. had made Bryan acting president, the Executive Council asked the House of Representatives to increase the duty on imported Negroes or to prohibit the trade altogether. The assembly had already been considering a bill to regulate the importation of Negroes, but shortly after receipt of the council's message, a member brought in a gradual abolition bill. This bill was tabled, however, and the importation bill emerged from committee so transformed that it merely provided for the collection of previously established duties.[32]

The council took up the cause of the Negro once more in November, this time endorsing the principle of gradual abolition. Emancipation of the present generation of slaves would create difficulties since most of them were "scarcely competent of freedom," but the manumission of Negro infants would provide for "the gradual abolition of Servitude for life . . . in an easy mode." Moreover, "no period seems more happy for the attempt than the present, as the number of [slaves], . . . ever few in Pennsylvania, has been much reduced by the practices & plunder of our late invaders." The abolition of slavery would not only be a proper way to thank God for His help (the British had evacuated Philadelphia only a few months earlier) but would also establish Pennsylvania's "character for Justice & Benevolence." But the council's eloquence failed to move the house.[33]

Three months later, the council took up abolition once more, arguing that slavery was especially disgraceful in a nation fighting for its liberty. Since it was so ardent for this

---

[31] *Journals of the House of Representatives of the Commonwealth of Pennsylvania* . . . , [1776–1781] (Philadelphia, 1782), p. 31; Peter Force (ed.), *American Archives*, 4th ser. (6 vols.; Washington, D.C., 1833–46), II, 172.

[32] Burton A. Konkle, *George Bryan and the Constitution of Pennsylvania, 1731–1791* (Philadelphia, 1922), p. 153; *Pennsylvania Archives*, 1st ser., VI, 685; *Pa. H. of R., 1776–1781*, pp. 213, 217, 218, 222, 225, 226.

[33] *Pa. Archives*, VII, 79.

reform, the council went beyond its constitutional role and offered to supply the draft of an abolition bill to the assembly. This time the house acted. Even before receiving the latest message from the council, the assembly had formed a committee to draft an abolition bill. The council's offer to submit its own draft, however, aroused the house's ire and precipitated an extended debate on the council's legislative role. The unicameral legislature, determined to resist the revival of bicameralism, resolved that any bills submitted by the council would be unacceptable. Shortly after this issue had been disposed of and the ruffled feelings of the assemblymen soothed, the committee on abolition reported a bill that was debated and, in accordance with the provisions of the constitution, ordered printed for public consideration.[34]

The bill's preamble denounced slavery as "highly detrimental to morality, industry, and the arts." It pointed out that those who were fighting for their freedom should be willing to grant it to others, and that the abolition of slavery would be a fitting means for thanking God for His aid during the war. The bill itself emancipated all Negro children born in the future but required them to serve their mothers' masters. These children would be entitled to all the privileges of indentured servants, and the girls would be unconditionally free at eighteen whereas the boys would serve until they were twenty-one. Slaveowners were required to register their slaves and unregistered Negroes would be considered emancipated, although masters could not escape financial responsibility for the care of their Negroes by refusing or neglecting to register them. The bill also repealed the slave code and required slaves to be tried in the same courts as freemen, but it limited the right of slaves to testify to cases involving other slaves. Marriage to whites would still be illegal, and Negroes who violated this ban could be fined £100 or bound out to serve for 7 years. The rights of free Negroes were further limited by a clause that permitted them to be bound out for service if they refused to support themselves. Finally, the bill prohibited the importation of slaves.[35]

[34] *Pa. H. of R., 1776–1781,* pp. 304, 307, 309–11, 317, 319.
[35] *Pennsylvania Packet,* March 4, 1779.

Although it was printed to elicit public discussion, the bill aroused little comment in the press. "A Citizen" suggested that requiring the freed Negroes to serve only during their minority would provide insufficient compensation to their masters for the expense of raising them; they should be required to serve until they were twenty-eight or thirty. Furthermore, the bill should require masters to educate their servants to prepare them for freedom.[36]

More serious opposition was expressed by a group from Chester County that asked the legislature to reject the bill. Despite the council's continued requests for speedy action, the house failed to complete action on the bill before adjourning and referred it, along with several other matters, to the attention of the next legislature. Accordingly, one of the first acts of the newly elected house was to appoint a committee (which included George Bryan, now a member of the assembly) to prepare an abolition bill. In November, 1779, the committee reported, the house debated the bill, and once more ordered its publication. At this point, in the first recorded vote on abolition, thirty-eight members voted in favor and only eight were opposed.[37]

The new version of the abolition bill had a much longer preamble that compared the condition of the Negroes to the British tyranny that Americans had so narrowly escaped. The abolition of slavery would not only demonstrate the sincerity of the American fight for freedom, but would also be a "substantial proof" of Pennsylvania's gratitude for being rescued from the British. The new bill was similar in many respects to the former measure, but with several significant differences. The Negroes emancipated by the bill would serve until they were twenty-eight (instead of eighteen or twenty-one). The bill also eliminated the ban on intermarriage. Although the new version of the abolition bill required a longer period of service of the freed Negroes, the withdrawal of the proposal that lazy Negroes could be bound out (which was similar to the Black Codes adopted by southern states after the Civil War) afforded them protection

[36] *Ibid.*, March 13, 1779.
[37] *Pa. H. of R., 1776–1781*, pp. 364, 365, 389–90, 392, 394, 398, 399.

against a possible abuse that might have rendered their freedom meaningless.[38]

Shortly after the bill was printed, George Bryan published a series of letters to a country clergyman, designed to win backcountry support for abolition. He pointed out that abolition had won widespread approval throughout the state and had met little opposition in the legislature. Although the proposed bill was eminently just and in full accord with the constitution's claim that "all men are born equally free," the mistaken belief that abolition might have an adverse effect on the other states had led the assembly to proceed cautiously. The only opposition had come from Chester County, and Bryan, a leader of the "Presbyterian" party, found it "irksome . . . that these few opposers of the bill should generally be members of the Presbyterian Churches, which are otherwise remarkable for their zeal, and for their exertions in the cause of freedom." He asked the clergyman to whom the letters were addressed to use his influence to gain support for abolition and to answer arguments against the bill. The "Quakers, who we think have but clouded views of the gospel, have nearly cleared their society of this opprobrium of America"; would Presbyterians "continue so void of charity and justice, as to . . . labour for the continuance of it [?]" He refuted the reasoning of the Chester County petitioners that slavery was compatible with the Bible and that freed Negroes would become lazy and refuse to work. In a general discussion of the wisdom of abolition, Bryan pointed out that slavery was incompatible with democracy, that it debased labor and endangered the community by providing a class of internal enemies. The war had demonstrated that even well-treated Negroes could be enticed to join America's enemies. The common argument that only slaves could perform certain types of work was inapplicable to Pennsylvania since freemen performed all the work for which slaves were used. Furthermore, with the cessation of hostilities an influx of European workers would eliminate the dangers of any future labor shortage. Since the Negroes would serve until they were twenty-eight with the knowledge

[38] *Pennsylvania Packet,* December 23, 1779.

that they would eventually be free, they would work harder, and there would be little loss to their masters. The abolition of slavery would strengthen Pennsylvania in relation to other states still hampered by that wasteful institution.[39]

"A Whig Freeholder" expressed "pleasure and satisfaction" with the bill, suggesting only an amendment to permit immigrants from other states to bring their slaves with them. Another commentator thought the bill could be improved by requiring masters to educate their Negroes. No master could consider himself "acquited either in law or conscience from the great duty of capacitating the child to receive instruction, especially in the great principles of religion." "Phileleutheros" believed that the bill did not go far enough because it would not emancipate the present generation of slaves. Furthermore, forcing Negroes to serve until they were twenty-eight was unjust. All the Negroes should be set free, and their former masters should be required to pay for the support of those who had grown old in their service. In answer to those who argued that the freed Negroes would form a vice-ridden element, he suggested that vice was not a monopoly of the Negroes. The Negroes' vices were the result of their debased condition and completely understandable in view of their lack of inducements to act otherwise. He could well understand that the Negroes, "feeling the horrors of their situation," should attempt to lose themselves in drinking. If the abolition bill, as its preamble suggested, was intended as an expression of gratitude to God for His aid, then the assembly should remember that God would accept only unblemished offerings. The proposed bill fell far short of this standard.[40]

When the assembly resumed in January, 1780, it found evidence of increasing public support for abolition. Five petitions in favor of the bill were presented in January and February while only one, from Bucks County, expressed opposition. On March 1, however, two petitions asked for the defeat of the measure. One of these, from Lancaster County, was dismissed "on account of its indecency." The house then

[39] *Ibid.*, December 25, 1779, January 1, 1780. Konkle, *Bryan,* p. 190, attributes these letters to Bryan.

[40] *Pennsylvania Gazette,* January 26, 1780; *Pennsylvania Packet,* January 27, 1780; *Pennsylvania Gazette,* February 2, 1780.

proceeded to a final vote, and by a vote of thirty-four to twenty-one Pennsylvania became the first state to enact an abolition law.[41]

The final version of the bill was essentially the same as the one printed in December, 1779, with a slight modification which made it easier to manumit slaves. The final date for the registration of slaves was established as November 1, 1780.[42]

There is no evidence that abolition had been a party issue. The assembly that enacted the abolition law was completely dominated by the radical party. The conservatives, who had been an active minority in the previous assembly, had lost even this slender hold in the October, 1779, elections. There is no indication, however, that the conservatives—normally the allies of the Quakers—would have opposed abolition. The issue was one that divided the radicals. The eastern counties were stronger in support of abolition than the western ones. Representatives from the city of Philadelphia supported the abolition bill unanimously. The only delegations in which the opponents of abolition were in the majority were those from Lancaster, Berks, Northampton, and Westmoreland counties. Bryan was correct in his assumption that the bulk of the opposition came from the Scotch-Irish Presbyterians of the backcountry. Although the Quakers had been rendered politically powerless by their opposition to the war, the members of the Society of Friends supported the abolition bill, and Anthony Benezet is said to have interviewed all of the members of the assembly in an effort to obtain votes for the measure. Bryan remarked that the abolition bill "astonishes and pleases the Quakers. They looked for no such benevolent issue of our new government, exercised by Presbyterians." [43]

Twenty-three of its opponents issued a stinging denunciation of the abolition bill. Abolishing slavery during war time

---

[41] *Pa. H. of R., 1776–1781,* pp. 412, 424, 425, 435.

[42] *Pennsylvania Packet,* March 30, 1780.

[43] Robert L. Brunhouse, *The Counter-Revolution in Pennsylvania, 1776–1790* (Philadelphia, 1942), p. 76; Allan Nevins, *The American States During and After the Revolution* (New York, 1924), p. 448; George Bancroft, *History of the United States of America* ("Centenary Edition"; Boston, 1879), VI, 307.

showed a callous disregard for the safety of the other states. It could only serve to weaken the unity of the nation while it was fighting for its life. As the site of battle shifted to the South, southern soldiers would be increasingly apprehensive about the safety of their families left "at the mercy of a superior force of slaves, which may from the sound of freedom, that may go forth from this law, . . . lead the negroes of these states, to a demand of an immediate and intire freedom, or to other disorders." Furthermore, the opponents of the abolition bill could not agree to permit Negroes to be "made free citizens in so extensive a manner as this law proposes." The dissenters specifically objected to permitting Negroes to vote, hold public office, marry whites, and serve as witnesses. The minority manifesto also predicted that the limited period of service required of Negro children would lead to the financial ruin of some families.[44]

A "Liberal," writing in the *Pennsylvania Packet,* answered these objections point by point. The supposed dangers to southern interests were imaginary and had not been urged by southerners. He held up to ridicule the idea "that when the British Generals every where proclaim liberty to the slaves, any relaxation of their bondage, on our part, should provoke the negroes against the Americans." Against the argument that the law was defective because it granted Negroes civil liberties, he pointed out that the constitution guaranteed these rights to all natives, including, of course, the Negroes who were born here. As for intermarriage, "Would it be consistent with natural rights for a legislature to prohibit a match of this sort?" There was no danger in allowing Negroes to serve as witnesses, for it had been allowed in Massachusetts for years "without inconvenience." Furthermore, if Negroes were denied the right to give evidence, white men could also be deprived of this basic right. Allowing Negroes the right to hold public office would not lead to any difficulties since the people could be relied on to elect the best men; they would "neither elect rascally whites, nor the debased blacks." [45]

[44] *Pa. H. of R., 1776–1781,* p. 436.
[45] *Pennsylvania Packet,* March 25, 1780.

The October, 1780, elections constituted a "minor revolution" in Pennsylvania politics. Sixty per cent of the members of the new assembly had not served in the previous house, and since most of the new members were conservatives, the two factions were now evenly balanced. The new house was subject to heavy pressure to alter the abolition law. Almost from the beginning of the session the assembly was inundated with petitions from slaveowners who had failed to register their Negroes before the November deadline, asking permission to keep these Negroes in slavery. Although the petitioners claimed that they had failed to register their Negroes only because they had not learned of the requirement in time, it was obvious that the Negroes were well acquainted with the provisions of the law, for they claimed their freedom in increasing numbers.[46]

In response to this flood of petitions, the assembly took up a bill to revise the abolition law in March, 1781. One of its purposes was to allow residents of that part of the state claimed by Virginia at the time the abolition law was enacted additional time to register their slaves. But in a test vote the assembly showed that it was ready to extend the registration period for the entire state until January, 1782. This meant that those Negroes who had been emancipated by their masters' failure to register them would be returned to slavery.[47]

Indications that the assembly was willing to modify the abolition law so soon after its enactment alarmed Negroes and abolitionists. A group of Negroes emancipated because of their masters' failure to register them begged the assembly to allow them to remain free. "Philotheuros" urged the assembly to reject demands for an extended registration period—the law had been frequently published and ignorance of the law was no excuse for its evasion. Although masters who had failed to register their Negroes would suffer a loss, "the injustice to the negroes, and discredit to the assembly, would infinitely overbalance such considerations." The unregistered Negroes were free "and it would be . . .

[46] Brunhouse, *Counter-Revolution,* pp. 89–90.

[47] *Pa. H. of R., 1776–1781,* pp. 537, 540, 547, 562, 570, 573, 576, 586, 591–95, 601, 604–5, 607, 679, 690–92.

[an] indelible . . . stain on the legislative annals of this state to deprive them of the blessings of liberty." [48]

Throughout the previous year's discussion of abolition the pro-slavery elements had failed to produce a spokesman. Now, however, a writer in the *Pennsylvania Journal* presented a comprehensive defense of slavery against the arguments of a generation of abolitionists. He began with a personal attack, asserting that many of those who had eagerly purchased slaves at an earlier time were now actively condemning those who defended slavery. Abolitionists now paid no heed to the dangers of emancipation, just as formerly they had ignored the dangers of importing slaves.

Slavery was justifiable, being based on the right to punish criminals and capture prisoners during wars. American slave traders had saved many African war prisoners who would have been put to death if they had not been bought as slaves. To those who argued that these reasons could not justify the slavery of the children of slaves, he said that wars created a national guilt, shared by unborn generations.

Slavery was justified in the Bible. Although some might maintain that this privilege was restricted to the Israelites, they would have a hard time proving it, for "it would be pure heathenism to say, that ever God granted any thing as a privilege that was unjust in itself." Several antislavery writers had asserted that since the Jews had been allowed to keep their bondsmen only six years, this same reasoning ought to limit the servitude of the Negroes. In this instance, however, the example of the Jews did not apply. Abolitionists had also argued that the cruelties of the slave trade made slavery unjustifiable. Addressed "to the passions of men," this argument was faulty because it could apply with equal force to all trades subject to abuse. If the trade was carried on with cruelty, it should be regulated, but this was no reason to abolish slavery.

Striking at the root of the current agitation for abolition, the writer suggested that "some are prejudiced against perpetual servitude, from a maxim they have received, that *all mankind are born alike free.* Oh flattering language! but not

[48] *Ibid.,* p. 607; *Pennsylvania Packet,* December 2, 1780.

true, unless taken in a very restricted sense." Men were not born equally free from disease or sin; they were born subject to the control of parents and governments. Regardless, it was absurd to apply this reasoning to the case of the enslaved Negroes. Furthermore, he ominously pointed out, this philosophy was "neither friendly to church or state, as it is frequently used."

In conclusion, this eloquent defender of slavery maintained that his espousal of the legitimacy of perpetual servitude did not mean that he was not aware of the cruelties inflicted on the Negro slaves. He urged laws to prevent masters from mistreating their bondsmen, to require slaveowners to educate their Negroes, and to allow slaves to change their masters. Legislatures should devote their energies, not to a general abolition of slavery, but to the gradual liberation of some Negroes so that the states would not become overstocked with slaves and so that justice would be tempered with mercy. Extreme caution should be exercised, however, lest the dangers of manumission lead to a new kind of slavery—a bondage of the whites to the fear of a corrupt Negro population. The only safe way to alleviate the condition of the Negroes would be to allow Congress to devise a national policy of purchasing Negroes from their masters and then setting them free on their own lands. "But our present circumstances seem to render it highly imprudent, if not impracticable . . . to enter upon so difficult an affair." In the meantime, "Christians have reason to complain, when their servants are forced from them without sufficient compensation." [49]

"Liberalis" wrote an extensive reply to this unabashed apology for slavery, but another abolitionist returned to the immediate issue—the proposed bill to allow masters to retain their unregistered slaves. He argued that allowing masters in the previously disputed territory a longer registration period was justifiable, but that a general extension of registration was not. This would involve the enslavement of free citizens. The problem was not whether the Negroes in question should be declared slaves, "but whether the legislature,

[49] *Pennsylvania Journal*, January 31, February 5, 21, 1781.

whose powers are wholly derived from the freemen of the state, can make a law to enslave any freeman." Such a law would jeopardize the freedom of all Pennsylvanians. The writer charged that the claim that the bill was necessary to protect the rights of masters who had failed to register their Negroes through ignorance of the law was specious. According to "Public reports" one of those who had petitioned for the bill was a member of the legislature who had voted against the abolition law, and another petitioner had discussed the bill in public *before* the registration deadline.[50]

A Negro, writing in *Freeman's Journal,* implored the assembly not to return him to the slavery he and his family had just escaped. "To make a law to hang us all, would be *merciful,* when compared with this law; for many of our masters would treat us with unheard of barbarity, for daring to take advantage (as we have done) of the law made in our favour." Slavery was bad enough, but it became unbearable after a short period of freedom.[51]

The storm of protest raised by the attempt to reenslave the unregistered Negroes had its effect. On September 22, 1781, pro-slavery legislators attempted to amend a bill exempting southern refugees from the abolition law. They proposed adding a clause allowing the former owners of unregistered Negroes to keep them in their service for a limited period. Although this measure, unlike its predecessor, would not have permanently reenslaved the Negroes, it was easily defeated. On September 26 the house went further and stipulated that the bill exempting the southern refugees could not be construed as allowing for the reenslavement of any Negroes freed by the abolition law. Those who had envisioned the gradual erosion of the benefits granted by the abolition law were soundly defeated.[52]

Masters of unregistered Negroes continued, nonetheless, to petition for permission to retain them in bondage. In March, 1782, a motion to appoint a committee to draft a bill for this purpose was defeated by only one vote. A month later,

[50] *Ibid.,* April 4, 1781; *Freeman's Journal,* June 13, 1781.
[51] *Freeman's Journal,* postscript, September 21, 1781.
[52] *Pa. H. of R., 1776–1781,* pp. 667, 684, 689, 690, 693–96.

however, the assembly decided to allow masters who were living in the territory that had been claimed by Virginia additional time to register their Negroes. Almost all of the members who voted against this special extension of the registration period had voted in favor of the general extension. The pro-slavery representatives obviously hoped that defeat of the special provision for masters in the formerly disputed territory would bring pressure for a general extension of the registration period. The strategy was obvious and antislavery men, who had resisted any general extension, now supported the request of the southwestern Pennsylvania slaveowners. As in the case of the abolition law, the vote on extending the registration period did not follow party lines, but eastern conservatives resisted a statewide extension while the Scotch-Irish radicals of the backcountry supplied the bulk of its support. Although individual masters continued to petition for permission to retain their unregistered slaves, no movement to revise the abolition law gained serious support in the assembly after April, 1782. Abolition had been accepted as a reality even by its enemies.[53]

THE REVOLUTION AND ABOLITION

The years of the Revolutionary War had brought great gains for northern Negroes. All the northern states, except New York and New Jersey, had taken steps to eradicate slavery. Vermont took the lead by abolishing slavery in her constitution of 1777; a combination of the bill of rights and judicial interpretation ended slavery in Massachusetts and New Hampshire. Pennsylvania, Rhode Island, and Connecticut adopted gradual abolition, guaranteeing freedom to future generations of Negroes. Undoubtedly the revolutionary élan was a moving force behind the policy of abolition.

[53] *Pa. 6 H. of R.*, pp. 568, 569, 582, 585, 604, 612, 633–34, 689; *Pa. 7 H. of R.*, pp. 892, 902, 912, 964; *Pa. 8 H. of R.*, pp. 44, 53, 110. (Whenever sessional journals or laws of a state or colonial legislature are cited the following abbreviated form has been used: e.g., *N.J. 17 Assembly 2*, or *N.J. 17 Laws 2*, to indicate the journals or laws of the seventeenth New Jersey Assembly, second session. When no session number is provided, the citation refers to the first session. Whenever reprinted or compiled editions have been used, a full citation has been supplied.)

The Revolutionary generation was sincere in its espousal of the Rights of Man; and men who were convinced that a three-penny duty on tea was a step to tyranny could recognize that slavery was a violation of natural rights. In the preamble to their abolition acts, both Pennsylvania and Rhode Island appealed to the ideology of the American Revolution to justify their actions. In both these states the success of abolition was also due to the efforts of the Quaker abolitionists, whose plea that slavery was incompatible with Christianity prepared the way for the Whig-abolitionists' argument that it was irreconcilable with the Rights of Man.

But the North had not been completely converted. Pennsylvania masters continued to press for the reenslavement of their unregistered Negroes, Massachusetts slaveowners grumbled about erroneous judicial decisions, and New York and New Jersey, with the heaviest concentrations of slaves, appeared unmoved.

The success of the abolitionists in New England and Pennsylvania focused attention on New York and New Jersey where slavery remained entrenched as firmly after the Revolution as before. New York and New Jersey were crucial to the success of the abolitionists. Of all the northern states, slavery was most important economically and socially in these two states. New York and New Jersey would be the testing ground for gradual abolition. But the difficulty of promoting gradual abolition in these important states was compounded by the fact that the pre-Revolutionary antislavery agitation, which had prepared the way for abolition elsewhere in the North, had had little impact in New York and in the non-Quaker areas of New Jersey.

THE NEW YORK CONSTITUTION AND ABOLITION

The strength of pro-slavery opinion in New York was demonstrated at an early date. In the spring of 1777 when the New York Provincial Congress was drafting a constitution, Gouverneur Morris suggested that it should contain a promise of eventual abolition. Morris maintained that "a regard to the rights of human nature and the principles of our holy religion, loudly call upon us to dispense the blessings of freedom to all mankind," but since "it would at present be productive of great dangers to liberate the slaves within this State," he suggested that the constitution recommend to a future legislature "to take the most effectual measures consistent with public safety, and the private property of individuals, for abolishing domestic slavery." After some debate, it became obvious that a majority of the delegates opposed the resolution and Morris offered a substitute, eliminating the assertion that slavery was contrary to human nature and religion. This proposal was at first accepted, with only Ulster County and New York voting against it, but a parliamentary maneuver resulted in an indefinite postponement of the question, and the 1777 constitution was adopted without any promise of eventual liberty to the slaves.[1]

In New Jersey, Quaker abolitionists had carried on a strenuous campaign to induce the legislature to modify the slave code, a campaign which reached its height shortly before the war. A Presbyterian minister, the Reverend Jacob Green, added his support to the antislavery forces in New Jersey in 1776 in a pamphlet opposing reconciliation with Great Britain. A strong advocate of independence, Green hoped that once the American states were free they would abolish slavery, since it was "a dreadful absurdity . . . that a people who are so strenuously contending for liberty, should at the same time encourage and promote slavery." In 1778 Samuel Allinson, a respected Quaker, expressed similar sentiments in a letter to Governor William Livingston, asking him to take the lead in working for the abolition of slavery in New Jersey. "I fear America never can or will prosper in a right manner; or receive & enjoy true peace . . . until she 'proclaims Liberty to the captives, and Lets the oppressed go free.'" Livingston replied that he shared Allinson's sentiments and that he had proposed that the assembly should "lay the foundation for . . . manumission." The house, however, "thinking us rather in too critical a situation to enter on the consideration of it at that time; desired me in a private manner to withdraw the message." He had complied with this request (there is no reference to abolition in the version of the governor's message printed in the assembly *Journal*) , but he told Allinson that he would continue to use all his influence to secure an end to slavery in New Jersey.[2]

---

[1] *Journals of the Provincial Congress, Provincial Convention, Committee of Safety and Council of Safety of the State of New York* (Albany, 1842) , pp. 887, 889.

[2] [Jacob Green], *Observations: on the Reconciliation of Great-Britain, and the Colonies* . . . (Philadelphia, 1776) , note 29; Allinson

The same session of the New Jersey Assembly that asked Livingston to withdraw his recommendation for abolition nonetheless objected to the proposed Articles of Confederation on the grounds that the requirement that troop quotas be based on a state's white population was a violation of the Declaration of Independence. Even if it was necessary or expedient to deny liberty to men of *"a particular Colour,"* they should still be counted in assessing troop quotas, since "all the inhabitants of every Society . . . are bound to promote the Interests thereof." [3] The New Jersey legislature obviously believed that men were born equal in respect to duties if not rights.

THE NEW JERSEY DEBATE ON SLAVERY

The abolition of slavery in Pennsylvania aroused great interest in New Jersey. The *New Jersey Gazette* expressed its approval of the step taken by Pennsylvania, calling it an "act of humanity, wisdom and justice." Several months later, the *Gazette* printed the abolition law in its entirety. In September, 1780, three petitions for gradual abolition were presented to the New Jersey legislature, but they were first postponed and then met with strong opposition. A routine motion to permit the petitions to be read a second time passed by only one vote, and after they were read again two-thirds of the house concurred in a motion to file them without taking any further action. [4] The New Jersey legislature was still not ready even to discuss the merits of abolition.

The failure of the assembly to take up the question did not reflect public apathy. To the contrary, beginning in the fall of 1780 New Jersey newspapers carried an increasing number of letters on slavery and abolition, constituting perhaps the most extensive newspaper debate of the subject before the 1830's. John Cooper (soon to be elected a member of the

---

to Livingston, July 13, 1778, Livingston to Allinson, July 25, 1778 (Allinson Letters, MS copies in the Rutgers University Library, Rutgers, N.J.) .

[3] *N.J. 2 Assembly,* 145, 148. (For explanation of legislative citations, see p. 137, n. 53.)

[4] *New Jersey Gazette,* February 23, May 17, 1780; *N.J. 4 Assembly 4,* 262; *N.J. 5 Assembly,* 11, 20–21, 27.

council from Burlington) opened the debate with a letter published in September. He pointed out that at a time when the Americans were spilling their blood in the defense of liberty, they should not neglect the enslaved Negroes. Having declared all men to be equal by birth, the Americans should be consistent and liberate their slaves or "our words must rise up in judgment against us." Americans could not expect God to listen to their prayers for victory "whilst the groans of our slaves are continually ascending mingled with them."

Cooper was unique among abolitionists of the Revolutionary generation in his disdainful rejection of gradualism: "if we keep our present slaves in bondage, and only enact laws that their posterity shall be free, . . . we save that part of our tyranny . . . which to us . . . is of the most value." This would be a most wicked policy. "It would be plainly telling our slaves, we will not do justice unto you, but our posterity shall do justice unto your posterity."

"If we are determined not to emancipate our slaves," Cooper urged, "let us alter our language; . . . let us . . . declare to the world, that tyranny is a thing we are not principled against, but that we are resolved not to be slaves, because we ourselves mean to be tyrants." But, "if . . . neither the love of justice, nor the feelings of humanity are sufficient to induce us to release our slaves from bondage, let the dread of divine retribution—of national calamities—induce us to do it." [5]

In reply, "A Whig" argued that Cooper's plan was utterly impractical and inappropriate. No defender of slavery, the "Whig" claimed to favor gradual abolition, but, he asserted, freeing the present generation of slaves at a time when much of the country was laid waste by war would be absurd. Moreover, since "all slaves are in reality as much the property of their masters as the gold and silver for which they were bought, . . . they cannot be deprived of them without being paid the value, which will be a new and heavy tax upon the publick." Furthermore, Negroes were unfit to be free because of the bad habits they had acquired as slaves.

[5] *New Jersey Gazette,* September 20, 1780.

There was no pressing need to liberate them because they were well treated and were "better off than the generality of the white poor, who are obliged . . . to work harder than the slaves in general in this state." The "Whig" urged caution; he had heard that the Pennsylvania abolition law would probably be repealed or altered "on the ground of inexpediency." [6]

"A Friend to Justice" rose to Cooper's defense. The "Whig" had prostituted the name because "A Whig . . . abhors the very idea of slavery." Since slaves were not a legitimate form of property (slavery being based on theft), there could be no injustice in liberating the Negroes. Compensation should be paid to the slaves for their years of involuntary service, not to their masters. As for the argument that the slaves were well treated, the "Whig" had ignored the true nature of slavery, "the intolerable mortification that must incessantly arise from being wholly subservient to the will of another." [7]

"Eliobo" undertook one of the most comprehensive statements of the pro-slavery argument ever heard in the North. He could not understand the cause of the sudden disposition in the minds of many to free the slaves but supposed it was based on the absurd notion that the Negroes were miserable in slavery. This was utterly false. The Negroes, born in slavery, expected nothing more. Accustomed to having all their needs cared for, they enjoyed "more happiness, and a state of superior felicity to their master's."

If the Negroes were freed, they would be unable to support themselves because of their "deep wrought disposition to indolence and laziness." In general, they did not earn enough for their masters to pay for their own support, and if they were free they would certainly be unable to support their families. Furthermore, "want of judgment and discretion is national in Negroes," and they exhibited a "general looseness of passions and [an] uncontrovertible propensity to gratify and satiate every thirst . . . without attending to the consequences." Their passion for liquor was uncontrollable and

[6] *Ibid.,* October 4, 1780.
[7] *Ibid.,* November 8, 1780.

would be even worse when they were free. Freedom would bring into full bloom every vice they showed even traces of while they were enslaved. He predicted that freeing the Negroes would be so disastrous that the whites would be forced to reenslave them.

"Eliobo" refused to accept the claim of most antislavery writers that Negroes could be improved by education. Furthermore, once they were free, the debased Negroes would be on an equal footing with whites, making it impossible to prevent miscegenation; consequently, "our land would swarm with mulattoes." The most important objection to emancipation, however, was the danger of the freed Negroes revolting against the whites and setting up their own kingdom. "None can deny that those are the natural consequences of making them free." [8]

"Eliobo's" extreme arguments readily lent themselves to ridicule. The Reverend Jacob Green substituted the word "slaveowner" for "Negro" in many of "Eliobo's" arguments, showing the ignorance and the dangers to be feared at the hands of this class. In a satirical piece, "Eliobo Secundus" described a meeting of slaves at which "Eliobo's" letters were read. When the Negroes were told that the slaves were happier than their masters, they jumped for joy, crying out: "Poor Massa!—Me wish you massa as happy as I; I pity you massa . . . I pity your poor unhappy children; . . . Oh massa! I could be willing to be master one week that you and your family might taste the superior happiness I now feel." The master's family was extremely depressed when it learned of its inferior position. "They most bitterly cursed their parents for being such enemies to their posterity as not to give them a Negro education." Not only were the slaves convinced that they should no longer seek liberty, but many whites had changed their minds on the value of freedom.

Those who fully adopted your scheme, have remarkably cleared up the disputes between Great Britain and America. . . . They remember the sweets of arbitrary government under George the Third . . . and mourn the sad effects of freedom under the

[8] *New Jersey Journal,* November 29, December 27, 1780.

Congress, who have vainly imagined that liberty is preferable before slavery.[9]

"Marcus Aurelius" issued a blistering attack on Green, accusing him of trying to expiate some hidden crime. And so the debate continued in the pages of the *New Jersey Journal* for several more issues, with each succeeding letter becoming more vituperative.[10]

Meanwhile, the pages of the *New Jersey Gazette* featured a letter from "Impartial," pointing out that slaves were a legitimate form of property, that the constitution protected men from being deprived of their property without due process of law, and that the legislators had sworn to uphold the constitution. Accordingly, they could take no action to free the Negroes without the consent of their owners. The Golden Rule required men to be kind to their Negroes, but no more enjoined masters to free their slaves than creditors to release debtors from their obligations. "Impartial" hoped that individual masters would emancipate their slaves or that the public, by subscription and not by law, would purchase their freedom. But all steps to end slavery should be postponed until the war ended and it was possible to settle the Negroes in a separate region.[11]

"A Lover of True Justice" rejected antislavery arguments based on the Declaration of Independence; the greater part of mankind was not in fact born free—children were subject to their parents, wives to their husbands—so that "arguments drawn from this topick prove too much; and therefore nothing." He was willing to envision an eventual emancipation of the slaves, providing it was done according to certain principles: men should not be deprived of their property without compensation, the interests of society should not be neglected (suddenly freeing all the slaves, who were unprepared for freedom, would be disastrous), and miscegenation should be prevented. The only way this could be done was for a group of philanthropic men to purchase the Negroes and allow

[9] *Ibid.*, January 10, 31, 1781.
[10] *Ibid.*, January 17, 24, 31, February 7, 28, 1781.
[11] *New Jersey Gazette*, January 10, 1781.

them to earn their freedom in manufacturing enterprises.[12]

These two pro-slavery pieces did not go unanswered. "E."
denied that slaves were a legitimate form of property, but
"Homo Sum" charged that these arguments had no application to the point at issue—a gradual, not an immediate,
abolition of slavery. "The freedom of those unhappy black
people, induced in so very gradual a manner as it is in
Pennsylvania, must remove every reasonable apprehension of
danger to the state, or private loss to individuals." He had
been a slaveowner for years, but reading the petition
presented to the legislature in September, 1780, had
convinced him of the justice of gradual abolition. Even this
moderate point of view was repugnant to pro-slavery men.
"Truth et Justice" charged that it would be just as illegal to
deprive masters of their property in twenty years as it would
be to do so immediately. A gradual abolition act would be "a
solemn act of publick ROBBERY." [13]

The great debate on slavery in New Jersey clearly demonstrated the strength and persistence of pro-slavery feeling.
Pro-slavery men were still convinced that Negroes were a
legitimate form of property, that slaveowners could not be
deprived of their property without compensation, and that
emancipation presented a grave danger to the public. But
ultimately, all pro-slavery arguments turned on the question
of property rights. As the "Lover of True Justice" put it,
abolitionists would have to devise a scheme that would guarantee that *"no one has his slave forced from him or* [is] *put to
necessary trouble and expence in bringing them up without
an equivalent."* [14] New Jersey abolitionists could find little
comfort in that challenge.

THE DEFEAT OF ABOLITION
IN NEW YORK

Except for a New York law emancipating slaves whose
masters allowed them to enlist in the Revolutionary army,
neither New York nor New Jersey had taken any steps
towards abolishing slavery by the time the Revolutionary

[12] *Ibid.,* February 14, 1781.
[13] *Ibid.,* March 14, 21, April 11, 1781.
[14] *Ibid.,* February 14, 1781.

War drew to a close.[15] In 1785 (a year after the abolitionists' success in Connecticut and Rhode Island), however, anti-slavery men made a concentrated effort to end slavery in New York and New Jersey. The Quakers, gradually freeing themselves from the taint of having opposed the war, took the lead in these campaigns.

Early in 1784 New York Friends were delighted to hear that the state senate was considering a gradual abolition bill, introduced by Ephraim Paine (who later represented New York in Congress). Although the Quakers sent a committee to meet with members of the legislature to urge them to support the measure, the Friends were soon disappointed. The senate postponed the bill to the next session. Edmund Prior, a leading New York Quaker, reported that the excuse given for postponement—the pressure of other business—might have been plausible for some senators but was merely an excuse for others who wanted to get rid of the bill. Nevertheless, "on conversing with divers of the members, we had the satisfaction to find a considerable number to be in favour of it, and those of the most active—and they announced to us a determination to pursue the matter." [16]

In January, 1785, the cause of Negro freedom received a great boost with the organization of the New York Manumission Society. Alarmed by a recent attempt to seize free Negroes and export them for sale as slaves, seventeen New Yorkers pledged themselves to aid defenseless Negroes. From the beginning, Quakers took great interest in the organization, and five of the seventeen founders were members of the New York Monthly Meeting. In its Declaration of Principles, the society promised to work for the liberation of the slaves, and one of its first acts was to petition the legislature for gradual abolition.[17]

[15] "An Act for Raising Two Regiments . . . ," *Laws of the State of New York* . . . (New York, 1792), I, 42. The legislative journals do not indicate any discussion about the clause of the bill emancipating Negro soldiers.

[16] *N.Y. 7 Senate,* pp. 38, 45, 54; Prior to James Pemberton, February 26, March 3, 11, 1784 (Pemberton Papers, MSS at the Historical Society of Pennsylvania), XL, 103.

[17] John Cox, Jr., *Quakerism in the City of New York, 1657–1930* (New York, 1930), p. 62; New York Manumission Society, "Minutes" (MSS, New-York Historical Society), I, 1–2, 3–4, 17.

Even before the manumission society acted, Paine had reintroduced his abolition bill, and the senate swiftly passed the measure. In the assembly, a committee appointed in response to a Quaker petition had already recommended a gradual abolition law, and the approval of the committee report, thirty-two to ten, must have led the friends of the Negro to see victory within their grasp.[18]

When the house took up the bill, a hostile motion by an Ulster County representative to postpone the bill to the next session was easily defeated. But now the opponents of abolition were clearly identified; representatives of Kings, Richmond, and Ulster counties, where there were many slaves and where Dutch slaveowners were zealous of their property rights, strongly opposed the bill. At this point Aaron Burr, a newcomer to politics but already adept at muddying political waters, offered an amendment. Instead of following Pennsylvania's example of gradual abolition, Burr suggested an immediate and total abolition of slavery. Pro-slavery assemblymen hastened to vote for the Burr proposal, realizing that making the bill more radical would make its defeat more certain. Antislavery members saw through the scheme, however, and rallied to reject this seemingly generous proposal. They also defeated an attempt to extend the period of enforced servitude required for the Negro children freed by the act. After their setback on this issue, pro-slavery men proposed that masters be freed from the obligation of supporting these children, assuming, no doubt, that an abolition bill that would require the public to assume the burden of supporting thousands of Negro children would be easily defeated. Once more, however, they failed. A section of the bill that required masters to educate the children of their slaves was also retained—and by a large majority. Abolitionists had cause to celebrate; it seemed as if New York was close to enacting an abolition statute more liberal than Pennsylvania's famed law.[19]

When the house resumed its consideration of the bill in March, however, it adopted three amendments designed to

[18] *N.Y. 8 Senate 2*, pp. 8, 15, 20, 21, 22, 23; *N.Y. 8 Assembly 2*, pp. 11, 14, 15.

[19] *N.Y. 8 Assembly 2*, pp. 48, 49, 53–57, 59.

relegate free Negroes to a position of permanent inferiority. These amendments made Negroes ineligible for public office and unable to serve as witnesses, deprived them of the right to vote, and made interracial marriages illegal. When the senate refused to concur, the assembly reconsidered and dropped the ban on officeholding but stood fast in its insistence on the other two amendments. After an assembly-senate conference, the lower chamber agreed to remove the ban on marriages while the senate accepted the denial of voting rights for Negroes. The bill was then sent to the Council of Revision, which vetoed the measure.[20]

The Council of Revision's sole objection to the bill was the disputed voting clause. The veto message argued that the denial of voting rights implied an exclusion of Negroes from the right to hold office, that it was unconstitutional and contrary to the Revolutionary principle of no taxation without representation, and that it would be dangerous since the Negroes might conspire to overthrow a constitution that provided benefits they could not enjoy. The senate voted to override the veto, but the assembly refused. Those who had supported the voting restriction now voted to sustain the veto, whereas those who had objected to the restriction voted to override a veto message which expressed their own feelings on Negro rights. The abolitionists preferred a bad bill to no bill at all, and pro-slavery representatives, having severely weakened the measure, now delivered the coup de grace.[21]

The narrow defeat of the abolition bill was extremely disheartening to the friends of the Negro but, according to a writer in the *New York Packet,* news of the bill's defeat was greeted with "great joy and rejoicing" by "all the slave mongers." He caustically noted that those who openly defended slavery were influenced by the spirit of he "who first enslaved mankind." But those assemblymen who, "under the pretext of passing a bill for manumitting slaves," worked so assiduously to put clauses into the bill to defeat its purpose exceeded the Devil, their father, "in wickedness and deceit." New Yorkers ought to refrain from electing slaveholders to

[20] *Ibid.,* pp. 62–64, 76, 77, 84, 86; *N.Y. 8 Senate 2,* pp. 39, 42, 44, 45, 47, 55–56.

[21] *N.Y. 8 Senate 2,* pp. 55–56; *N.Y. 8 Assembly 2,* pp. 119, 120.

the legislature, "for those who make slaves of the blacks," he warned, "will likewise of the whites." [22]

A few days later another writer replied with a stinging attack on the abolitionists and their motives. Emancipation, he charged, would lead to "the total subversion of our liberties." The Negroes, "in combinations with their friends the Quakers, would give every assistance to our enemies, as . . . in the late contest, when they fought against us by whole regiments, and the Quakers at the same time supported every measure of Great-Britain to enslave us." The Friends, he sarcastically noted, were much more zealous for the liberty of the Negroes now than they had been for the freedom of white men in 1776 and 1777. Their motives were obvious; with the aid of the Negroes they would be able to obtain a greater influence in the government. [23]

Discouraging as the defeat of the abolition bill was, it did not spell a complete failure to obtain relief for New York's Negroes. Shortly after the veto, the legislature tacked a rider to a financial measure that reinstated some of the clauses of the defunct abolition bill. It prohibited the importation of Negroes into New York and emancipated illegally imported Negroes. The bill also allowed masters to free their slaves without posting bonds if the overseers of the poor certified that the Negro was under fifty years of age and capable of supporting himself. Finally, the bill provided for jury trials for slaves accused of capital crimes. [24]

The manumission society continued active in its concern for New York Negroes. The society's standing committee reported in the summer of 1785 that it had succeeded in persuading several masters to manumit their slaves and that others, convinced of the injustice of their former treatment of the Negroes, might be induced to treat them with less severity, if not to liberate them. Although "a great number of Persons are violently opposed to the Emancipation of their

[22] *Loudon's New York Packet,* March 31, 1785.

[23] *Ibid.,* April 4, 1785.

[24] *N.Y. 8 Assembly 2,* pp. 59, 60, 124, 126, 128, 142, 153; *N.Y. 8 Senate 2,* pp. 66, 68; "An Act granting a bounty on hemp . . . and for other purposes . . . ," *Laws of the State of New York . . .* (Albany, 1886), II, 120–21.

Slaves," the committee hoped that the good example set by others as well as the force of true religion would eventually "dispel the mist which Prejudice, self Interest and long Habit have raised." Nonetheless, "the period of compleat Freedom" was still "considerably remote." [25]

In February, 1786, the standing committee reported several cases of "glaring Oppression" and noted that some masters were exporting their slaves to the plantation colonies. A few months later the committee reported that a "very considerable" number of Negroes had been exported and, to make matters worse, some of them were undoubtedly kidnapped free Negroes. In an effort to put a halt to this evil, the society petitioned the legislature to prohibit the sale of Negroes outside the state. The senate passed a bill for this purpose but the measure failed in two sessions in the assembly.[26] The abolitionists had to be content with a law emancipating slaves who had become state property as a result of the confiscation of Tory estates.[27]

New York abolitionists were dealt another cruel blow by the legislature in 1788 when, in the course of a general revision of the state's laws, it enacted the first comprehensive slave code since 1730. The first section, which held that every Negro who was a slave at the time the act was passed would continue to be held in slavery, clearly provided a firm legal basis for the continuance of bondage. Three years after the abolitionists had thought the goal within their grasp and twelve years after the Declaration of Independence, New York riveted more firmly than ever the fetters of slavery on her Negro population. After this, New Yorkers could no longer argue that slavery was merely an unwelcome legacy of colonial rule. The independent state of New York had put its seal of approval on the institution. The new code did contain one concession to the pleas of the manumission society,

[25] N.Y. Manumission Soc., "Minutes," I, 21–23.

[26] *Ibid.*, I, 35, 37, 39, 41–45; *N.Y. 9 Senate,* pp. 34, 42, 56, 57, 77, 86; *N.Y. 9 Assembly,* pp. 153, 154; *N.Y. 10 Assembly,* pp. 70, 71.

[27] "An Act to Further Amend . . . An Act for the Speedy Sale of Confiscated Estates . . . ," *N.Y. Laws* (1792), I, 278. The legislative journals do not indicate any discussions of the clause that emancipated the Negroes.

however, by making it illegal to buy or receive a slave with the intent to export him. Violators were to pay a fine of £100 and the Negro was to go free.[28]

THE DEFEAT OF ABOLITION
IN NEW JERSEY

The *New Jersey Gazette* had followed the progress of the New York abolition bill of 1785 with great interest. "We feel for the honour of New-Jersey," the *Gazette* commented, "lest she should be behind in adopting a measure so replete with justice and humanity." David Cooper, a New Jersey Quaker who had written two antislavery pamphlets, took the lead in a campaign to persuade New Jersey to abolish slavery. Working tirelessly, he drafted a petition, presented it to the Quaker Meeting for Sufferings, and sent copies to all the New Jersey monthly meetings. In November, 1785, Cooper brought eleven other Friends with him to the legislature and presented the petition. "The speaker, and sundry other members appeared pleased with this move, and the Governor is a warm advocate for the measure," Cooper noted in his diary. A supreme court judge immediately drafted another petition to support the Quaker appeal. This petition was signed by "the most respectable names in the State." "Nevertheless," Cooper observed, "such an opposition was likely to be made as to leave little room to expect much immediate result." [29]

Cooper's assessment of the legislature's mood proved completely accurate. A motion to appoint a committee to prepare a bill for the gradual abolition of slavery and to prohibit the importation of slaves was immediately amended to restrict the committee to consider only the importation of Negroes. Even then it took the tie-breaking vote of the speaker to pass the motion. In February, 1786, the legislature

[28] *N.Y. Laws* (1792), II, 85–87. The legislative journals reveal very little about the bill, indicating only that it was amended several times without indicating the nature of the amendments: *N.Y. 11 Assembly*, pp. 54, 56, 69, 70, 79, 85, 88; *N.Y. 11 Senate*, pp. 36, 38.

[29] *New Jersey Gazette*, March 7, 28, 1785; [William J. Allinson], "Notices of David Cooper," *Friends' Review*, XVI (1862–63), 21.

passed an act that, to grant justice to the Negroes and protection to the laboring population, ended the importation of slaves. But the justice and protection meted out by the law were slight. The fines imposed on violators were low and illegally imported Negroes were not emancipated. Slaves were granted some safeguards by a clause making it illegal for masters to mistreat their bondsmen, but the penalties were very small. Manumissions were made somewhat easier. Masters could free their slaves without having to assume any financial responsibility if their Negroes were in the prime of life and certified as capable of supporting themselves. This feature of the law, however, was rendered distasteful by other clauses restricting free Negroes to second-class citizenship. If convicted of any crime more serious than petty larceny, they could be banished from the state. They could not travel outside of the county in which they had been manumitted without a certificate proving their freedom. Negroes freed in any other state were absolutely prohibited from entering New Jersey.[30] Notwithstanding the few concessions the law made to their aims, the abolitionists had only to read the law to realize how far they still had to go.

OPPOSITION TO SLAVERY IN THE NATION

Despite the reluctance of New York and New Jersey to abolish slavery, the postwar period brought new groups into the antislavery camp. Although the Quakers continued to be the mainstay of the movement, other religious groups now added their influence to efforts for abolition.

In New England members of the Congregational clergy had been active since the beginning of the struggle with Great Britain in persuading their communities of the evils of slavery. John Allen, William Gordon, Levi Hart, and Jonathan Edwards, Jr., had written pamphlets denouncing slavery as incompatible with the ideals of the American Revolution. Samuel Hopkins had used his pulpit in slave-trading Newport to preach the evils of slavery and the African trade. In 1774 Hopkins had failed to persuade the Presbyterian

[30] N.J. 10 Assembly, pp. 15, 24, 34; N.J. 10 Assembly 2, pp. 6, 11, 14, 22, 25–27; N.J. 10 Council 2, pp. 7, 9, 11; N.J. 10 Laws 2, pp. 239–42.

Synod of New York and Philadelphia to take a stand on the issue, but he continued firm in his belief that the clergy and churches of the nation should provide moral leadership in condemning slavery. In 1786 he suggested that the Congregational clergy of Boston and Connecticut join the Synod of New York and Philadelphia in denouncing the slave trade. A year later, the Presbyterians debated a statement that the doctrine of universal brotherhood required church members to promote abolition and the education of Negroes, but ultimately they adopted a much milder pronouncement. It approved the interest many states had taken in abolition and noted that since it might be "dangerous to the community" to allow men without education and "previous habits of industry" to participate fully in "all the privileges of civil society," church members should educate their slaves and allow them to earn money to purchase their own freedom. The meeting also urged Presbyterians to "use the most prudent measures, consistent with the interests and state of civil society, in the counties where they live, to procure eventually the final abolition of slavery in America." [31] Although this was hardly a radical call to arms in the cause of Negro freedom, it clearly put the church on the side of liberty and placed slavery on the defensive.

Individual Presbyterian congregations went further. The Reverend Jacob Green's congregation in Morris County, New Jersey, followed the example of the Quakers and barred slaveholders from membership. Samuel Hopkins' congregation decided that slavery and the slave trade were "a gross violation of the righteousness and benevolence . . . inculcated in the gospel; and therefore we will not tolerate it in this church." [32]

Although the Methodist church in its early years drew

[31] *A Collection of Acts, Deliverances, and Testimonies of the Supreme Judicatory of the Presbyterian Church* . . . (Philadelphia, 1886), p. 806; Hopkins to Levi Hart, February 10, 1786, in Edwards A. Park (ed.), *The Works of Samuel Hopkins* . . . (3 vols.; Boston, 1852), I, 121; *Records of the Presbyterian Church in the United States of America* . . . (Philadelphia, 1841), pp. 539, 540.

[32] "Rev. Jacob Green, of Hanover, N.J.," (*Proceedings of the New Jersey Historical Society*, 1893), 2d ser., XII, 224; Park, *Hopkins*, I, 157.

most of its membership from the South, it followed the example of its leader, John Wesley, and took a forthright stand against slavery. In 1780 American Methodist ministers resolved that "slavery is contrary to the laws of God, man and nature, and hurtful to society." Traveling ministers were told that they would have to manumit their slaves. In 1784 the Methodist Conference, which established the independent American church, required all members to make provision within the year for freeing their slaves—the Methodists, like the Quakers, would bar slaveholders from membership. This rigorous antislavery policy was very unpopular in the South. When Thomas Coke, who had been selected by Wesley to be the first bishop of the American church, visited Virginia in 1785 he encountered violent opposition. Although he hesitated for some time, he finally agreed to suspend the antislavery rules. The church leaders regarded this as merely a strategic retreat and pointed out that they still abhorred slavery and would not "cease to seek its destruction." [33] Nonetheless, the Methodists remained silent on slavery for the next twelve years.

Despite the hostility of the Virginia Methodists, abolitionists could detect signs that antislavery feeling was even spreading to the South. Maryland and Delaware debated gradual abolition plans in the winter of 1785–86, and by the end of the decade both had active abolition societies. Virginia revised her slave code to permit benevolent masters to manumit their slaves. Several leading southern statesmen condemned slavery. In one of the most often quoted passages from his *Notes on Virginia*, Thomas Jefferson pointed out the deleterious effects of slavery. "The whole commerce between master and slave is a perpetual exercise of the most boisterous passions, the most unremitting despotism, on the one part, and degrading submissions on the other." But, he was pleased to note, since the Revolution there had been a

[33] *Minutes of the Methodist Conferences, Annually Held in America, From 1773 to 1794, Inclusive* (Philadelphia, 1795), pp. 38, 62, 71, 83; Methodist Episcopal Church, *Minutes of Several Conversations . . . At a Conference Begun in Baltimore . . . 1784. Composing a Form of Discipline . . .* (Philadelphia, 1785), pp. 15–17; Samuel Drew, *The Life of the Rev. Thomas Coke . . .* (New York, 1818), pp. 135–39.

gradual change in attitudes on slavery and "the way [is] I hope preparing, under the auspices of heaven, for a total emancipation." George Washington also hoped "to see some plan adopted, by which slavery in this country may be abolished by slow, sure, imperceptible degrees." [34]

THE ABOLITIONIST ATTACK ON THE SLAVE TRADE

Although abolitionists were pleased to learn that southern statesmen approved of abolition, they were deeply disappointed with the new federal constitution, which, in deference to southern demands, denied Congress the power to end the slave trade for twenty years. "How does it appear in the sight of Heaven," Samuel Hopkins asked in despair, "that *these states,* who have been fighting for liberty . . . , cannot agree in any political constitution, unless it indulge and authorize them to enslave their fellow-men!" [35]

The limitations placed on the federal government led the Quakers and other abolitionists to accelerate their widespread attack against the slave trade that was reviving on the state level. In the summer of 1787 Moses Brown persuaded the Yearly Meeting to petition the Rhode Island legislature "to prevent that cruel and unjust trade, and finally to abolish that barbarous custom of holding mankind as slaves." As soon as Samuel Hopkins saw the petition, he tried to persuade ministers of other faiths to support it. Although Hopkins was extremely pessimistic (he and the other ministers had little respect for the paper money party in control of the legislature), he was soon able to report that Rhode Island had taken the lead in outlawing the slave trade. Hopkins gleefully announced the result to the Reverend Levi Hart,

[34] Jeffrey R. Brackett, *The Negro in Maryland* (Baltimore, 1889), pp. 52–55; Helen B. Stewart, "The Negro in Delaware to 1829" (Master's thesis, University of Delaware, 1940), pp. 62–66; Mary S. Locke, *Anti-Slavery in America From the Introduction of African Slaves to the Prohibition of the Slave Trade* (Boston, 1901), pp. 74–75; Thomas Jefferson, *Notes on the State of Virginia* . . . ([Paris, 1785]), pp. 298, 300–301; George Washington to John F. Mercer, September 9, 1786, in *The Writings of George Washington,* ed. John C. Fitzpatrick (39 vols.; Washington, D.C., 1931–44), XXIX, 5.

[35] Hopkins to Hart, January 29, 1788, in Park, *Hopkins,* I, 158.

whom he urged to secure a similar law in Connecticut. "Is it not extraordinary, that this State, which has exceeded the rest of the States in carrying on this trade, should be the first Legislature on this globe which has prohibited that trade?" Especially remarkable was the fact that there had been only four votes in opposition. Moses Brown was elated because the bill had been passed not "upon mere commercial views but the more noble and enlarged principles exprest in the memorial and act." [36] Nevertheless, the law would be a dead letter if neighboring states did not close their ports to Rhode Island slave traders.

A Quaker petition to prohibit the slave trade produced no results in Massachusetts in 1787. The next year, however, a notorious case involving the kidnapping of free Negroes aroused a public storm. Jeremy Belknap took advantage of the furor and persuaded the Boston Association of Ministers to support demands for a law providing heavy penalties for kidnappers and making participation in the slave trade a crime. Massachusetts Negroes supported these measures in their own petition and were gratified to see the General Court comply with their requests. [37]

Quakers from New York and New England as well as representatives of the Presbyterian clergy urged Connecticut to follow the lead of Massachusetts and Rhode Island and outlaw the slave trade. Accordingly, Connecticut lawmakers approved a bill in 1788 that forbade Connecticut citizens to participate in the trade and also prohibited the kidnapping of free Negroes. [38]

Pennsylvania Quakers, who had been unable to participate

[36] Mack Thompson, *Moses Brown* (Chapel Hill, N.C., 1962), pp. 190–95; Hopkins to Moses Brown, August 13, October 22, 1787, Hopkins to Hart, November 27, 1787, in Park, *Hopkins*, I, 121–23.

[37] George H. Moore, *Notes on the History of Slavery in Massachusetts* (New York, 1866), pp. 224–27; "Queries Respecting the Slavery and Emancipation of Negroes in Massachusetts, Proposed by the Hon. Judge Tucker of Virginia, and Answered by the Rev. Dr. Belknap," (*Collections of the Massachusetts Historical Society*), 1st. ser., IV, 204–5.

[38] "Extracts from a Letter from New York" (Misc. MSS of the Pennsylvania Abolition Society, Hist. Soc. of Pa.), I, 179; *Public Records of the State of Connecticut* (9 vols.; Hartford, 1894–1953), VI, 472–73.

directly in the great triumph of 1780, had sufficiently recovered their prewar position to press for further gains for the Negro in 1788. Supported by a petition signed by nearly two thousand Philadelphians, they asked the assembly to revise the abolition law to prevent slave traders from fitting out their ships in Philadelphia and to plug the loopholes through which unscrupulous men could evade the purpose of the act.

In response, a legislative committee recommended a comprehensive revision of the abolition act that would prohibit the separation of slave families, punish kidnappers of free Negroes, prevent masters from sending children of slaves (who would be free at twenty-eight) out of the state to cheat them of their freedom, and prohibit masters from sending pregnant slaves out of the state with the intent of denying their children the benefit of the abolition law. The committee agreed with the Quakers' contention that fitting out slave vessels in Pennsylvania ports violated the spirit of the state constitution and the congressional resolve of 1774 to end the importation of slaves. The legislature acted with great dispatch in implementing these suggestions. On March 24, two weeks after approving the report, a bill embodying all of its recommendations was brought before the assembly. The next day, it was read a second time and ordered published for public consideration. Although the constitution required postponing important legislation to the session following publication, the house agreed with the arguments of William Lewis that any delay would only encourage unscrupulous men to continue to evade the intent of the 1780 act. Accordingly, the assembly took up the bill for a third reading March 28. In deference to the objection that prohibiting masters from separating slave families would violate sacred property rights, the house approved an amendment to allow a ten-mile separation, and then passed the bill by a large majority.[39]

The new abolition law enabled Pennsylvania to retain its reputation for being in the forefront in establishing and protecting Negro rights. Not only had Pennsylvania provided

[39] *Pa. 12 Assembly,* pp. 104, 108, 109, 128, 133–35, 137, 159, 164, 170, 177–79, 197; Thomas Lloyd, *Proceedings and Debates of the General Assembly of Pennsylvania Taken in Short-Hand* (4 vols.; Philadelphia, 1787–88), III, 219–25, 231.

for the eventual extirpation of slavery, but it now protected those Negroes who would spend the rest of their lives in bondage from one of the greatest evils they faced—the separation of families.[40]

And in New Jersey the Quakers, who had been so bitterly disappointed with the results of their petition in 1785, returned to the attack three years later. James Pemberton, a prominent Philadelphia Quaker and a leader of the newly revived Pennsylvania Abolition Society, urged Governor William Livingston to support the Quaker attack on slavery and the slave trade. David Cooper, who had spearheaded the earlier Quaker effort, traveled to Princeton, addressed the legislature, and presented a bill drafted by the Quakers. Members of a large committee appointed to consider the bill assured Cooper that they approved of the Quakers' aims. When the bill was brought to the floor, however, "it was pulled to pieces and the most essential parts left out." Nevertheless, Cooper noted, "the disposition of the Assembly is exceedingly changed and softened on this subject since we addressed them in . . . 1785. So that I have little doubt that a law to the Friends' liking may before long be obtained." [41]

The law that finally emerged did not provide for gradual abolition as the Quakers had requested, but it did prohibit participation in the slave trade and afforded slaves an important safeguard by making it illegal to remove them from the state without their consent. It also granted Negroes, bond and free, the same procedural rights in law courts as white men, and repealed the clause of the 1786 law that allowed the courts to banish free Negroes. Furthermore, the act required masters to teach their slaves to read before the Negroes became twenty-one. This was a step in preparing them for freedom (there was no reason why a slave should be able to

---

[40] James T. Mitchell and Henry Flanders (compilers), *The Statutes at Large of Pennsylvania from 1682 to 1801* (16 vols.; Harrisburg, 1908), XII, 52–56; *Pa. 14 Assembly*, pp. 51, 53, 56, 86, 106, 109.

[41] Pemberton to Livingston, November 4, 1788 (Livingston MSS of the Mass. Hist. Soc., Rutgers University Library, Rutgers, N.J.) microfilm copy, reel 9; Allinson, "David Cooper," XVI, 135; *N.J. 13 Assembly,* pp. 15, 17, 19, 27, 54, 59, 68, 72, 75; *N.J. 13 Council,* pp. 15, 17, 19, 20, 24. There is a copy of the Quaker petition in a box of misc. MSS of the Pa. Abolition Soc.

read) and indicated the degree to which the New Jersey legislature had "changed and softened on this subject." Livingston regretted that the assembly would go no further but, he explained to the Quakers, "however desirous the western part of New Jersey may be . . . there are some of the northern counties whom too rapid progress in the business would furnish with an excuse to oppose it altogether." [42] For many years the opposition of these northern counties would continue to prevent the abolitionists from securing the freedom of the Negroes.

New York antislavery men faced a similar difficulty. Although the abolitionists had achieved great success in their short, concentrated campaign to close northern ports to slave traders, New York still allowed them to prepare ships for the nefarious trade in her harbor. When James Pemberton urged the New York Manumission Society to ask the legislature for a law similar to those passed by the other northern states, John Murray, Jr., explained the realities of New York politics.

I have to lament the many obstacles & embarrassments, which the Advocates for Freedom in this State, have to encounter with, and none perhaps of a more potent nature than the circumstance of a great body of Dutch, who hold Slaves in this government, & seem, as it were startled, & in arms, whenever a proposition comes forward touching that People, so that we have but little to hope for from our Legislature at this time, as I expect a large proportion of the Assembly, is constituted of Dutch Men. [43]

Murray's analysis of the temper of the assembly proved correct. When Matthew Clarkson, vice-president of the New York Manumission Society, introduced a gradual abolition bill, the house refused even to refer it to the committee of the whole, usually a routine and uncontested step. A Quaker petition, asking that slave traders be prohibited from fitting

---

[42] *N.J. 13 Laws,* pp. 486–88; Livingston to James Pemberton, October 20, 1788, in Richard P. McCormick, *Experiment in Independence* (New Brunswick, N.J., 1950) , p. 65.

[43] [Pemberton] to N.Y. Manumission Soc., sent with covering letter to Murray, January 11, 1790, Murray to Pemberton, February 4, 1790, in misc. MSS of the Pa. Abolition Soc., II, 81, 85.

out their vessels in New York, was rejected by the assembly on the grounds that the constitution vested sole control over commerce in the hands of the federal government. With the pro-slavery elements in firm control, the assembly proceeded to undo some of the gains the abolitionists had won previously. The assembly narrowly defeated a move to repeal the prohibition on exporting slaves but approved a bill to permit the export of any slave guilty of certain misdemeanors. When the senate balked at this and amended it to allow the export only of slaves convicted of a crime, the house refused to concur. It soon became clear that the senate would not back down and that the house would have to choose between the senate version or no bill at all, so the assembly acquiesced to the version of the bill that was less likely to be abused by avaricious masters who would try to sell their slaves in the South.[44] But the friends of the Negro had, nevertheless, met with a resounding defeat.

The report of a committee of the New Jersey legislature, appointed to consider a petition for gradual abolition in 1790, appeared to sum up the attitude of New York and New Jersey legislators toward abolition. The committee argued that Negroes were sufficiently protected by the existing laws, which prevented their export without their consent, and penalized masters who abused their slaves. And voluntary manumissions were encouraged. Although the legislature could pass a law, freeing Negroes born thereafter at twenty-eight, the committee observed that "from the state of society among us, . . . and progress of the principles of universal liberty there is little reason to think that there will be any slaves at all among us 28 years hence." Furthermore, "experience seems to show that precipitation in the matter may do more hurt than good, not only to the citizens of the state in general, but to the slaves themselves." Therefore, the report concluded, "it is not necessary nor expedient at this time, to make any new law upon the subject."[45] Abolitionists drew little comfort from a document that proclaimed that the

[44] *N.Y. 13 Assembly 2,* pp. 12–15, 21, 37, 39, 52–54, 65, 69, 70, 79, 81–82, 89; *N.Y. 13 Senate 2,* pp. 26, 28–30, 35–37; *N.Y. Laws* (1792), II, 312.

[45] *N.J. 14 Assembly 2,* pp. 17, 20.

inevitable success of their principles made any action on the part of the legislature not only unnecessary but also inexpedient.

It would have been difficult for abolitionists to find evidence to support the sanguine hopes of the New Jersey legislative report. According to the 1790 census, there were over 11,000 slaves in New Jersey, and despite liberalized manumission procedures, less than twenty per cent of the Negro population was free. There were still large concentrations of slaves in the Dutch counties of northeastern New Jersey—over eighteen per cent of the Bergen County population was slave. In New York slavery was even more firmly entrenched. Over 21,000 of the nearly 26,000 Negroes in the state were slaves in 1790. As before the war, slavery was heavily concentrated in certain areas; nearly one-third of the population of Kings County was made up of slaves. In the city of Albany, only 238 out of 1,146 heads of families reported that they owned no slaves.[46] An analysis of the 1790 census reports for New York and New Jersey would have given scant comfort to those who believed that slavery would gradually disappear if it were left alone.

ABOLITION SOCIETIES

Although abolitionists had been stymied in their efforts to persuade New York and New Jersey to abolish slavery, they were able to aid the Negroes in several significant ways. The early abolition societies had aims that encompassed more than obtaining abolition laws. When Pennsylvania antislavery men had first organized in 1775, they formed The Society for the Relief of Free Negroes Unlawfully Held in Bondage; and when they reorganized in 1784, after the Quakers emerged from their wartime obscurity, the abolitionists put three aims in their title: "the Abolition of Slavery, the Relief of Free Negroes," and "Improving the Condition of the Colored Race." Both the New York and the Pennsylvania

[46] Thomas F. Gordon, *A Gazeteer of New Jersey* . . . (Trenton, N.J., 1834), p. 30; United States Bureau of the Census, *Heads of Families at the First Census of the United States Taken in the Year 1790* (Washington, D.C., 1908), pp. 9–10, 12–14.

abolition societies devoted a great deal of painstaking effort to securing compliance with existing laws to protect Negroes. With the assistance of a staff of legal advisers, the societies prosecuted stubborn masters who refused to liberate Negroes entitled to freedom. Pennsylvania masters who had neglected to register their slaves were forced to liberate them, if they failed to yield to persuasion. The New York Manumission Society secured the freedom of Negroes who had belonged to confiscated estates and had been emancipated by the legislature. Despite difficulties in detecting clandestine slave traders who preferred to work on dark and foggy nights, New York abolitionists were able to save several slaves and free Negroes destined to be sold illegally in the South. Although New Jersey abolitionists did not organize an antislavery society until 1793, they were aided by sympathetic attorneys and representatives of the Pennsylvania Abolition Society in securing the freedom of several illegally enslaved Negroes.[47]

Both the New York and Pennsylvania abolition societies considered the supervision and protection of free Negroes a major responsibility, believing that the progress of abolition would depend on convincing the reluctant whites that their fears of free Negroes were groundless. At one of its first meetings, the New York Manumission Society urged its standing committee to watch over the conduct of free Negroes and to prevent them "from running into practices of Immorality or Sinking into Habits of Idleness." In 1786 the standing committee recommended the establishment of a free school for Negroes, a project that was to become the most successful activity of the society. Two years later, a special committee appointed to consider ways to "prevent the irregular behavior of Free negroes" suggested using admission to the African Free School as an inducement. Only those free Negroes who had registered with the society would be admitted to the school and to retain the approval of the society, free Negroes would have to stay sober, live clean lives, and refuse to entertain slaves. The freedmen were warned against "allowing Fiddling, Dancing or any noisy Entertainments in

[47] The MS records of the N.Y. Manumission Soc. at the N.Y. Hist. Soc. and of the Pa. Abolition Soc. at the Hist. Soc. of Pa. give evidence of the extensive legal activities of the abolitionists.

their houses." The Pennsylvania Abolition Society instituted a comprehensive plan to aid and supervise free Negroes in 1789. It appointed an elaborate system of committees to supervise morals, to promote education, to secure employment, and to arrange apprenticeships for free Negro children.[48]

The abolitionists carefully followed the proceedings of their state legislatures and promptly intervened when the rights of Negroes were endangered. In 1791 when the Pennsylvania Abolition Society learned of a bill that would allow officers of the federal government to hold slaves in Pennsylvania (as an exception to the abolition law), the society's acting and corresponding committees immediately petitioned for its defeat.[49]

When, shortly after the formation of the new federal government, abolitionists turned to Congress in an attempt to secure Negro rights, they rapidly discovered that Congress was not only unwilling to take any steps towards abolition, but would not even exercise its constitutional powers to regulate the slave trade. In 1790 New York and Philadelphia Friends petitioned Congress to restrict the slave trade, but a petition from the Pennsylvania Abolition Society went further. It urged Congress to exercise its powers under the general welfare clause of the Constitution to "Countenance the Restoration of Liberty" to the Negroes and to "devise means for removing this inconsistency [slavery] from the Character of the American people." The petitions aroused a storm of protest. Pro-slavery congressmen accused the Quakers of advocating bloodshed and insurrection and used the Quakers' refusal to defend American rights during the Revolution to discredit them. One southern congressman was so aroused that he threatened to hang any Quaker who dared venture into his state. But, as a colleague pointed out, the abolition society's petition—signed by the respected Benjamin Franklin, its president—was much more radical than the Quakers' memorial. A southerner remarked that Franklin's signature on the document only proved his senility. (But

[48] N.Y. Manumission Soc., "Minutes," I, 24, 39, 92, 99–101; misc. MSS of the Pa. Abolition Soc., II, 41.

[49] Pa. Abolition Soc., "Minutes," I, 147–48.

Franklin proved he still had his wits about him by publishing a stinging parody of the southern congressmen's arguments.) [50]

Contrary to their expectations, the abolitionists were learning that antislavery sentiment did not advance at a steady pace. It must have been particularly disappointing to those who hoped that their goals would be advanced with the passage of time that while the New York legislature had passed an abolition act in 1785, it refused even to discuss such a measure in 1790. Far from finding increased public acceptance of their aims, the abolition societies were often forced to combat increasing criticism. In 1792 the New York Manumission Society had to call a special meeting to consider the necessity of publishing the aims of the society "in order to remove prejudices and misapprehensions which had arisen, and which if suffered to continue might influence the public against the Society." Two months later the standing committee noted that the society's effectiveness had been reduced because "the Principles and designs of the Society have been grossly misrepresented or extremely misunderstood [and] . . . much opprobrium has been cast" upon the members "and the passions of many raised against them." [51]

The gubernatorial campaign of 1792 heightened opposition to the manumission society. John Jay, one of the candidates, had served as president of the society and his opponents made the most of it. They accused him of wanting to "rob every Dutchman of the property he possesses most dear to his heart, his slaves." Not satisfied with that, they proclaimed that Jay wanted to force "masters to educate the children of those slaves in the best manner, even if unable to educate their own children." Jay issued a diplomatic reply: he believed that all men had a right to freedom, and he would always be "an advocate for the manumission of slaves

---

[50] *Ibid.*, I, 111–13. Congressional reaction to the petitions is vividly described in a series of letters from John Pemberton to his brother James, February 11, March 8, 14, 16, 17, 20, 1790, in misc. MSS of the Pa. Abolition Soc., II, 93, 113, 117, 121, 123, 127. Franklin's parody is in Albert H. Smyth (ed.), *The Writings of Benjamin Franklin* (10 vols.; New York, 1907), X, 87–91.

[51] N.Y. Manumission Soc., "Minutes," I, 161, 165.

in such way as may be consistent with the justice due to them, with the justice due to their master, and with regard due to the actual state of society." [52]

The hostility aroused by the abolition societies was remarkable in view of their moderate aims, restrained conduct, and conservative membership. Leading members of the New York Manumission Society included Alexander Hamilton and his political ally, Congressman Egbert Benson. Melancton Smith, an Anti-Federalist and Clintonian, and Matthew Clarkson, a prominent Federalist, were also members. The most active Quaker member, John Murray Jr., was a leading merchant and a director of the Bank of New York. The New York society was so conservative that after an extended period of debate it could not agree to exclude slaveholders from membership. Both the Pennsylvania and New York societies, although dominated by members of the Society of Friends, sought to gain public acceptance by electing prominent non-Quakers as their first presidents. Benjamin Franklin was never active in the affairs of the Pennsylvania society, but he lent the abolitionists the great prestige of his name by agreeing to serve as president. John Jay was elected president of the New York Manumission Society despite the fact that he continued to own Negroes. (Jay freed his Negroes after they had served a reasonable period to pay for their purchase price.) The Quakers, aware of the lingering legacy of hatred resulting from their failure to support the Revolution, were careful to play down their own roles in the abolitionist movement. Thus the Pennsylvania Abolition Society's 1790 petition to Congress opened with a statement that the society had been formed by "Citizens of various religious denominations." In modern terminology, the abolition societies were often "front" organizations through which members of the Society of Friends could gain wider support for their antislavery policies. The interests of the Quakers and the abolition societies were inexorably intertwined. When James Pemberton, a Quaker member of the Pennsylvania Abolition Society, corresponded with

[52] J. C. Dongan to Jay, Jay to Dongan, February 27, 1792, in *The Correspondence and Public Papers of John Jay*, ed. Henry P. Johnson (4 vols.; New York, 1890–93), III, 413 n., 413–15.

John Murray Jr., they discussed attacks against slavery by both the Quakers and the abolition societies.[53] Although attempts to dissociate abolitionism from the taint of the Quaker war record may have diverted some criticism, the 1790 congressional debate demonstrated that the pro-slavery forces could always condemn abolitionism by identifying it with the allegedly unpatriotic Society of Friends.

Increasingly abolitionists found themselves on the defensive. The wave of Revolutionary enthusiasm for the sacred Rights of Man had receded; even those who had been genuinely caught up in the enthusiasm of the moment, who had been willing to sacrifice private interest for the common good, had long since resumed their ordinary perspectives. If they still thought that slavery was wrong, the thought did not disturb them. They were not reconciled to the destruction of property rights involved in abolition, nor were they prepared to face the possible dangers and competition of a free Negro population. In the twenty-five years since Americans had solemnly resolved that all men were created equal and were equally entitled to liberty, the Negro had made limited gains in the North. But New York and New Jersey strenuously resisted all abolition proposals and as long as they resisted, the cause would falter. All hopes of convincing the South to let the oppressed go free would wither. New York and New Jersey were the great stumbling blocks to the triumph of gradual abolition.

[53] N.Y. Manumission Soc., "Minutes," I, 16, 29, 36, 40, 56. In 1798 Jay listed slaves in an account of his taxable property, noting: "I purchase slaves, and manumit them at proper ages, and when their faithful services shall have afforded a reasonable retribution," William Jay, *The Life of John Jay* (2 vols.; New York, 1833), I, 335. For an example of combining Quaker and abolition society business, see Pemberton to Murray, cited above, note 43.

By the close of the eighteenth century, it had become clear to antislavery men that the completion of their task would require new and intensive efforts. The wartime enthusiasm for the Rights of Man that had contributed to the abolition of slavery in Pennsylvania and in New England seemed to have lost its momentum and could not be counted on to achieve the same goal in New York and New Jersey, not to mention the southern states, unless the abolitionists redoubled their efforts to convince Americans that slavery was immoral and impolitic. Thus in 1792 the New York Manumission Society's acting committee, reporting on means of furthering the aims of the organization, emphasized that "a general diffusion of the principles" of the society was essential to promoting the cause of freedom.[1]

THE SPREAD OF ANTISLAVERY FEELING

Ever since the beginning of the Revolution, the publication of antislavery essays had been increasing. Benjamin Rush recalled in 1787 the great opposition he had encountered in 1773 when he had first spoken in behalf of Negro rights and how, only a few years before, John Woolman and Anthony Benezet had stood alone in their opposition to slavery. Now, however, antislavery sentiment had spread. "The cloud which a few years ago was no larger than a man's hand has descended in plentiful dews and at last covered every part of our land." Although Quakers continued to be prominent

[1] New York Manumission Society, "Minutes" (MSS at the New-York Historical Society), I, 164.

in the ranks of antislavery writers, they tried to remain as anonymous as possible because their sect's attitude toward the war was so unpopular and because they wanted to avoid having to show their works to the Quaker Overseers of the Press. (The Society of Friends had apparently become increasingly cautious in approving antislavery pamphlets and probably refused to permit the publication of a major work by Anthony Benezet.) [2]

Quaker antislavery writers (as well as those of other religious persuasions who now joined them) relied increasingly on arguments derived from principles of Enlightenment thought. Whereas the early Quaker abolitionists had argued that slavery was incompatible with the Golden Rule, antislavery writers now emphasized the inconsistency of slavery with the Rights of Man. As one antislavery writer put it, Americans who had subscribed to the Declaration of Independence and continued to hold slaves condemned themselves by their own words.

If . . . we persevere in this wicked practice . . . , when we have done so much to rescue ourselves from the hands of oppression, will not the world call us liars and hypocrites? Was it for this . . . that half the world was agitated with an eight years war? Was it for this that a hundred thousand men were killed? [3]

Throughout the war, abolitionists had warned that God would not permit Americans to win their freedom until they had liberated their slaves. After the successful conclusion of the war, antislavery writers argued that the American victory should not be interpreted as a sign that God approved of slavery—the steps already taken toward emancipation were "one reason why the . . . Governor of the world has spared and prospered us." But "evil *may*, and we have reason to fear it *will* come upon us, if we do not proceed to a thorough

---

[2] Rush to John Coakley Lettsom, September 28, 1787, in Lyman H. Butterfield (ed.), *Letters of Benjamin Rush* (2 vols.; Princeton, N.J., 1951), I, 441–42; Henry J. Cadbury, "Quaker Bibliographical Notes, II, Anti-slavery Writings," *Bulletin of the Friends' Historical Association*, XXVI (1937), 52–53; Anthony Benezet to George Dillwyn, [1783], David Cooper to Samuel Allinson, June 15, 1783, in George S. Brookes, *Friend Anthony Benezet* (Philadelphia, 1937), pp. 372–75, 457–58.

[3] *American Museum*, I (1787), 210.

reformation of this sin." A later refinement of the argument that God would punish Americans for the sin of slavery maintained that although the war had been won, God now revealed his anger by bringing drought and pestilence to the land.[4]

The depredations of the Barbary pirates who enslaved American seamen enabled abolitionists to draw a meaningful parallel. "Humanus" noted that "Negro masters doubtless shudder at the idea of slavery among the Algerines, and execrate them as barbarous tyrants . . . but are they less barbarous than the followers of Mahomet?"[5]

Abolitionists did not rely only on appeals to reason. Drawing on other Enlightenment themes, such as the cult of the noble savage, antislavery writers published several sentimental pieces, purportedly written by slaves, showing the misery they endured. "The African's Complaint" pictured a slave lamenting:

Oh, ye aged parents: what were your feelings . . . when your child . . . was torn from you by the cruel unfeeling Christians —forced into a floating dungeon more terrible than death itself —bartered as a slave—exposed to contempt and scorn—unjustly marked with the whip of tyranny—his labour unjustly extorted from him . . . —trampled on by a monster whose avaricious heart [is] . . . unsusceptible of the tender feelings of soft humanity!

An "Address to the Heart, on the Subject of American Slavery" reminded readers of the *American Museum* that "The doom of the children of Africa is fixed: their lot is dreadful bondage! O christianity! thou whose mild teacher taught self-denial to the world . . . can thy professors make captive and destroy their brethren?" Abolitionists were also aware of the uses of irony. A New Jersey newspaper printed an account of a Negro who was brought before a justice of the peace for having purchased stolen property. When the

[4] [Samuel Hopkins], "Appendix to the Second Edition . . . ," *A Dialogue Concerning the Slavery of the Africans* (New York, 1785); John Parrish, *Remarks on the Slavery of the Black People* (Philadelphia, 1806), pp. 3–5.

[5] *New Jersey Gazette,* September 18, 1786.

Negro was told that *"the receiver is as bad as the thief,"* he asked the judge if this did not also apply to white men. If it did, then the constable should arrest the owner of the slave Tom, who was standing nearby, because "he buy Tom as I buy de . . . knife . . . He know very well that *poor Tom* be [s]tolen from his old fadder and mudder." [6]

Although most antislavery writers of the period were remarkably moderate, Abraham Bishop, later to become the stormy petrel of Connecticut politics, struck a note that would have gladdened the heart of John Brown. While most Americans were shocked by the bloody revolt of the Negroes of Santo Domingo, Bishop compared their fight for freedom to the American Revolution. "Let us be consistent, Americans, and if we justify our own conduct in the late glorious revolution, let us justify those, who, in a cause like ours, fight with equal bravery." [7]

Noah Webster (Bishop's Yale classmate) employed arguments drawn from liberal economics in his dissertation on the *Effects of Slavery, on Morals and Industry*. Assuming that men might condemn slavery in principle but would not give it up unless it was proved to be against their interests, Webster enumerated the disadvantages of slave labor. Slavery provided a hostile and lazy laboring class; it turned masters into cruel tyrants; it created the danger of insurrections; and its most deplorable effect was "checking or destroying national industry." Webster asserted that a slave was worth only $58 per year (hire plus subsistence), whereas a free laborer was worth $110. Furthermore, a slaveowner had to invest in his labor force, and he ran the risk of losing his slave property through sickness or death, as well as his other possessions through the thievery and negligence of the Negroes. Therefore, slavery was "much the most expensive mode of cultivation." [8]

[6] *New York Weekly Magazine,* II, (1797), 353; *American Museum,* I (1787), 466; *New Jersey Journal,* November 12, 1788.

[7] "J. P. Martin," "Rights of Black Men," *American Museum,* XII (1792), 299–300. "J. P. Martin" was the pseudonym of Abraham Bishop: see Franklin B. Dexter, "Abraham Bishop, of Connecticut, and his Writings" (*Proceedings of the Massachusetts Historical Society*), 2d ser., XIX (1905), 192.

[8] Noah Webster, Jr., *Effects of Slavery on Morals and Industry* (Hartford, Conn., 1793), pp. 5–8, 14, 22–23, 53–54.

ORGANIZING FOR ABOLITION

The abolitionists recognized the importance of influencing public opinion by disseminating antislavery propaganda, but they also realized that achieving their aims would require strengthening the organized opposition to slavery. In the same report in which the New York abolitionists stressed the need for spreading the antislavery argument, they also recommended new organizational efforts. The New York Manumission Society, which had confined its activities largely to the city of New York, was the only antislavery society in the state and there was none at all in New Jersey. The acting committee suggested that the society recruit corresponding members in other areas of the state and promote the formation of a sister society in New Jersey. Although the Pennsylvania Abolition Society included citizens of New Jersey in its membership and had been active in several freedom cases in that state, it also saw the need for a separate New Jersey society and in 1793 appointed a special committee to organize a New Jersey antislavery society. The committee told New Jersey abolitionists that "every State (excepting yours) from Rhode Island to Virginia" had already formed antislavery societies, and it urged the New Jerseymen to follow their example to "complete the Connection." If this were done, all the abolition societies could cooperate and together they could "defy the Influence of Interest or Avarice." Representatives of the Pennsylvania society traveled to Burlington on January 26, 1793, and supervised the birth of the New Jersey Society for Promoting the Abolition of Slavery.[9]

Ever since 1790, the Pennsylvania Abolition Society had urged other antislavery societies to join it in petitioning Congress to regulate the slave trade. By 1792 eight petitions, beside that from the Pennsylvania abolitionists, were presented to Congress. Recognizing the importance of cooperative action, the New York Manumission Society sought a more efficient means of promoting it, and in the fall of 1792

---

[9] N.Y. Manumission Soc., "Minutes," I, 164–67; Pennsylvania Abolition Society, "Minutes" (MSS at the Historical Society of Pennsylvania), I, 175, 177, 185, 189; Pa. Abolition Soc., misc. MSS, III, 208.

issued a call for a convention of antislavery societies to meet in Philadelphia in 1794.[10]

The first abolitionist convention brought together representatives of antislavery societies from Connecticut, New York, New Jersey, Pennsylvania, Delaware, and Maryland. The delegates petitioned Congress to regulate the slave trade, and they also drafted petitions to the states that had not yet abolished slavery. The delegates urged the abolition societies to continue to petition their legislatures for measures to aid the Negro, to facilitate the formation of local antislavery societies, and to take steps to improve the conduct of the free Negroes. On this last point, the convention observed, "We are all too much accustomed to the reproaches of the enemies of our cause, on the subject of the ignorance and crimes of the Blacks, not to wish that they were ill-founded." Although the misbehavior of the free Negroes was attributable to the fact that they had been brought up as slaves, the convention urged the abolition societies to promote the education of free Negroes to prepare them to be good citizens. Recognizing the utility of a periodic exchange of views, the delegates recommended annual conventions.[11]

Delegates to the 1795 convention heard reports of mixed progress. The petition to Congress had resulted in palliative legislation, but of the petitions to the states, only the one submitted to the Connecticut legislature had produced any results. (The Connecticut Assembly had passed a total abolition bill, but it had been defeated in the legislative council.) The convention renewed its appeal to the abolition societies in an address that exhibited a naïve faith in the efficacy of reason, which was so characteristic of much late eighteenth-century thought. It maintained that many men continued to hold slaves and to acquiesce in the pro-slavery argument "merely from want of reflection, and from an habitual attention to their own immediate interest. If to such were often applied the force of reason, and the persuasions of eloquence,

---

[10] Pa. Abolition Soc., "Minutes," I, 167; N.Y. Manumission Soc., "Minutes," I, 172; Pa. Abolition Soc., misc. MSS, III, 232, 234.

[11] *Minutes of the Proceedings of a Convention of Delegates from the Abolition Societies* . . . (Philadelphia, 1794), pp. 3–5, 8, 13–16, 19–21. (Hereafter. *Convention Minutes*).

they might be awakened to a sense of their injustice."
Accordingly, the abolition societies should establish frequent
public orations on the evils of slavery.[12]

ABOLITION DEBATES IN NEW JERSEY
AND NEW YORK

New Jersey abolitionists continued to meet steadfast opposition in their efforts to aid the slaves. In the spring of 1792
they presented several petitions to the legislature, asking for
further reforms of the law on manumissions. The petitions
were referred to the following session and then sent to a
committee that reported a gradual abolition bill. Consideration of the bill was postponed until May, 1793, when the first
section of the bill providing for a total abolition was read,
debated, and rejected.[13] Shortly thereafter, abolitionists were
put on the defensive when the assembly passed a bill making
it more difficult for Negroes to secure their freedom by law
suits. This had been prompted by slaveowners who were
angered at the success of abolitionists in securing the freedom
of Negroes in cases where there were legal imperfections in
their masters' titles. The slaveowners' plans were stymied,
however, when the legislative council failed to act on the
bill.[14]

Another gradual abolition bill advanced through several
readings in the spring of 1794, but it was defeated in the
assembly by a single vote. Joseph Bloomfield, a former officer

[12] *1795 Convention Minutes*, pp. 14, 17, 26–30.

[13] *N.J. 16 Assembly 2*, pp. 21, 34; *N.J. 17 Assembly*, pp. 10, 13, 81, 83;
N.J. 17 Assembly 2, pp. 105, 106, 114, 116–17. (Whenever sessional
journals or laws of a state or colonial legislature are cited the following
abbreviated form has been used: *N.J. 17 Assembly 2*, or *N.J. 17 Laws 2*,
to indicate the journals or laws of the seventeenth New Jersey Assembly, second session. When no session number is provided, the citation
refers to the first session. Whenever reprinted or compiled editions have
been used, a full citation has been supplied.)

[14] *N.J. 17 Assembly 2*, pp. 138, 142, 143, 144; *N.J. 17 Council 2*, p. 18.
Slaveowners had unsuccessfully petitioned for such a bill in two
previous sessions of the Assembly: *N.J. 16 Assembly*, pp. 12, 24, 75; *N.J.
17 Assembly*, pp. 24–25, 69.

of the Revolutionary army and current president of the New Jersey Abolition Society, told Philadelphia abolitionists that "every prudent effort" had been made to support the bill, and although it had been defeated, "the friends . . . to the general emancipation of Blacks are not discouraged, but think their labor in a short time will be blessed with their desired object." Despite Bloomfield's optimism, no action was taken on a petition for gradual abolition presented to the assembly in November, 1794.[15]

The prospects for a rapid abolition of slavery in New York were no more hopeful than in New Jersey. A committee appointed by the manumission society to consider asking the legislature for a gradual abolition law reported in 1793 that such a request "would, in the *present situation of things,* be premature, and therefore *at this time,* it would not be advisable." In 1795, however, in accordance with the recommendations of the convention of antislavery societies, the manumission society appointed a committee to petition for a gradual abolition law. The election of John Jay, former president of the society, to the governorship of New York may have made the abolitionists more optimistic. A few days after the opening of the 1796 legislature a close friend of Jay, James Watson, asked for permission to introduce a gradual abolition bill. The opposition immediately asserted itself and Watson's request was granted only after a roll call vote. The committee to which the bill was referred reported favorably. Its report observed, however, that it would be "unjust and unconstitutional to deprive any citizen or citizens . . . of their property . . . without making them a reasonable compensation," and that therefore the state should pay masters for the loss of the lifetime services of the children of their slaves. This recommendation was accepted in a close vote and then the bill was referred to a special committee and not reported again. The abolitionists probably realized that a program of compensated abolition would be impossibly

[15] *N.J. 18 Assembly 2,* pp. 28, 49, 50, 61; Bloomfield to Samuel Coates, June 30, 1794 (Bloomfield MSS at the New Jersey Historical Society, Newark, N.J.) ; *N.J. 19 Assembly,* pp. 28, 95. Although the petition was referred to the next session, it was not brought up as old business, *N.J. 19 Assembly 2,* pp. 6–9.

expensive and that it would be best to wait a year and try again.[16]

A writer in the New York *Argus* was "mortified at the *death wound*" the abolition bill had received with the adoption of the compensation resolution. Ever since the bill had been introduced, its supporters could see that abolition had "*mortal* enemies." When one representative, remarking that the idea of sitting next to a black representative disgusted him, suggested that a separate area be set aside for the Negroes, "the supporters of the bill *saw clearly,* that there was a plan in view *to defeat the bill!*" Many resolutions had been offered to test the temper of the house, but not "until charges of *illiberality,* and refusals to bring forward *amendments,* or to *meet* upon any ground, were *liberally* dispensed, did friends to the bill agree to this *death wound.*" [17]

The Duc de la Rochefoucauld-Liancourt, who visited New York at this time, was equally shocked by the attitude of New Yorkers toward abolition. Although he could understand that the great number of slaves in the South would make emancipation there extremely difficult, he could not comprehend why abolition could not proceed rapidly in New York. He found out that "The respect due to *property*" was the slogan with which every proposal for abolition was attacked. An eminent attorney, liberal in most of his views, told the duke "that it would be an attack upon property, to declare even the children of female slaves free; for . . . the masters who have purchased or inherited slaves, possess them under the idea that their *issue* shall be their property." Thus, La Rochefoucauld observed, while Virginians argued that slavery could not be abolished without banishing all the Negroes, New Yorkers maintained that no steps toward emancipation could be taken unless masters were fully compensated. "This is certainly throwing every possible

[16] N.Y. Manumission Soc., "Minutes," I, 173, 207, 217–18, 220; "Report of the Committee on Ambiguities in the Confiscation Act and to Consider a Petition for Gradual Abolition," N.Y. Manumission Soc., "Committee Reports" (MSS at the New-York Historical Society), February 19, 1793; William Jay, *The Life of John Jay* (New York, 1833), I, 390; *N.Y. 19 Assembly,* pp. 27, 28, 35, 40, 41, 51, 52, 64–65.

[17] *Argus,* February 12, 1796.

obstacle in the way of the abolition of slavery." [18]

The abolition bill aroused considerable interest in the New York press. "Justice" claimed that the bill was a product of "Quaker influence and Quaker principles." The Friends, he pointed out, considered abolition a religious duty and they would not rest until they had forced all others to adhere to their views. Having identified the abolition bill with Quaker fanaticism, the author appealed to class feelings. Even if the abolitionists were motivated by benevolence, "uninfluenced by any sinister views," still their principles would be misapplied since the law would operate unequally. "The poor man, whose only dependence is on domestics, must, with his numerous offspring, be reduced to penury and want, while the rich are wallowing in every luxury and pleasure." Uncompensated abolition would be "an outrage of justice and liberty." [19]

A "Consistent Democrat" warned his fellow Democrats that in the future he would support only those candidates who supported abolition, regardless of party. "Another Democrat" castigated the "Consistent Democrat." His beliefs that "The principles of liberty are *superior* to laws" would ultimately lead to "a community of goods" and a requirement that the rich share their property with the poor. [20]

"An invariable Friend to the equal Rights of Man" was pleased that in the course of the legislature's debate on abolition "the doctrine of perpetual slavery was universally admitted to be unprincipled." But he was distressed that the bill might founder because of possible inconveniences arising from abolition: "Private right and convenience always ought . . . give way to public good." Slavery was incompatible with the Declaration of Independence and therefore *"Every negro in America is this moment of right, a freeman."* If any Negro were to sue for his freedom in the Supreme Court, he would undoubtedly be declared free. He reminded Americans that Negroes had died "on the field of battle

---

[18] François Alexandre Frederic duc de la Rochefoucauld-Liancourt, *Travels Through the United States of North America,* trans. H. Neuman (2 vols.; London, 1799) , II, 449–50.

[19] *Argus,* January 23, 1796.

[20] *Ibid.,* January 26, 30, 1796.

bravely fighting for that liberty and independence we this day enjoy, and which we not only withhold from the present generation, but would, from nothing but sordid motives of gain rob from thousands of innocents, yet unborn." [21]

"Benevolus," in a long and exhaustive article, demonstrated that slavery was incompatible with several sections of the state constitution and that the legislature had erred in not realizing this. He argued that although the legislature could not deprive masters of their property, neither did it have to protect their property rights. If, therefore, the legislature would merely repeal the fugitive slave laws, the courts would refuse to return fugitives to their masters and slavery would end. The *American Minerva* approved this argument but maintained that simpler reasoning could produce the same conclusion:

Property in the persons and labors of other men, is a thing in itself absurd—it is a direct violation of the law of nature and society—and of course every constitutional declaration and every law, authorizing such violation, is *ipso facto* void.

Two days later, however, the *Minerva,* apparently alarmed at its own boldness, warned that although slavery was "one of the degrading badges of our old colonial situation," its removal required great caution. "The friends of freedom in the United States see the danger of taking too deep hold of *principles.* They dread the consequences of making the slaves know the *extent* of their rights." Therefore, "expediency and public safety induce them to treat the subject with uncommon caution. A *gradual* restoration of the blacks to their rights is all that is desired or can with safety be hazarded." But "this they have a right to *expect* from the legislature." [22]

The legislature's failure to enact gradual abolition and the interjection of the compensation issue did not discourage the abolitionists. The committee appointed to promote passage of the bill reported to the manumission society that the circumstances under which the bill had been rejected left "little doubt" of success at the next session. But although the New York City representatives in the legislature assured the

[21] *Ibid.,* February 3, 1796.
[22] *Ibid.,* February 6, 1796; *American Minerva,* February 6, 8, 1796.

society that an abolition bill would be introduced at the next session, they refused to commit themselves to support it—an ominous sign since no abolition bill could be successful without solid support from the city of New York.[23]

The senate debated a gradual abolition bill several times in the early months of 1797 without result. The next year the assembly took up the issue again. This time, however, an amendment for compensated abolition was easily defeated. The vote reflected the fact that the bill already contained a compromise on the troublesome compensation issue. Since slaveowners had argued against uncompensated gradual abolition on the grounds that the limited period of service required of the Negro children freed by the act would not pay for the cost of raising them, the bill allowed masters to abandon these Negro children and required the towns to support them. Slaveowners could raise the Negro children of their slaves and have their labor as a reimbursement, but if they thought this was a bad bargain, as they loudly maintained, then they could rid themselves of the children and the expense. With the compensation issue settled by compromise, the house passed the bill by a large majority.[24] But now the senate became the brake, refusing to refer the bill to the committee of the whole and thereby killing it.[25]

With their goal clearly in sight, the abolitionists did not relax their efforts. In 1799, for the fourth time in as many years, gradual abolition was the topic of heated debate in the legislature. Early in the session, the assembly took up a bill similar to the one rejected by the senate in the previous year.

[23] N.Y. Manumission Soc., "Minutes," I, 228, 240; "Report of the Committee Appointed to Consult with the Representatives of New York City . . . ," N.Y. Manumission Soc. Committee Reports (January 12, 1797) .

[24] N.Y. 20 Senate, pp. 32, 33, 46, 56, 58, 63, 67–68, 88, 90; N.Y. 21 Assembly, pp. 112–14, 261–68, 274.

[25] The senate did, however, approve another house bill passed in response to a Quaker petition and confirming the emancipation of slaves in cases in which masters had not complied with all legal requirements. (Quaker slaveholders, under pressure from their meetings to free their slaves, had sometimes neglected to post the required bonds. Their non-Quaker creditors or heirs could, before the enactment of this law, reenslave these Negroes) . N.Y. 21 Senate, pp. 108, 109, 135; N.Y. 21 Assembly, pp. 90, 96, 98, 103–4, 182; N.Y. 21 Senate, pp. 39, 40, 74; N.Y. 21 Laws, pp. 289–90.

Erastus Root, a vigorous debater and adamant opponent of slavery, unsuccessfully attempted to amend it so that the children of slaves would be freed at the same age as white apprentices on the grounds that the Negroes were already free "both by the constitution and laws of this state, and by the Divine Law." [26]

The clause of the bill that permitted masters to abandon Negro children led to complicated maneuvering. By a two-to-one margin, the house defeated an attempt to delete this compromise. But then the assembly accepted an amendment that put the burden of supporting abandoned children on the state rather than on the local communities. This was a significant alteration. It would distribute the costs of the abandonment program throughout the state, requiring taxpayers in areas where slaveholding was rare to help pay for supporting Negro children in other parts of the state. The adoption of this amendment led the house to reconsider its earlier vote and to eliminate the abandonment clause altogether. It then sent the bill to the senate.[27]

At first it seemed as if the upper house would continue to block abolition when it rejected a motion to discuss the bill in the committee of the whole. Several days later, however, the senate took up the bill and reinstated the controversial abandonment clause, making the state responsible for supporting abandoned Negro children. In this form the bill readily withstood a motion to reject it. The senate then added another clause designed to please slaveowners, allowing them to manumit any slave immediately after the passage of the law. By rejecting a motion to exclude old and sick slaves, the senate openly invited slaveowners to escape the responsibility for supporting and caring for their old or disabled Negroes. With adjournment less than a week away, the house had no choice but to accept the senate's amendments.[28]

That the gradual abolition law implicitly recognized the

---

[26] Erastus Root, "Notes," in Jabez D. Hammond, *The History of Political Parties in the State of New-York . . .* , (2 vols.; 4th ed.; Sacracuse, N.Y., 1852) , I, 580–81.

[27] *N.Y. 22 Assembly 2*, pp. 47, 49, 77–81, 94, 95, 99.

[28] *N.Y. 22 Senate 2*, pp. 41, 43, 76, 102, 107–9; *N.Y. 22 Assembly 2*, pp. 264, 265, 272.

connection between abolition and the principles of the Declaration of Independence was evidenced by the fact that the act would take effect on July 4, 1799. All Negro children born after that date would be free, but would have to serve the masters of their mothers until they were twenty-eight (males) or twenty-five (females). Slaveowners could abandon these Negro children a year after their birth, and they would be considered paupers, bound out to service by the overseers of the poor. The state would reimburse the towns for the support of abandoned children at a monthly rate of up to $3.50 per child.[29] Since the law did not prohibit overseers of the poor from binding out an abandoned Negro child to the same master who had "abandoned" him, masters could be paid up to $3.50 per month for every Negro child, over one year old, born to one of their slaves. Because the overseers of the poor would be inclined to bind out the child to the owner of the child's mother, masters could expect to derive a lucrative income from abandonments. This abandonment clause was, therefore, a disguised scheme for compensated abolition, and it undoubtedly served to make gradual abolition more acceptable to slaveowners conscious of their property rights.

Many years later Erastus Root recalled the struggles over the abolition bill. "The slaveholders . . . were chiefly Dutch. They raved and swore by *dunder* and *blixen* that we were robbing them of their property. We told them they had none, and could hold none in human flesh . . . and we passed the law." Although it is clear that most of the opposition to abolition came from the Dutch settlers of the Hudson River region, the political division on the issue is not at all clear. According to a leading New York historian, the vote on the bill was strictly according to party lines, with the Federalists in favor and the "party of the small tradesman and mechanic, for reasons of economic jealousy," opposed. A close examination of the votes on abolition shows this to be incorrect. Thirty-four of the representatives who supported abolition were Federalists and thirty-three were Republicans. Fourteen of the opponents of abolition were Federalists

[29] *N.Y. 22 Laws,* pp. 721–23.

while nine supported the opposition party. In the senate, nineteen Federalists and three Republicans supported abolition and seven Federalists and three Republicans tried to defeat the bill. In other words, the Republicans supported abolition twenty-three to nine in the assembly, and in the senate they split evenly on the issue.[30] It is clear, therefore, that abolition was not an issue identified with either of the two major parties, but rather one that split the parties themselves.

The abandonment clause, which had been put back in the bill by the senate, became the subject of immediate and

[30] Root, "Notes," 580–81; Dixon R. Fox, "The Negro Vote in Old New York," *Political Science Quarterly*, XXXII (1917), 254. In a footnote (p. 254), Professor Fox explains that he arrived at this conclusion by using the names of those who voted for Addison and Haight, "the candidates of the opposition," for the Council of Appointment, citing Hammond, *Political Parties*, I, 122, as evidence that Addison and Haight were members of the opposition. Professor Fox has misinterpreted Hammond on this point. Since there were five candidates for the council and only three were elected, two were defeated and in this sense Addison and Haight were the "opposition candidates," i.e. they were the opponents of the successful candidates. As a matter of fact, these men belonged to different parties: Hammond (I, 122) identifies Addison as an Anti-Federalist and the *Daily Advertiser* (April 11, 1796) lists Haight as a Federalist.

To determine party affiliations in the assembly, I have used the vote for U.S. senator which, according to Hammond (I, 122), "probably" reflects the strength of the two parties in the house during the extra session in 1798. Since there was no election between the date of that vote and the vote on the abolition bill, this generalization must hold true for the session of the assembly that passed the abolition bill. To determine the political affiliation of senators, I have used Hammond (*passim*), as well as the vote on a resolution strongly condemning the Virginia and Kentucky resolutions, assuming that Federalists supported it and Republicans opposed it. My conclusions, therefore, are based on comparing the vote of the assembly on January 31, 1799, on the first clause of the abolition bill (*N.Y. 22 Assembly 2*, p. 77), with the assembly's vote for senator on August 17, 1798 (*N.Y. 21 Assembly*, p. 22), and on comparing the senate's vote to reject the abolition bill on March 27, 1799 (*N.Y. 22 Senate 2*, p. 107), with the vote on the Virginia and Kentucky resolutions on March 5, 1799 (*N.Y. 22 Senate 2*, p. 67).

For another interpretation, see Edgar J. McManus, "Antislavery Legislation in New York," *Journal of Negro History*, XLVI (1961), 214.

184

continuing attack and continued to divide the two branches of the legislature. Governor De Witt Clinton's message to the legislature in 1802 predicted that the abandonment program would prove a "growing expence" if it were not altered.[31] The assembly had already tried to repeal the clause only to be turned down by the senate.[32] Now a house committee recommended repeal once more, claiming that the services performed by the children freed by the abolition law would "make ample satisfaction" for the costs of bringing them up. The senate rejected repeal again, but this time approved a sustitute bill reducing payments for abandoned children and eliminating all payments for children over four years old. The house rapidly concurred in this compromise.[33] By this time the cost of maintaining abandoned Negro children was rising at an alarming rate. In 1801, the total cost had been only $1,359, but by 1804 it had risen to over $20,000 per year, and it was obvious that it would continue to rise. Accordingly, the senate, which had rejected repeal again in 1803, finally capitulated the next year.[34]

NEW JERSEY REJECTS ABOLITION

In New Jersey, antislavery men were still unable to make any headway in face of the determined opposition of the eastern counties. Moreover, the abolitionists were extremely disorganized. The abolition society, which had required the service of Philadelphia abolitionists to assist in its formation, had never been well organized. Since May, 1793, various committees had been instructed to prepare a petition for gradual abolition, but committee members could never seem to get together. Changes in personnel made no difference,

[31] *N.Y. 25 Assembly*, p. 6.

[32] *N.Y. 23 Assembly*, pp. 36–38, 44, 48–50; *N.Y. 23 Senate*, pp. 23, 55, 57.

[33] *N.Y. 25 Assembly*, pp. 24, 78, 86, 128, 174, 177; *N.Y. 25 Senate*, pp. 61, 63, 71–73, 77, 93, 99; *N.Y. 25 Assembly*, pp. 210–12, 217, 231–32, 235; *N.Y. 25 Laws*, pp. 82–83.

[34] *N.Y. 25 Assembly*, p. 17; *N.Y. 28 Assembly*, p. 35; *N.Y. 26 Assembly*, pp. 181, 186, 200, 202; *N.Y. 26 Senate*, pp. 91, 103–4; *N.Y. 27 Assembly*, pp. 54, 57, 66–67, 151, 156–58, 223, 232–35, 237; *N.Y. 27 Senate*, pp. 50, 51, 61, 62, 67, 70, 79; *N.Y. 27 Laws*, p. 145.

and it was not until 1797 that the society was able to print and circulate copies of a petition asking the legislature to abolish slavery. The legislature had already been considering a revised slave code and, in January, 1797, the abolitionists attempted to amend it to provide that all Negro children born thereafter would be freed when they became twenty-five. This was defeated in a close vote. But when a new motion was offered changing the age for emancipation to twenty-eight, Elias Dayton changed his vote, producing a tie that was broken by the speaker's vote for abolition. Before taking further action, the house decided to publish the bill for the information of the public. (Many of those who had voted against abolition also voted against publishing the bill, believing, perhaps, that public agitation would strengthen the antislavery men.) [35]

Abolitionists viewed the slavery bill with mixed emotions. Joseph Bloomfield, president of the abolition society, noted that the bill "re-enacts in one law, the severe acts, which to the disgrace of our State have been long in force together with the acts of March 1786 & Nov. 1788, *without any additional penalties.*" But, since the bill did contain a gradual abolition clause, "the friends to manumission will not oppose the present Bill, as nothing will be lost, but a great deal gained." Bloomfield hoped for the bill's passage, leaving it to a future law to eliminate its "disgraceful penal sections." [36]

"Howard," who wrote a blistering attack on the bill in the *State Gazette,* was so repulsed by the bill that he hoped it would be rejected by the legislature as "too disgraceful."

The severity with which it is so replete, and the barefaced injustice which many of the sections display, is surprising indeed. Had this bill been formed in the dark ages of the world, when the rights of man were neither known, acknowledged or understood, it would have been more excusable.

[35] New Jersey Abolition Society, "Minutes" (MSS in the Quaker Collection, Haverford College, Pa.), pp. 6–7, 8, 14, 19, 21–22, 25, 31. Copies of the petitions with nearly 800 signatures are in the New Jersey State Library, Trenton; *N.J. 21 Assembly,* pp. 25, 26, 32; *N.J. 21 Assembly 2,* pp. 10, 20, 29–30, 32–34, 36, 37, 51–53.

[36] Bloomfield to Samuel Coates, January 27, 1797, in the Bloomfield MSS.

He pointed to clauses that confirmed the slavery of the Negroes, prevented them from serving as witnesses, and permitted whippings for minor offenses as examples of the measure's barbarity. Although the bill did provide for gradual abolition, this would not begin until 1800. The promise of freedom implied that slavery was unjust; why then delay emancipation? The opponents of abolition no longer tried to defend slavery as justified in principle but now relied on the argument that abolition was inexpedient, citing the misconduct of free Negroes. "Howard" suggested that they really opposed emancipation for another reason, "which has much greater weight . . . but . . . is generally kept out of sight"—Negroes "make excellent slaves, and in that capacity are very valuable." Avarice was the real basis of the pro-slavery argument. He pointedly reminded New Jersey slaveowners that although abolition had produced no great evils in Pennsylvania and Massachusetts, the slaves of St. Domingo had massacred their unyielding masters.[37]

Like pro-slavery men in New York, New Jersey opponents of abolition made use of the prevalent hostility to the Quakers in their attempts to discredit emancipation. They charged that during the Revolution "a certain class of people" had not only refused to take up arms in defense of American liberty and property, but had actually employed all their efforts "to fix the chains of British slavery on the virtuous inhabitants of the United States." After the war, "they resolved to bring about their destructive purposes in another line. This extremely selfish and double-faced people," having disposed of their own slaves at a profit, "immediately poisoned the minds of the slaves throughout our whole country," making them useless and thereby depriving slaveowners "of their sacred property." This was merely a continuation of the Quakers' wartime conspiracy. If the Negroes were freed, the Friends would control their votes and run the state, which would be "worse than British tyranny." The legislature should

be watchful of such men as once endeavoured to enslave us and now want to strip us of the fruits of our labour, to sow the seeds

[37] *State Gazette* (Trenton, N.J.), February 14, 1797.

of dissension in our states, by which they may involve us in the most serious disputes, when they will again plead that they cannot in conscience take up arms.[38]

When the legislature took up the slavery bill again in the fall, the prospects for abolition had dimmed. This legislature was the first elected under a new apportionment system. Previously each county had three representatives in the assembly, but under the new system the three most populous counties, Hunterdon, Burlington, and Sussex, were granted four representatives each. At the same time, the representation of the two counties with the fewest inhabitants, Cumberland and Cape-May, was reduced to two and one, respectively. The net effect of this change was a slight loss for the abolitionists since both of the counties with reduced representation were antislavery. Although there is no evidence to support the charge of one New Jersey historian that reapportionment was aimed at defeating abolition, the assembly was so closely divided on the issue that the change in representation contributed to the demise of the abolition section of the bill. On November 2, 1797 the committee of the whole struck out the abolition clause by a margin of three votes.[39]

According to "Howard" (probably a member of the legislature), pro-slavery assemblymen had argued against abolition primarily as an unconstitutional confiscation of property. They had also used such arguments as "the general misconduct of free negroes, the danger to which the state would be exposed from the manumission of so great a number (notwithstanding the gradual manner in which it was to be performed)," and the Negroes' "incapacity to obtain a livelihood." "Howard" patiently answered these arguments although he confessed he had "little hopes for making the impression he would wish upon those who differ with him." He realized that those who were subject to preju-

[38] *Ibid.*, February 21, 1797.
[39] *N.J. 21 Laws*, p. 212; Francis B. Lee, *New Jersey as a Colony and as a State* (4 vols.; New York, 1903), III, 272: "In 1797 gerrymander was attempted when . . . the representation of members of the Assembly . . . was so adjusted as to defeat a bill providing for the abolition of slaves [*sic*]. *State Gazette*, November 14, 1797; *N.J. 22 Assembly*, pp. 8, 9, 21, 66.

dice and interest would not be overcome "by the weapons of reason and truth." [40]

In the spring of 1798, in the course of another debate on the revised slave code, abolitionists tried again to insert a gradual abolition clause. Speaking in its support, William Stockton maintained that slavery was incompatible with the Declaration of Independence and unauthorized by law. This contention was strenuously opposed by Jonas Wade. He argued that the slaves were a "hundred times more happy" here than in their native land. Although he doubted whether the principle of slavery was right, he concluded that God had seen fit to allow the Africans to be enslaved. Ultimately, however, this was a question of property rights. He challenged the abolitionists in the assembly: if they wanted to promote the happiness of men, why stop at emancipation? They could "introduce the agrarian system at once" and vote for a general redistribution of property. Wade cited the Lockian justification of private property: "Upon the same principle we claim a right to slaves." Freeing Negroes after only twenty-eight years of service would be unjust since it would not fully compensate masters for the expense of raising them. "Where is the boasted rights of property in this case?" [41]

The abolitionists' last ditch effort to reinsert the abolition clause lost by one vote in the assembly, and an attempt to amend the bill when it reached the legislative council was also defeated. As in previous votes on abolition, the eastern counties were solidly aligned against it while the Quaker-dominated counties of West Jersey favored the measure. [42]

Although the "Act Respecting Slaves" did not abolish slavery, it did improve the status of the slaves in several respects. Slaves were now allowed to own real estate; the age at which Negroes could be manumitted without requiring the posting of bonds was raised from thirty-five to forty; freed Negroes could reside in any county; free Negroes

[40] *State Gazette,* November 7, 1797.

[41] *Ibid.,* April 10, 1798.

[42] *N.J. 22 Assembly 2,* pp. 5, 35, 57–58, 66; *N.J. 22 Council 2,* pp. 70–71.

from other states were allowed to come to New Jersey; and the penalties for abusing slaves or failing to educate them were raised. Furthermore, the sections of the bill that had authorized the whipping of fugitive slaves or slaves who assembled in groups without permission had been altered.[43]

New Jersey abolitionists reported to the 1798 abolitionists' convention that the new law had reenacted most of the favorable provisions of the old laws while eliminating many of their harsh features. The report noted, however, that public opinion in New Jersey was more divided on abolition than on any other issue. The annual orations recommended by a previous convention had not been instituted by the New Jersey Abolition Society because "in East Jersey such orations would not be tolerated, in West Jersey they are unnecessary." Although gradual abolition had been defeated by one vote in the house, the abolitionists claimed that among those who had voted against it were men who were against slavery in principle but were afraid to offend their slaveholding constituents, as well as men who feared the results of abolition "from the effects experienced from the ungovernable rage and violence of the Blacks on St. Domingo." Characteristically, the report ended on an optimistic note (the abolitionists were always reassuring themselves) : "Time and the silent operation of truth and justice are . . . making numerous proselytes and it cannot be doubted but a short time will ensure the object of our wishes, a gradual abolition of this pernicious practice." [44]

PUBLIC OPINION AND SLAVERY

The revolt of the Negroes of St. Domingo, accompanied by a reign of terror, had had a serious effect on American public opinion. The 1798 abolitionists' convention undoubtedly had this in mind when it noted that

The situation of public affairs . . . renders the present time unsuitable for the adoption of any new measures of importance. In

[43] William Patterson (compiler), *Laws of the State of New Jersey* (New Brunswick, N.H., 1800), pp. 307–13.

[44] "Report of the New Jersey Abolition Society," Pa. Abolition Soc., misc. MSS, V, 147.

many of the United States a peculiar degree of caution in the management of the business becomes necessary; and on this ground it is deemed more prudent to persevere in the steps which have already been so judiciously taken, than to attempt at this juncture, any material variation or extension of them.[45]

There were, however, grounds for optimism. At the same time that legislatures debated the wisdom of abolition, slavery was gradually being undermined by an acceleration of voluntary manumissions. Despite the limitations imposed by colonial slave codes, even in the colonial period some masters had rewarded faithful slaves by emancipating them in their last will. After the Revolution, when manumissions were made somewhat easier, there was a slight increase in testamentary manumissions. But after 1796, the number of wills emancipating slaves increased rapidly. Between 1786 and 1796, for instance, only four out of thirty-two New York wills mentioning slaves provided for manumission. But between 1976 and 1800, twenty out of thirty-four wills that included slaves freed them. Manumissions in New Jersey followed a similar pattern. Between 1796 and 1800, 40 per cent of wills mentioning slaves provided for emancipation.[46] Some benevolent masters not only freed their Negroes but established funds for their support and gave them personal gifts. Joseph Towers, a New York City shopkeeper, provided that after his wife's death his "mulatto boy" would go free and receive £12 per year as well as his master's clothes. Sometimes testamentary manumissions were made conditional—the Negro would have to serve faithfully for a number of years or he would have to make provisions to support himself and not be an encumbrance on the estate. Occasionally a master would set down the reasons for his decision to free his Negroes. Cornelius Clopper freed his Negro woman and her two children, gave them a house and lot and an annual income "for and in consideration of their faithful service to me." Far less frequently slaveowners cited more abstract considerations. Abijah Holbrook, a Connecticut miller, freed his slaves

---

[45] *1798 Convention Minutes,* 11.
[46] See Appendix, Table 3.

because he was "influenced by motives of humanity and benevolence, believing that all mankind by nature are entitled to equal liberty and freedom." Martha Waln of Philadelphia had mixed motives. She freed her Negro woman "for divers good causes, and out of a pious principle As Well as in the Consideration of the sum of Twenty-Five pounds . . . paid by my black woman." [47]

Although the abolitionists were silently aided by the increasing number of voluntary manumissions, they were also gratified that the Methodist church was returning to its former antislavery position. The new church *Discipline,* adopted by the 1796 General Conference included "regulations . . . for the extirpation of the crying evil of African slavery." The Methodists proclaimed themselves as "more than ever convinced of the great evil of African slavery" and recommended that the subordinate meetings be cautious in admitting slaveholders to official stations in the church. Members of the church who sold slaves were to be immediately suspended, and those who purchased them were to agree to manumit the Negroes after a reasonable period of service to pay for their cost. Although the 1800 General Conference rejected a motion to exclude all slaveholders from membership, as well as a proposal that would have required members to manumit all slaves born after 1800, the conference agreed to instruct the subordinate conferences to petition their state legislatures for gradual abolition laws. By 1804, however, the antislavery forces in the Methodist church had been severely weakened. The petition clause was eliminated from the *Discipline,* and in 1808 all sections of the *Discipline* relating to slaveholding by private members were eliminated; instead, the regional conferences were instructed to make their own regulations on the sale or purchase of slaves by members.[48]

[47] *Abstracts of Wills on File in the Surrogate's Office, City of New York (Collections of the New-York Historical Society, 1892–1908)*, XV, 15, 54; Samuel Orcutt, *History of Torrington, Connecticut . . .* (Albany, 1878), 212; Pa. Abolition Soc., misc. MSS, I, 19.

[48] *Minutes of the General Conference of the Methodist Episcopal Church, Begun at Baltimore, on the 20th of October, 1796* (Baltimore, 1796), pp. 23–24; *Journals of the General Conference of the Methodist*

NEW JERSEY ADOPTS GRADUAL ABOLITION

Although the prospects for gradual abolition in New Jersey seemed dim in the closing years of the century, the assembly was quite receptive when a gradual abolition bill was brought up in 1803. The change in the assembly's attitude was marked; only two years earlier the legislature had weakened the legal position of the slaves when it agreed to allow the courts to send convicted slaves out of the state, thereby permitting unscrupulous masters a chance to evade the ban on the export of slaves.[49] Now, however, the assembly seemed prepared to accept abolition. It turned down a motion to require emancipated Negro children to serve until they were twenty-eight, and ended their servitude at twenty-five instead. Nonetheless, the assembly was still deeply divided on abolition. An attempt to vote on the first section of the bill aroused a long debate that was finally cut off only by a decision to postpone the question. Five days later the house was still unable to agree and postponed it again, ordering the bill published for public consideration in the meantime.[50]

When the assembly convened in February, 1804, the abolition society presented an eloquent plea for gradual abolition, pointing out that slavery was indefensible "in a land of freedom, and by a people distinguished for reason and humanity." Although it was alleged that to "emancipate those now living" would violate property rights, this argument could not apply to the proposed emancipation of unborn Negroes. Even those who judged the issue from a purely economic viewpoint would have to agree "that to enslave Children to the latest posterity for the cost of the parent . . . is a satisfaction vastly disproportionate." The years of servitude required of the emancipated Negro children would amply

Episcopal Church (New York, 1855), I, 37, 40, 41, 44, 60, 61, 64; Robert Emory, *History of the Discipline of the Methodist Episcopal Church* (New York, 1845), pp. 276–78.

[49] *N.J. 25 Assembly 2*, pp. 9, 11–12, 35, 55, 58, 60, 73, 74; *N.J. 25 Council 2*, pp. 69, 70; *N.J. 25 Laws 2*, pp. 77–78.

[50] *N.J. 27 Assembly*, pp. 64, 93, 99, 117; *N.J. 28 Assembly*, pp. 8, 20, 21, 24, 27–28, 34. The *True American* (Trenton, N.J.), November 21, 1803, prints the bill as of November 8, 1803.

compensate masters for the expense of raising them, except in a very few cases. "If then the principle is admitted that perpetual slavery, is politically wrong, and morally a departure from the great laws of nature and humanity, certainly this question of profit and loss may be adjusted." The abolitionists asked the assembly:

> Will nothing short of the *servitude of children to the end of time satisfy the owner, for the price paid for . . . the parent?* . . . We ask you . . . for no *law* to touch property *in possession* however acquired; neither for the disannulling of that by which twelve thousand human beings are doomed to die as they were born—*vassals in a land of freedom!* We supplicate you for the unborn . . . .[51]

The assembly debated the abolition bill for two days and then added a clause allowing New Jersey masters, like those in New York, to abandon the children of their slaves to the care of the overseers of the poor at the expense of the state. (A similar provision had been included in the abolition section of the 1797 slavery bill). The house then approved the bill by the overwhelming majority of thirty-four to four. The legislative council concurred, twelve to one. After July 4, all Negro children born in the state would be free, although they would have to serve until twenty-five (males) and twenty-one (females).[52] New Jersey had joined the other states of the North in providing for an end to slavery. Henceforth, slavery was fated to become increasingly an institution peculiar to the South.

The final vote on the bill was astounding. For years New Jersey legislatures, like the state, had been deeply split on the issue. Only a few months earlier abolition had been the subject of acrimonious debate and repeated postponements; now the vote for abolishing slavery was nearly unanimous. What had happened? Although the membership of the legislature had changed considerably since previous debates on the question, this alone did not explain the result. Eight men

---

[51] The petition is in the N.J. State Library; it is reprinted in the *True American*, February 6, 1804.

[52] *N.J. 28 Assembly 2*, pp. 91, 94, 99, 111, 113–16, 118; *N.J. 28 Council 2*, pp. 280, 283, 288; *N.J. 28 Laws 2*, pp. 251–52.

who had voted against abolition during the 1797–98 debates were members of the 1804 legislature; six of them switched and supported abolition in 1804.[53] It would also be impossible to ascribe the overwhelming victory for abolition to a complete reversal of public opinion in New Jersey; there is no evidence of such a drastic change. Although the legislature which passed the abolition law, unlike that of 1797–98, had a Republican majority, the abolition of slavery was not a party issue. A majority of the members of both parties in the legislature supported the bill—fifteen Federalists and twenty-nine Republicans voted for it, whereas four Federalists and one Republican opposed it.[54] Furthermore, the fact that the bill was postponed many times suggests that the legislature was not as united in support of the measure as the final vote might imply. It would seem rather, that the abolitionists, having finally attained enough votes to pass the bill, were able to persuade their opponents either to abstain or to vote for it to give the impression of the great unanimity necessary to secure public acceptance of the new policy.

The inducement the abolitionists offered the pro-slavery legislators in return for their votes was probably the inclusion of the abandonment clause, similar to the one that had proved so expensive in New York. Perhaps the abolitionists could have passed the bill without this clause but agreed to include it to get the overwhelming vote essential to public acceptance of abolition. An article written in defense of the abolition law supports this interpretation, asserting that the abandonment clause "was inserted, in order that those coun-

[53] The two members of the legislature who voted against abolition in the 1797–98 session and also in 1804 were James Van Duyn and Peter De Vroom, both of Somerset County. The six who changed their vote in favor of abolition in the 1804 session were: Gershom Dunn and Ephraim Martin (Middlesex), Aaron Kitchell and David Welsh (Morris), John Outwater (Bergen), and John Lambert (Hunterdon).

[54] Walter R. Fee, *The Transition from Aristocracy to Democracy in New Jersey, 1789–1829* (Somerville, N.J., 1933), p. 137. To determine the political affiliation of members of the legislature, I have used the vote for Joseph Bloomfield and William Stockton, the Republican and Federalist candidates for governor, in the joint session of the legislature (*N.J. 28 Council*, p. 40).

ties who had no slaves in them, might assist the counties in which slavery still existed in gradually getting rid of it also." This "generous concession" was "salutary in securing the passage of the law." [55]

The nearly unanimous vote for abolition became an important argument for the defenders of the new law. "A Republican," who wrote a comprehensive defense of the abolition law, pointed to the final vote on the bill as evidence of the widespread acceptance of the principle of abolition, demonstrating to those opposed to the law that they were members of a powerless minority. After arguing the incompatibility of slavery with Christianity and with the philosophy of the Declaration of Independence, he proceeded to answer specific objections to the law. The argument of pro-slavery men that the law was the product of "the *spirit of party*" was without foundation. Men of both parties had signed petitions in favor of the bill and several prominent Federalists had spoken for the bill in the legislature. (This attention to Federalist support indicates that those who castigated the law as a party measure were directing their fire at the Republican party.)

The "Republican" pointed out that the abolition law was not a radical measure: "While it lays a sure foundation for the abolition of that iniquitous system of human degradation and misery, it prudently avoids touching property in that species now held." But every slaveholder should be "thankful for the tenderness with which he has been treated by the present Legislature" and not condemn the law, he warned, "lest some future Legislature indulge his desire for its repeal, and enact one in its stead much more injurious to his interests."

Fears that the abandonment program "would prove highly burthensome to the state," he dismissed as "groundless," ignoring the fact that New York had finally been forced to repeal a similar provision of its abolition law for that reason. He predicted that no more than a half a dozen Negro children would ever be abandoned by New Jersey masters, but even if six hundred were released by their masters, it would

[55] *True American,* April 30, 1804.

probably not cost the state a penny since many people would be glad to assume the expense of raising these children without any other compensation than their labor. "Were abandonments to become general, there would I am confident be more applications for children than those abandonments would satisfy." Moreover, masters would be well aware of the value of the services of these children and would not abandon them. But "an opinion has by some means got footing, that when masters abandon their children . . . the overseers [of the poor] will return them to the masters, and allow them three dollars a month for their maintenance; and that this will induce masters generally to throw their [Negro] children upon the town or county—This opinion," he maintained, "is not warranted by the law." [56] Nonetheless, this proved to be an accurate prediction of how the law would operate.

As early as December, 1805, a New Jersey newspaper reported that a petition for the repeal of the third section (the abandonment clause) of the abolition law had been circulated in several counties. The petitioners contended that "it is becoming a common and increasing practice in this county for Slave-holders to abandon the children of their slaves . . . and then to receive from the Treasury for supporting these children *three dollars per month* or *thirty-six dollars per year*." This constituted "a very heavy tax," paid by the state "to men who have always enjoyed all the benefit and grown rich by the labor of Slaves, which must be mostly drawn from those who never owned any Slaves nor received any advantage from Slavery, but earned their own bread." "A Hunterdon Farmer" agreed, pointing out that

Even many Slave-holders who think it unjust that the public should be burthened with the support of the children of their Slaves, will yet fall into the practice unless it is put a stop to; for, say they, we shall have to pay our parts of the tax for supporting

[56] *Ibid.*, September 10, 17, 1804. Another defender of the abolition law (*ibid.*, April 30, 1804) reported that the abandonment clause had been copied from the New York law and that "the children which have been abandoned in that state, if I am rightly informed, have been so very few as never to make any sensible addition to the taxes of the State." He was certainly not "rightly informed."

such children as others abandon . . . This will make abandonments general, and extremely numerous.

He estimated that even if only one hundred children were abandoned per year, at the end of seven years the cost of supporting them would be $25,000 per year. "Are the People of New Jersey prepared to pay such a monstrous tax as this—and for so unprofitable an object?" [57]

While some New Jerseyites grumbled about the expense of the abandonment clause, others sought the repeal of the entire abolition law. One petition widely circulated in Bergen County charged that the abolition law was not only "unconstitutional, impolitic, and unjustly severe," but predicted that the law would endanger the community. Slaveholders, having a right to the unlimited services of their slaves, had "an equal right to the unlimited services, of their issue." The petitioners sarcastically noted that "it is easy for such of our Citizens as have no such species of property to Cry out freedom, away with Slavery, and in the fever of their zeal, imagine they can contrive laws, to rid the country of the opprobrium, and the people of the expence." But the abolition law had already proved deficient: "the evil with which it is fraught . . . strikes consternation, and gives alarm." What was this terror-producing fault? The law made no provision for the maintenance of children born to free Negro girls while these girls were still servants. These grandchildren of slaves might, therefore, become chargeable to the town and this would lead to great expense!

A petition from Morris County revealed the desperation of pro-slavery men as it frantically attacked the abolition law from all sides. First, it challenged the constitutionality of the law on the grounds that it deprived individuals of their property without consent. But then it complained that the law required freeborn inhabitants to serve until they were twenty-five. Since the law would not allow masters to abandon their Negro children until they were one year old, the law was discriminatory—in effect it taxed masters the thirty-six dollars it cost to maintain a Negro child for one year.

[57] *Ibid.,* December 16, 23, 1805.

The Morris County petitioners were not satisfied with the abandonment clause either, deeming it impractical because of the heavy taxes it would require. On the other hand, repeal of this clause alone would provide no equitable solution: if the burden of supporting the children of slaves was "more than the State could bear, how much more grievous & Hard will it be (from any Change of said Law short of Repeal thereof) for a County, Town, or an individual to bear." Although the petitioners claimed that they were willing to "ameliorate Slavery in any Plausible way or Manner that the Burden might be made Equal," they thought it "inexpedient to make the Slaves free at This time." The legislature should repeal the abolition law.[58]

In response to public demands, a bill to repeal the third section of the abolition law was introduced in the assembly in the fall of 1804, but it was defeated. A year later the assembly was inundated with petitions. Some petitioners sought the repeal of the controversial abandonment clause, others its retention, and a third group demanded repeal of the entire abolition law. After a great deal of complicated parliamentary maneuvering the two houses concurred in repealing the third section of the law. The legislative council also passed a bill that would have required the children of slaves to serve for a longer period, but this was rejected by the assembly.[59]

Despite the repeal of the abandonment clause, the state remained responsible for the maintenance of children abandoned before the policy had been altered. The support of these children proved to be an enormous financial burden. In the fiscal year November, 1807 to November, 1808, the state paid over $12,000 for the support of abandoned Negro children. This represented fully thirty per cent of the state budget (excluding the separate prison and militia budgets). In the next fiscal year, the support of abandoned children accounted for over forty per cent of the budget, with Bergen

---

[58] Copies of the pro-slavery petitions are in the N. J. State Library.

[59] *N.J. 29 Assembly*, pp. 223–24, 238, 289–90; *N.J. 29 Council*, pp. 382, 386, 390; *N.J. 30 Assembly*, pp. 404, 420; *N.J. 30 Assembly 2*, pp. 490, 501, 503, 510, 533, 549, 550–52, 555, 556, 558–59, 581, 604; *N.J. 30 Council 2*, pp. 502, 503, 507–9, 511, 517; *N.J. 30 Laws 2*, p. 668.

County alone receiving over $7,000 for this purpose.[60] To correct this growing evil, the legislature in 1808 required the overseers of the poor to advertise the availability of abandoned Negro children and to bind them out wherever possible to persons who, without requiring any payments, would take care of them in return for their services. The next year the legislature noted that "large and unusual sums of money have been drawn from the treasury . . . for maintaining abandoned blacks which has caused suspicions" of fraud. Accordingly, it tightened the law to insure that money for abandoned children could only be obtained in bona fide cases of abandonments. Finally, in 1811 the legislature terminated all payments for abandoned children after observing that in some instances the state maintenance payments had exceeded the price of the lifetime services of a slave.[61]

THE TRIUMPH OF GRADUAL ABOLITION

The problem of maintaining abandoned Negro children, which plagued New York and New Jersey, was the legacy of the pro-slavery argument. In both states that argument had shed its coating of biblical justification and historical precedent and stood revealed as the armor of property, defending its interests. New York and New Jersey slaveholders, and more especially those of Dutch ancestry, stood firm in defense of what they deemed their legitimate property rights and refused to consent to the emancipation of unborn generations of Negroes unless they received some compensation. The abandonment programs adopted by New York and New Jersey were thinly disguised schemes for compensated abolition. Although masters were deprived of the benefits of the abandonment program within a few years, their losses were probably very small. No slaveowner lost a single Negro in his possession at the time the abolition laws were passed.

---

[60] *N.J. 33 Assembly,* pp. 75–97; *N.J. 34 Assembly,* pp. 213–35.

[61] *N.J. 33 Assembly,* pp. 117, 125, 138–40; *N.J. 33 Council,* p. 812; *N.J. 33 Laws,* p. 112; *N.J. 34 Assembly,* pp. 188–89; *N.J. 34 Council,* p. 193; *N.J. 34 Laws,* pp. 200–201; *N.J. 35 Assembly 2,* pp. 398, 440, 503, 506, 537, 542; *N.J. 35 Council 2,* pp. 1037, 1056, 1060–61; *N.J. 35 Laws 2,* pp. 313–14.

Furthermore, as long as their female slaves continued to bear children, masters could have the services of young Negroes merely for the expense of raising them to working age.[62]

The history of the movement to abolish slavery in New York and New Jersey had significance that extended beyond the time and the place. The long debates over abolition had revealed a fundamental division within the American creed, a contradiction in a simultaneous devotion to human rights and to property rights. The basic right of men to life and liberty was challenged by the equally basic human right of men to their property. It was not until this conflict was resolved by compromise on the tangled issue of property rights that the abolitionists' appeals to national and religious ideals achieved their aims. The record of the protracted conflict over abolition in these northern states boded ill for those abolitionists who hoped that their principles would gradually conquer the rest of the nation. If New Yorkers steadfastly opposed uncompensated abolition, Virginians would not surrender; if a form of compensated abolition was impossibly expensive in New Jersey, it would be foolhardy to even attempt it in South Carolina.

The immediate effects of the gradual abolition laws adopted by New York and New Jersey were slight. No Negroes would be emancipated until twenty years after the enactment of the laws that promised them freedom. But in the long run these laws marked the beginnings of a new system of race relations and labor in the North. And even beyond this, the triumph of gradual abolition in New York and New Jersey marked the point at which the sections began to tread diverging paths, the point at which the nation became a house divided against itself.

[62] These years of service were valuable. Masters could sell the services of these children for a number of years and obtain a good price. For instance, the estate of a New Jersey farmer who died in 1809 included a sixteen-year-old girl who would serve until she was twenty-five and was valued at $100, and a thirteen-year-old boy with fifteen years of service who was worth $225. Andrew D. Mellick, *The Story of an Old Farm* (Somerville, N.J., 1889), p. 611.

The adoption of gradual abolition laws by all of the northern states that had not ended slavery through judicial interpretation met the immediate and most pressing demands of the abolitionists. Nonetheless, many of the opponents of slavery realized that their labors were not yet ended. The freed Negroes would continue to require the advice and protection of the abolition societies. If they were to be accepted by the dominant white society, they would have to be guided and educated, and who would provide the required counsel and aid if not the abolitionists? Furthermore, some antislavery men continued to urge improvements in the abolition laws, hoping either to secure a total abolition of slavery or at least to reduce the period of service required of freed Negro children to put them on an equal footing with white apprentices.

ABOLITION IN CONNECTICUT

The Connecticut Abolition Society, founded in 1790, petitioned for an immediate and total abolition law in 1792, only eight years after the enactment of the state's gradual abolition law. The abolitionists were gratified at the attention given their request, "considering the greatness & novelty of the object." Although the legislature postponed action on the petition, it did provide additional protection for slaves by making it illegal to sell them out of the state.[1]

[1] Jonathan Edwards, Jr., to James Pemberton, February 19, 1793 (Misc. MSS of the Pennsylvania Abolition Society, at the Historical Society of Pennsylvania), III, 226. *Minutes of the Proceedings of the Second Convention of Delegates from the Abolition Societies . . .* (Philadelphia, 1795), p. 17; *Public Records of the State of Connecticut* (9 vols.; Hartford, Conn., 1894–1953), VII, 379; VIII, xviii.

When the legislature met in May, 1794, the abolitionists were prepared. They scheduled a public meeting aimed at stimulating abolitionist sentiment to coincide with the opening of the legislative session. The assembly's response to the abolitionists' demands was extremely gratifying; it passed an abolition bill that was unparalleled in its generosity to the slaves. Its preamble castigated slavery for its "direct and necessary tendency" to keep the slaves in ignorance and as being "productive of immorality, degrading to the dignity of human nature, and destructive of the natural Rights which every member of an equal and just Government ought to enjoy." The bill would have freed all slaves on April 1, 1795, and required slaveowners to care for old and disabled Negroes. It also provided for the education of Negro children. But the council refused to give its consent.[2]

With the defeat of this remarkable bill, interest in the question declined and in October, 1794, abolitionists could not even persuade the assembly, hitherto so responsive to their demands, to pass an abolition bill. Early in 1797, however, abolitionists induced the legislature to reduce the period of servitude required of Negro children from twenty-five years to twenty-one. In the fall the legislature went even further and repealed the entire colonial slave code. Finally, in 1848 (perhaps to justify her stance in the sectional controversies of the day), Connecticut enacted complete and total abolition, freeing the few remaining slaves who had been born before the beginnings of gradual abolition.[3]

EFFORTS FOR TOTAL ABOLITION
IN PENNSYLVANIA

Pennsylvania abolitionists were amazed to discover in 1792 that the legislature had made an important move toward complete abolition. It began, strangely enough, when a group of refugees from the bloody St. Domingo slave revolt sought permission to keep their slaves in Pennsylvania as an exception to the abolition law. The report of the committee that considered their request went far beyond the

[2] *Public Records of Conn.*, VIII, xix.
[3] *Ibid.*, VIII, xx; IX, 38–39, 92; 91–92 n.

point at issue. It recommended that the legislature reject the refugees' petition because slavery was "obviously contrary to the . . . Constitution of this state."[4] This was indeed a radical statement; if slavery was unconstitutional, then all Negroes (not only those born since March 1, 1780) were legally emancipated.

Following the lead of the committee report, Representative John Shoemaker proposed a bill to modify the abolition law so that no child would be forced to serve beyond the age of twenty-one. The implications of the report of the committee on the refugees' petition was also clear to antislavery men outside the house. The Quakers petitioned the legislature to implement the philosophy of its committee's report and to provide for total abolition. The committee on the Shoemaker resolution agreed that "slavery is . . . repugnant to the spirit and express letter of the Constitution of this commonwealth" and recommended the preparation of an immediate abolition bill. Unfortunately, the onset of a dreadful yellow fever epidemic forced a curtailment of the legislative session, and the assembly did not find time to take up the committee report before hastily adjourning.[5]

In 1797 a new outbreak of yellow fever brought an abrupt end to the legislative session before the house could complete action on a new bill providing for total abolition and compensation for slaveowners. After that the legislature lost whatever enthusiasm it had had for total abolition and merely shunted the bill from one session to the next. Early in 1799, however, the Quakers petitioned for abolition and in the winter of 1799–1800 a series of petitions indicated a revival of public interest. Two groups of free Negroes not only urged the house to pass the bill, but offered to pay a special tax to purchase the freedom of their enslaved brethren. The house adopted this proposal with alacrity, viewing

[4] *Pa. 3 H. of R.,* pp. 39, 42, 45, 55, 60. (Whenever sessional journals or laws of a state or colonial legislature are cited the following abbreviated form has been used: e.g., *N.J. 17 Assembly 2,* or *N.J. 17 Laws 2,* to indicate the journals or laws of the seventeenth New Jersey Assembly, second session. When no session number is provided, the citation refers to the first session. Whenever reprinted or compiled editions have been used, a full citation has been supplied.)

[5] *Ibid.,* pp. 195–96, 201, 205, 291; *Pa. 3 Senate,* pp. 150–51.

204

it as a method of providing for compensated abolition at no cost to the taxpayers.[6]

A special abolition society committee that lobbied for the bill failed to win senate approval. But the society soon realized that despite its declared purpose, the house's bill was dangerous. Accordingly, when the senate resumed consideration of the bill in 1801, the abolition society petitioned for its alteration or rejection. What the abolitionists had hoped for was a simple declaratory statute, asserting that slavery was unconstitutional. Instead, the pending bill implicitly recognized the legitimacy of slavery by providing for compensated emancipation. Although the bill allowed Negroes to purchase their own freedom, this had always been possible. And since the abolitionists refused "to be instrumental in paying for that which they believe incapable of purchase or sale," they would not help slaves buy their freedom. If the legislature expected to finance abolition through the charity of the abolitionists, it was completely mistaken. The proposed tax on free Negroes was foolish, for many of the freedmen had already spent their most productive years in slavery and found it hard to support their families; a new tax would only add to their difficulties. Moreover, a special and discriminatory tax was probably unconstitutional. Finally, the abolitionists objected that the bill would enact "unequal and severe discriminations" against free Negroes by requiring them to carry special passes. The senate agreed and rejected the bill as unnecessary and inexpedient, since its passage would cast doubt "on the principles of equal liberty, dispensed to all men by the . . . constitution."[7]

Although the failure of the legislature to pass a satisfactory total abolition law disappointed them, the abolitionists had already begun another attack on slavery. Taking its cue from the house's declaration that slavery was unconstitutional, the

[6] *Pa. 7 H. of R.*, pp. 283, 308–9, 354–55; Pa. Abolition Soc., "Minutes," I, 305; *Pa. 8 H. of R.*, pp. 75, 94, 268–69; *Pa. 9 H. of R.*, pp. 20, 49, 256, 353, 461; *Pa. 9 Senate*, p. 149; *Pa. 10 H. of R.*, pp. 23, 49, 76, 93, 123, 127, 133, 153, 159, 160, 162, 172, 176, 190, 236, 239, 300, 303, 304, 306, 309, 312, 320, 330, 358, 366–68, 374–76; *Pa. 10 Senate*, pp. 221, 223, 233, 235.

[7] Pa. Abolition Soc., "Minutes," I, 336, 350, 355–56; II, 16; *Pa. 11 Senate,* pp. 14, 31, 41, 119, 134–35, 140, 175, 278; *Pa. 12 Senate*, pp. 24, 32.

abolition society brought a test case before the courts in 1794, hoping for a verdict similar to the ones that had ended slavery in Massachusetts. The case dragged on for many years. In 1798 it was removed from the lower courts to the High Court of Errors and Appeals. The abolition society continually urged the committee entrusted with the prosecution of the case to press the matter, but it was not until 1802 that the court issued its verdict. After hearing the arguments of Jared Ingersoll, William Lewis, and William Rawle, the distinguished attorneys engaged by the abolition society, the court decided for the defendants, thereby establishing that "slavery *is* consistent with the Constitution." Although the prosecuting committee deplored the verdict, it assured the other members of the society that the termination of the case could serve as a means of directing the society's energies "to more successful means" to achieve the ultimate goal.[8]

The abolitionists' failure in the courts led to a new effort to persuade the legislature to implement its declaration that slavery was unconstitutional. In 1803 a Quaker petition pointed out that despite the beneficent results of the gradual abolition law, many Negroes still languished in slavery. A house committee agreed with the Friends' contention that slavery was incompatible with the natural rights philosophy incorporated into the constitution. Nonetheless, the committee ruefully noted, despite "the most solemn obligations to support this constitution," great numbers of men were held in slavery "under the immediate observation of every Member of this House." The committee challenged the complacency of the legislators: "Is there nothing obligatory in the constitution of this state, and of the United States? . . . Or in the religious principles we profess?" The house evaded the issue, tabling the committee's resolution for the immediate emancipation of all Negroes over twenty-one. The report of the senate committee on the Quaker petition was much more conservative and probably more nearly

[8] Pa. Abolition Soc., "Minutes," I, 210, 214–15, 305; II, 1, 14, 35–36, 47; Edward R. Turner, "The Abolition of Slavery in Pennsylvania," *Pennsylvania Magazine of History and Biography*, XXXVI (1912), 138–39. The case was Negro Flora *v.* Joseph Graisberry; the records of the case have been lost.

reflected public opinion on the question. Although regretting that it had been impossible completely to abolish slavery at the time of the gradual abolition law (this would have caused "too great [a] sacrifice of private right established by law"), the committee noted that there were very few slaves in the state and liberation would probably not be conducive to their interests. It was clear that the legislature was not willing to speed the process of gradual abolition, a view that was confirmed a year later when both houses rejected total abolition proposals.[9]

The attitude of the legislature reflected growing public apathy. The decline of abolitionist fervor can be traced in the minutes of the abolition society. In 1804 the society not only did not initiate the request for total abolition, but it failed to present a petition in support of the measure before the senate rejected the bill. (The committee appointed to present the petition made the best of it, telling the society "that such progress had been made in the matter by the members of the Legislature as precluded the necessity of forwarding the memorial.") The minutes for succeeding years are extremely sparse; frequently the correspondence and acting committees, which were responsible for most of the society's activities, failed to report. In 1808 a member pointedly suggested that the chairman of the correspondence committee call a meeting as soon as possible. And several times the society was unable to hold its regular quarterly meetings because of the lack of a quorum. The meeting scheduled for the fall of 1805 was postponed a month, but efforts to obtain a quorum at a later date were equally fruitless and the meeting was permanently adjourned. Both the president and vice-president were absent at the July, 1807, March, 1808, and January, 1809, meetings and only eight members attended the meeting scheduled in July, 1810. As the numbers of slaves in Pennsylvania declined through the operation of the gradual abolition law, the society increasingly suffered from a "decline of energy, and [a] gradual tendency to a state of apathy." [10]

[9] *Pa. 13 H. of R.*, pp. 218, 360–63; *Pa. 13 Senate*, pp. 170–71, 229–30; *Pa. 14 Senate*, pp. 158, 183, 193, 212, 443–44; *Pa. 15 H. of R.*, p. 61.

[10] Pa. Abolition Soc., "Minutes," II, 79, 87, 123–45; Edward Needles,

Nonetheless, the society was able to rise from its somnolent state when faced with concrete problems that required the intervention of the friends of the Negroes. In 1813 the abolitionists were aroused by a powerful movement to curtail the rights of free Negroes. A group of Philadelphians, complaining that the great number of free Negroes and fugitive slaves within the city were "becoming nuisances," asked for legislation to require all Negroes to register, to provide for binding out to service convicted Negroes "for the purpose of compensating the persons they may have plundered," and for a special tax on free Negroes to provide for impoverished Negroes. The abolition society strenuously resisted. It admitted that in some cases free Negroes had been guilty of crimes but charged that the bill proposed by the Philadelphia petitioners would be unconstitutional as well as impolitic. Despite the errant ways of some freedmen, "a large portion of them are entitled to the reputation of respectable, industrious, and useful Members of Society." Philadelphia free Negroes also petitioned for the defeat of this bill designed to limit their rights, but a memorial signed by the mayor, aldermen, and various citizens of Philadelphia reiterated the demand for discriminatory legislation. At the same time, the legislators, alarmed at the increasing number of fugitive slaves who sought refuge in Philadelphia, considered prohibiting Negro immigration into the state. Both bills, however, were ultimately defeated.[11]

By this time the issue of total and immediate abolition had become an increasingly moot point; the 1820 census reported only 211 slaves in the state and all must have been over forty. Nonetheless, abolitionists continued sporadic efforts to secure the completion of their task, none of which had any success. But antislavery men were still able to prevent retrograde action. On the eve of the Civil War, thirteen petitions

An Historical Memoir of the Pennsylvania Society, for Promoting the Abolition of Slavery . . . (Philadelphia, 1848) , 54.

[11] Pa. Abolition Soc., "Minutes," II, 178–82; *Pa. 23 H. of R.*, pp. 216, 417, 432, 484, 566–67, 588–89; *Pa. 23 Senate,* p. 540; *Pa. 24 H. of R.,* pp. 84, 101, 264, 448, 458, 493–95, 498; *Pa. 24 Senate,* pp. 417, 504. The legislature considered proposals to limit the rights of free Negroes in 1805–7, 1813–14, 1819–20, 1831–32, and 1860.

asked for a restriction of Negro immigration; the petitioners suggested that if this request were not granted, then the legislature should provide that immigrant Negroes "be reduced to the condition of slaves." The house indignantly rejected this proposal, pointing out that Pennsylvania had long been in the forefront of the antislavery movement. The last federal census to list any slaves in Pennsylvania had been in 1840.[12] Pennsylvania had long since been following the path of Benjamin Lay and Anthony Benezet; it had removed "the accursed thing" from its midst and would never reestablish it.

NEW YORK ABOLITIONISTS' SUCCESS

New York abolitionists, although pleased with the passage of the gradual abolition law in 1799, did not relax their efforts. The New York Manumission Society remained more active than its sister society in Pennsylvania, devoting itself to the education of freed Negroes in its African school and seeking improvements in the state's slave laws.

Less than a year after the passage of the abolition law, the society noted a sinister development—the export of Negroes, slave and free, to the southern states and the West Indies "had become very general." Not only that, but New Yorkers were also violating the ban on slave importations. An assembly committee assigned to study a manumission society petition substantiated the abolitionists' claims. The existing laws were riddled with loopholes. For instance, the slave code did not prohibit the export of slaves, only their sale with intent to export, leaving prosecutors the impossible task of proving the intent of a master who sold his slave to an exporter. Consequently, the exportation of slaves was increasing "to an alarming magnitude," and "Slaves to a number not to be credited, and with circumstances of great barbarity, have been exported from the city of New-York to the West India Islands." The legislature responded by strengthening the

[12] U.S. Bureau of the Census, *Negro Population, 1790–1915* (Washington, D.C., 1918), p. 57; *Pa. H. of R., 1860*, I, 124, 209, 237, 265, 280, 327, 375, 440, 481, 771–74, 835. The legislature considered requests for total abolition in 1811–12, 1820–21, 1826, 1829, and 1840.

prohibitions on slave imports and exports. Nonetheless, the standing committee of the manumission society was forced to exercise continual vigilance to prevent violations of the law. In 1807 the committee regretfully reported that "the illegal Transportation of Slaves is . . . carried on to an alarming extent from this [state] to the Southward, particularly to New Orleans." [13]

The manumission society sought to aid Negroes in another important area, supporting legislation to prevent cruel treatment of slaves. The senate passed a bill for this purpose in 1808 but failed to convince the assembly to concur. (The assembly did accept a bill to prohibit the kidnapping of free Negroes.) The failure of the assembly to pass the law to prevent abusive treatment of slaves prompted the abolitionists to collect evidence of inhuman treatment to present to the next session of the legislature.[14] In the meantime, the society attacked another evil. Despite the laws prohibiting the importation of slaves, unscrupulous masters continually brought Negroes into the state, after buying them in another state (usually New Jersey) and manumitting them subject to their agreeing to serve their new masters for an inordinate length of time. The society sent a committee to the legislature to secure a bill to prevent this and also to require masters to educate the Negro children who would be free when they were twenty-eight. Although the senate passed bills to prohibit importation of Negroes and to prevent cruel treatment, the measures were lost in the assembly.[15]

Despite the recalcitrance of the assembly, the abolitionists remained undaunted and immediately set to work on a new

[13] New York Manumission Society, "Standing Committee Minutes, 1791–1807," (MSS at the New-York Historical Society), pp. 158–62; N.Y. Manumission Soc., "Minutes," II, 40, 48, 50–58; *N.Y. 24 Assembly,* pp. 53, 55, 73, 79, 102, 178, 233, 278–79, 290, 300, 303, 321; *N.Y. 24 Senate,* pp. 135, 141, 142; *N.Y. 24 Laws* (Albany, 1887), pp. 547–52; N.Y. Manumission Soc., "Minutes," II, 169–70.

[14] N.Y. Manumission Soc., "Minutes," II, 176–77, 188; *N.Y. 31 Senate,* pp. 132, 174, 176, 186, 225–27; *N.Y. 31 Assembly,* pp. 277, 282, 335, 339, 344, 380, 395.

[15] N.Y. Manumission Soc., "Minutes," II, 201, 205–6; *N.Y. 32 Senate,* pp. 103, 106, 109–10, 127, 130, 131, 161, 168, 170; *N.Y. 32 Assembly,* pp. 275, 356, 361.

petition that not only reiterated their previous requests but also asked for the repeal of the provision of the slave code that allowed the courts to deport convicted Negroes. Even life imprisonment, they pointed out, was preferable to "the uncertain horrors of slavery in regions where ingenuity is tortured to heighten Cruelty." Over one hundred slaves had been sent into "such hopeless bondage" under this provision from New York City alone; this was "an evil of no inconsiderable magnitude." Once more the society dispatched a committee to attend the legislature and lobby for their cause. The senate, still amenable to the society's arguments, passed a bill strengthening the ban on importation of slaves, making out-of-state indentures illegal, and requiring masters to teach Negro children to read. A clause that would have permitted the courts to emancipate slaves who were the victims of cruel treatment was rejected by the assembly, which then passed the amended bill.[16]

Although the new law marked an important gain for Negro rights, the legislature had not repealed the deportation clause of the slave code. An abolition society committee set to work visiting judges in an effort to dissuade them from exercising their discretionary power to deport slaves. At the same time, another committee prepared a new petition. This memorial went far toward explaining the resistance to repeal. The abolitionists charged that the law led to "prosecutions for mercenary motives"; masters often prosecuted their slaves "from no other motives than to be enabled to obtain for them in a foreign country a higher price than they would produce at home." The society also repeated earlier requests for legislation to protect slaves from cruel masters by permitting the courts to emancipate victims of abuse. Since the committee assigned to procure signatures for this petition failed to report at two meetings, it is doubtful whether it was ever presented to the legislature.[17]

[16] N.Y. Manumission Soc., "Minutes," II, 226, 229–32, 237; *N.Y. 33 Senate*, pp. 79, 81–82, 94–95, 97, 126, 146; *N.Y. 33 Assembly*, pp. 94, 243, 249, 260, 267, 284, 288, 290, 295; *N.Y. 33 Laws*, pp. 32–33.

[17] N.Y. Manumission Soc., "Minutes," II, 243–44, 266, 267–69, 274, 278.

The laxity of the petition committee was symptomatic of a general decline in the enthusiasm of the members of the manumission society. In 1809 the standing committee had remarked on the "great lukewarmness on the part of some of the members of the society in forwarding the great cause in which we are engaged." Four years later the standing committee again complained of the lack of zeal exhibited by the society's members. "Are the objects for which we are associated of less importance now than when the society was first incorporated? or have our minds become callous to a long and familiar acquaintance with the enormities of the evils with which we have had to contend?" Nonetheless, the decline of the New York Manumission Society was not as complete as that of the Pennsylvania Abolition Society. Despite the waning enthusiasm among the rank and file members of the New York society, a small group of abolitionists serving on the standing committee continued to aid distressed Negroes and spurred the society's campaign for ameliorative legislation.[18]

Although the ardor of the abolitionists had cooled, political developments favored their aims. In 1810 Daniel D. Tompkins, long a member of the manumission society, was reelected governor. Tompkins was noted for his support of humanitarian reforms, and since he knew that the legislature would soon take up a revision of the slave code, it may have been his suggestion that prompted the manumission society to call a special meeting in November, 1811, to draft a petition for total abolition. Two months later Tompkins took up the subject in his annual message, recommending that in the course of the legislature's revision of the laws it provide for the "gradual and ultimate extinction of . . . slavery, that reproach of a free people." Although an assembly committee approved the governor's sentiments, it claimed that neither "the peace of society, [n]or the happiness of those slaves themselves, would be promoted by . . . a law for their entire emancipation." Although the persistence of slavery in New York was regrettable, the committee pointed out that

[18] *Ibid.*, II, 217, 330.

"such regret should not induce the adoption of measures calculated to violate private rights, or disturb the quiet of the community." [19]

But in the course of a general revision of the statutes, the next session of the legislature enacted a new slave code. An attempt to amend the bill to reduce the servitude of Negro children from twenty-eight to twenty-one years was defeated, and the new law differed little from the previous slave code. Nonetheless, a manumission society committee noted several objectionable amendments, omissions, and inaccuracies in the new law, and the committee drafted a new bill. After a month the house had taken no action on the society's bill, so the abolitionists sent a delegation to Albany to lobby for it. At this point the assembly's actions exceeded the fondest hopes of the abolitionists. The house not only approved the revisions the society had recommended, but by a large majority adopted an amendment freeing all Negro children born after May 1, 1814, at twenty-one instead of twenty-eight. The assembly passed the amended bill with only two dissenting votes. The manumission society delegation returned to New York convinced that the senate would give its unanimous approval to the measure. But the abolitionists were mistaken. The senate decided that the bill contained "principles which are too great an innovation on private rights, and too doubtful on the ground of public policy, to be acted upon without mature deliberation," and postponed the bill to the next session.[20]

The 1815 assembly passed again the liberalized gradual

[19] Tompkins was elected a member of the manumission society on June 19, 1801 ("Minutes," II, 60) ; Julius W. Pratt, "Daniel D. Tompkins," *Dictionary of American Biography,* ed. Allen Johnson *et al.* (New York, 1928–58) , XVIII, 583–84; *N.Y. 35 Assembly,* pp. 6–7, 23–24, 46, 61, 150–51. The assembly did pass a bill to ameliorate the condition of the state's Negroes. Although this bill was lost in the rush of adjournment, the assembly tacked a rider to an appropriation bill repealing the transportation clause of the slave code, but the senate refused to concur: *ibid.,* pp. 279, 311, 339, 409, 474–75, 486; *N.Y. 35 Senate,* pp. 279, 284, 287–88.

[20] *N.Y. 36 Senate,* pp. 165, 170, 223–24, 237, 246, 248, 249, 285, 354; *N.Y. 36 Assembly,* pp. 423, 454, 466–67, 477; *N.Y. 36 Laws,* II, 201–9; N.Y. Manumission Soc., "Minutes," II, 362–63; *N.Y. 37 Assembly,* pp. 180, 345, 361, 415, 454, 455, 467; *N.Y. 37 Senate,* pp. 199, 231, 237.

abolition law, but the measure continued to encounter great opposition in the upper chamber. First the bill was referred to a hostile committee. Then, the senate adopted an amendment to reestablish the discredited abandonment program that allowed masters to surrender Negro children for state support. The adoption of this proposal sealed the fate of the bill.[21]

Governor Tompkins, however, continued to give firm support to the movement for Negro rights. On January 28, 1817, shortly before his departure to assume his new duties as vice-president of the United States, he sent a special message to the legislature asking it to consider "whether the dictates of humanity, the reputation of the state, and a just sense of gratitude to the Almighty" did not demand the total abolition of slavery within a decade. A joint senate-assembly committee balked at endorsing total abolition, recommending instead a general revision of the slave laws to "accelerate the effect of . . . [the] wise system of gradual emancipation." The committee's bill eliminated the transportation clause of the slave code and provided that Negro children born after the bill was adopted would be required to serve only twenty-one years. The assembly went beyond this, however, adopting an amendment that followed Tompkins' suggestion, emancipating all Negroes born before July 4, 1799, as of July 4, 1827. The senate added an amendment relieving masters of the obligation to support aged Negroes emancipated by the bill, and then passed the measure by an overwhelming majority. New York had become the first state to pass a law for the total abolition of slavery.[22]

New York's abolition law of 1817 went further than any previous abolition statute. It was retroactive and provided for the uncompensated emancipation of approximately 10,000 Negroes who were slaves at the time the law was

[21] *N.Y. 38 Assembly*, pp. 189, 198, 233, 281–82, 291, 295, 298, 302, 304; *N.Y. 38 Senate*, pp. 176, 192, 218–20, 234, 270–73. The assembly passed another revised slave bill in 1816, but it also failed to win senate approval: *N.Y. 39 Assembly*, pp. 241, 370, 382; *N.Y. 39 Senate*, pp. 137, 229.

[22] *N.Y. 40 Assembly*, pp. 126–27, 239, 389, 425–26, 525–27, 539, 546, 556–63, 568, 693, 713; *N.Y. 40 Senate*, pp. 67–68, 193, 222, 236, 239, 245, 251. *N.Y. 39–41 Laws*, IV, 136–44.

enacted.[23] Like gradual abolition laws, however, the law did not emancipate any Negroes until they had spent many years in servitude, providing their masters some compensation for the expense of raising them to working age. The youngest slaves freed by the act would be twenty-eight before their emancipation and many of the newly freed Negroes would be near the end of their working lives.

Despite the promise of total abolition, a few abolitionists urged further action. James Tallmadge, whose antislavery resolution had opened the Missouri compromise debates, proposed that the New York Constitutional Convention of 1821 go one step further and provide for immediate as well as total abolition. When his opponents accused him of reviving the passions of the Missouri debates, Tallmadge replied that although he did not anticipate that any of his fellow delegates would oppose him on the principle he espoused, he would not shrink from controversy. "While my life lasts," he pledged, "the oppressed people who gave rise to that discussion, shall receive my support in every place, and every situation." Peter Jay, who had supported the abolition bill in the legislature and who had fought all attempts to disenfranchise free Negroes, nonetheless opposed the Tallmadge proposal. He argued that although he was "zealous in the cause of emancipation," he thought that "the law as it now stands, was more wise and expedient than an immediate freedom." The convention agreed and rejected Tallmadge's amendment as well as a proposal that the legislature's promise to emancipate all the slaves in 1827 be protected from the actions of future legislatures by being incorporated into the constitution. The promise of abolition was not made part of the new constitution, but the legislature did not repeal the 1817 law and July 4, 1827, marked the end of slavery in New York.[24]

---

[23] A New York State census of 1814 reported 11,375 slaves (*N.Y. 38 Assembly*, pp. 234–74).

[24] Nathaniel H. Carter and William L. Stone, *Reports of the Proceedings and Debates of the Convention of 1821* . . . (Albany, N.Y., 1821), pp. 167, 171–72, 485–87, 497–98; *Journal of the Convention of the State of New-York* . . . (Albany, N.Y., 1821), 268–73. There were still a few slaves in New York after 1827 since non-residents could bring

ABOLITION IN NEW JERSEY

In New Jersey abolition advanced at a much slower pace than elsewhere in the North; by 1810 New Jersey was the only northern state in which the number of slaves still exceeded that of free Negroes.[25] The New Jersey Abolition Society had never been strong or influential. Faced with implacable hostility in the northeastern part of the state and with widespread acceptance of abolition in the southwestern areas where little proselytising was required, the New Jersey abolitionists were easily discouraged. Moreover, New Jersey's lack of a great metropolitan center made it difficult to maintain a strongly centralized society similar to those in New York and Philadelphia. Although the New Jersey antislavery organization had been active in obtaining the release of free Negroes illegally kept as slaves and had lobbied for the gradual abolition law as well as other ameliorative legislation, it never succeeded in building up a loyal and devoted membership. In 1806 the society reported to the convention of antislavery societies that it was unable "to make any considerable effort" to comply with the convention's previous recommendations. Two years later, the society decided to meet only in the years preceding conventions, which were triennial occurrences now. In 1809 the New Jersey society held its last meeting, having to confess three years later "with some degree of sorrow and of shame" that the society had not even been able to hold a meeting to elect convention delegates. Their letter noted the "abatement of zeal" among members but hoped that the society would be revived in the near future. This proved to be a vain hope.[26]

---

slaves into the state. This practice was outlawed in 1841. Edgar J. McManus, *A History of Negro Slavery in New York* (Syracuse, N.Y., 1966), pp. 178–79.

[25] *Negro Population*, p. 57.

[26] The history of the New Jersey Abolition Society can be traced through its MS minutes in the Quaker Collection, Haverford College. The minute books of the Burlington and Salem branches of the society are also at Haverford. *Minutes of the Proceedings of the Eleventh American Convention for Promoting the Abolition of Slavery . . .* (Philadelphia, 1806), pp. 9–11; *1812 Convention Minutes*, p. 12; *1817 Convention Minutes*, p. 20.

New Jersey's proximity to the slave states, the lack of an efficient abolition society to protect free Negroes, and a law establishing very low fines to prevent the export of slaves, tempted many unscrupulous slaveowners to sell their Negroes in the booming slave markets of the South. In 1812 the legislature increased the penalties for the crime at the request of a member of the abolition society. But the new law still did not provide adequate protection since it allowed the export of slaves who had consented to their removal.[27] This provision opened the way for widespread fraud. Masters could obtain the consent of their Negroes by deceptive promises of freedom after a limited period of service in the South. Once the slave reached his destination, however, he was left without recourse. An Englishman who visited the United States in the 1820's reported that since slaves were selling for $300 in New Jersey while they would bring $700 to $800 in New Orleans, there were great temptations to circumvent the law; therefore "the traffic of slaves . . . became considerable." Some justices of the peace were "base enough . . . to attest that slaves consented to be removed, when in many instances they had never examined them." [28]

In 1818 New Jersey newspapers reported some particularly flagrant violations of the law. Several groups, aroused by these reports, asked the legislature for remedial action. The petitioners asserted that "No less than four vessels have cleared from the Port of Perth Amboy for New Orleans since March last with cargoes of human beings of all ages and conditions shipped as Merchandise." Some of these Negroes "were taken by force," many were too young to have given legal consent for their removal, "and most, if not all, of those who are certified to have consented, have been induced to go by threats from a master they dreaded or by illusive promises

[27] *1812 Convention Minutes*, pp. 12–13; *N.J. 36 Assembly 2*, pp. 94, 132, 163, 169–70, 188; *N.J. 36 Council 2*, pp. 1192, 1203, 1204; *N.J. 36 laws 2*, pp. 15–17.

[28] Gerrebrandt Van Houten, *The Van Houten Manuscripts . . .* (Paterson, N.J., 1894), p. 28; William Nelson and Charles A. Shriner, *History of Paterson and its Environs* (3 vols.; New York, 1920), I, 180; Isaac Holmes, *An Account of the United States of America* (London, [1823]), p. 324.

of Freedom and wealth." Shocked by these revelations, the legislators unanimously approved a new law absolutely prohibiting the export of slaves and providing increased penalties. Just before the new law took effect, however, Nicholas Van Wickle, who had been implicated in previous violations of the law, obtained certificates permitting the removal of more than sixty slaves for sale in Louisiana.[29]

The movement for the total abolition of slavery, which had periodically agitated the Pennsylvania legislature and had received such striking success in New York, did not gain momentum in New Jersey until the birth of the new antislavery movement of the 1830's. In 1839 a group from Bergen County, which had always been a center of pro-slavery feeling, petitioned for total abolition; a year later the New Jersey Anti-Slavery Society asked for a revision of the slave code, and five other groups petitioned for immediate abolition. But, as a convention of New Jersey abolitionists noted, these petitions were "treated with cold neglect," not because "our statesmen approve of slavery, nor on account of the interests of a few dozen slaveholders," but because politicians were afraid to jeopardize "the interests of their party at the South." [30]

Indicative of the revived interest in Negro rights was a series of petitions for granting the franchise to Negroes presented to the assembly in 1842. The legislature refused to grant this request, defeating by a large majority a motion to refer a franchise petition to the election committee. Despite this rebuff, New Jersey Negroes continued to press their

[29] *True American* (Trenton, N.J.), June 22, 1818; *Times: and New-Brunswick General Advertiser,* May 28, 1818; *Fredonian* (New Brunswick), June 4, 1818; two undated petitions, New Jersey State Library, Trenton; *N.J. 43 Assembly,* pp. 7, 8, 11, 13–15, 41, 42; *N.J. 43 Council,* pp. 11, 12; *N.J. 43 Laws,* pp. 3–5; George J. Miller, "County Records Reveal Efforts to Abolish Slavery," *New Brunswick Sunday Times,* January 1, 1932. New Jersey continued to allow the deportation of convicted slaves, a practice that had led to widespread abuse in New York.

[30] *N.J. 63 Assembly,* p. 415; *N.J. 64 Assembly 2,* pp. 262, 270, 294, 370, 418; *An Address to the People of New Jersey, By the Abolitionists of the State Favorable to Political Action Against American Slavery . . .* (New York, 1841), p. 2.

demands for the right to vote.[31] In addition, the 1842 legislature was faced with twenty-seven petitions ranging from requests to modify the slave code to demands for complete abolition. The assembly had appointed a committee to study the slave code in 1841, but the committee's bill was merely shunted from one session to the next, without any substantive action. The abolitionists refused to be discouraged. In 1843 ninety-six citizens of Bloomfield asked the assembly to "make this state in reality, (what it is nominally,) a free state." The abolitionists presented a new series of petitions in 1844. Later in the session, however, they told the legislature that they "did not wish to press the objects of their petitions, at this late stage of the session, and asked leave to withdraw their papers." [32] This did not, however, indicate hesitancy on the part of the opponents of slavery. They probably withdrew their petitions because they hoped to press their attack on slavery at the forthcoming constitutional convention.

If the abolitionists had any hope that the new constitution would abolish slavery, they were bitterly disappointed; the document did not even mention slavery.[33] Nonetheless, the abolitionists decided to follow the example of antislavery men in Massachusetts and Pennsylvania and ask the courts to determine whether slavery was compatible with the equal rights doctrine that had just been incorporated into the constitution. The abolitionists brought the issue before the Supreme Court in a series of cases in 1845.

The case for the Negro plaintiffs was argued by Alvan Stewart, a leading New York abolitionist who had gained a national reputation for his eloquent attacks on slavery. Stewart's arguments, totaling eleven hours, covered wide grounds. Going beyond the immediate point at issue, Stewart maintained that since slavery was a violation of the due process

[31] *N.J. 66 Assembly 2*, pp. 226–28, 313, 314; *N.J. 67 Assembly 2*, pp. 295, 307–8, 325–26, 384.

[32] *N.J. 65 Assembly 2*, pp. 298–99, 368, 585, 612; *N.J. 66 Assembly*, pp. 68, 226–28, 232, 282, 287, 301, 310; *N.J. 67 Assembly*, p. 62; *N.J. 67 Assembly 2*, pp. 265, 268, 394; *N.J. 68 Assembly 2*, pp. 475, 478, 485, 486, 669, 670.

[33] *Proceedings of the New Jersey State Constitutional Convention of 1844,* edited under the auspices of the New Jersey Writers' Project of the Works Projects Administration (n.p., 1942), pp. 614–44.

clause of the Constitution, it was not only unconstitutional in New Jersey but in all of the United States. He further argued that Congress could and should abolish slavery everywhere, since the federal government was required to guarantee the states a republican form of government. Slavery, Stewart held, was contrary to both the Bible and natural law. The New Jersey Constitution of 1844 had recognized the natural rights of all persons to life and liberty and automatically had put an end to slavery. Stewart pointed to the close resemblance between the first articles of the New Jersey Constitution and the Massachusetts Constitution of 1780 and argued that the New Jersey court should follow the precedent set by Massachusetts.

The opposing attorneys contended that the bill of rights was not intended to free the slaves, that it was "a mere abstraction, a rhetorical flourish, and . . . not a *part* of the Constitution." Furthermore, if the court accepted a literal interpretation of the disputed clause, it would allow wives and children to sue their husbands and parents. The opposition attempted to link abolitionists with "Fouriers, Anti-Renters, Socialists, Owenites, Fanny Wrighters, Non-Resistants, and No-Human Government-men, Dissolvers of the Union, Nullifiers, and Infidels." Stewart pointed out in rebuttal that these charges were irrelevant to the point at issue: "whether slavery in the State of New Jersey, is a *legal* and *lawful* institution or not." [34]

Despite Stewart's eloquence, the majority of the court ruled in favor of the slaveholders, maintaining that the framers of the constitution had not intended to apply the equal rights doctrine "to man in his private, individual or domestic capacity; or to define his individual rights or interfere with his domestic relations, or his individual condition." If the convention had intended to abolish slavery, "no one can doubt but that it would have adopted some clear and definite provision to effect it, and not have left so important and grave a question . . . to depend upon the doubtful

[34] The State *v.* Post, the State *v.* Van Beuren, *20 N.J. Law Rep.*, 368; Alvan Stewart, *A Legal Argument Before the Supreme Court of the State of New Jersey . . . for the Deliverance of Four Thousand Persons from Bondage* (New York, 1845), pp. 5–6, 26–27, 31–43, 45–47.

construction of an indefinite abstract political proposition." [35]

While awaiting the court decision, the abolitionists had continued to petition the legislature for abolition. But they achieved no success until 1846 when, in the course of a general revision of the laws, the judiciary committee reported "An Act to abolish slavery." The assembly now moved with astonishing speed, suspending the rules so that the bill could receive both its first and second reading on the same day. Within five days the bill received the unanimous approval of the assembly and ten days later the senate gave its unanimous vote for the bill.[36]

Although the bill's title promised a great deal, in effect the new law provided for a modified form of slavery. All New Jersey slaves were emancipated by the first sentence of the law, but the rest of the statute limited their freedom and relegated them to the status of apprentices. The children of these apprentices were to be maintained by their parents' masters until they were six years old, when they could be bound out to service as paupers. The children of slaves born before the passage of the revised law would continue to serve their mothers' masters as provided by the gradual abolition law. But the apprentices did have more legal protection than slaves. They could sue for their freedom in instances of abusive treatment; they could not be sold without their written consent; and under no circumstances could they be sold to a non-resident. In addition, the new law provided severe

[35] State *v.* Post, p. 375. It is difficult to determine whether the abolitionists had any real hope of success in these cases or merely prosecuted them to focus public attention on the evils of slavery. Slavery was not discussed at the constitutional convention, and there is no evidence that the adoption of the first clause of the bill of rights was intended to abolish slavery (*Convention Proceedings,* pp. 51, 129–40, 169, 409, 583).

[36] *N.J. 69 Assembly,* pp. 225–26, 272, 656, 682; *N.J. 70 Assembly,* pp. 138, 142, 344, 720, 725, 726, 740, 749, 847, 862, 872, 902; *N.J. 2 Senate,* pp. 642–45, 725–32, 738, 741, 756, 758, 759. Much of the discussion in the senate was taken up with efforts of four senators from Bergen, Sussex, Hudson, and Passaic counties who attempted to weaken the bill.

penalties for the export or attempted export of an apprentice out of the state, and the victims of these attempts were to go free.[37]

The abolition act was clearly a compromise measure. As the convention of New Jersey abolitionists had pointed out in 1841, the reluctance of the legislature to abolish slavery was not purely out of consideration for the property interests of "a few dozen slaveholders . . . who are as well able to pay for the labor they require as the rest of us." By 1846 there were fewer than seven hundred slaves in the state but, as the Supreme Court noted in its decision in the 1845 freedom cases, over half of these slaves were over fifty-five years old. These Negroes had a legal claim upon their masters for support if they became incapacitated—a risk that increased with age. A total abolition of slavery, the court pointed out, would free the slaveowners from this obligation and would force the public to support these aged Negroes. Although the court hastened to add that this consideration could have "no legitimate influence" on a judicial decision, this was undoubtedly an important factor in the minds of the legislators who passed the abolition bill. The new law solved the problem of ending slavery without requiring the state's taxpayers to support aged Negroes by substituting apprenticeship for slavery and by requiring masters to provide for the support of their servants. The apprenticeship system also solved a second problem—abolishing slavery without confiscating the property of the slaveholders. As the court reporter noted when the New Jersey freedom cases came before the Court of Errors and Appeals in 1848, "the distinguishing feature" of the abolition law was "that it abolishes all the odious disabilities of the Slave, while it leaves untouched the vested rights of the master to his service." The new law ended slavery without endangering the property interests of either the slaveholders or the state's taxpayers.

But despite the fact that the legislature had formally abolished slavery, Negroes remained subject to involuntary servitude. Accordingly, the United States census continued

[37] *Statutes of the State of New Jersey. Revised* . . . (Trenton, N.J., 1847), pp. 380–90.

to list them as slaves, and the last eighteen Negroes held in bondage in New Jersey in 1860 were liberated by death or by the thirteenth amendment.[38]

FREE NEGROES

By 1830, when there were over 2,000,000 slaves in the United States, fewer than one per cent were found in the New England and Middle Atlantic states, and most of these were in New Jersey. Only 2,780 Negroes remained in bondage in the northern states, and the free Negro population increased rapidly from just over 27,000 in 1790 to well over 122,000 by 1830.[39] Each federal census revealed that freedom, rather than slavery, was rapidly becoming the normal condition of northern Negroes as gradual abolition laws and voluntary manumissions reduced the number held as slaves.

Although most northern Negroes had gained their freedom, they were still members of a despised race, subject to countless indignities, denied the equal rights promised by the Declaration of Independence, and restricted to the most menial occupations. Jeremy Belknap, describing the conditions of free Negroes in Massachusetts in 1790, noted that "many of them are in a far worse condition than when they were slaves, being incapable of providing for themselves the means of subsistence." But, as the Duc de la Rochefoucauld-Liancourt observed, no matter how poor the freed Negroes were, none of them chose to move to the South to take advantage of the slavery that still existed there. Although several Massachusetts freedmen, disillusioned with the results of abolition, did petition the legislature to aid them in returning to Africa, most Negroes regarded the United States as their home and rejected all colonization schemes. But they continued to suffer from the prejudice of white Americans. Frances Kemble, who visited Philadelphia in 1838, noted that the free Negroes were "marked as the Hebrew lepers of old . . . They are not slaves indeed, but

[38] *Address*, p. 2; State v. Post, p. 372; The State *v.* Post, *21 N.J. Law Rep.*, 699; *Negro Population*, p. 57.
[39] *Ibid.*

they are pariahs; debarred from all fellowship save with their own despised race . . . They are free certainly, but they are also degraded, rejected." [40]

The freedmen were not completely friendless. At least in the first years after the gradual emancipation acts, the abolition societies regarded themselves as the protectors of the Negroes whose freedom they had advocated. In 1805 when the enthusiasm of the abolitionists was beginning to wane, the convention of antislavery societies urged local societies to continue this work. "Shall we, by lukewarmness or neglect, give the enemies of our institutions the triumph of reproaching us with indifference?" The Negroes still needed protection and aid. "Shall we now desert them? after teaching them that they belong to the rank of man? . . . Let us decide . . . whether we will continue our parental care over them, or leave them friendless and abandoned to their own weakness and ignorance." [41]

The abolitionists were forced to concede that many of the freedmen did not make good use of their liberty. William Dunlap remarked in 1806 that for the most part Philadelphia free Negroes were "degraded and vicious," although many of them, he hastened to add, were "useful and respectable." Burlington, New Jersey, abolitionists reported to the 1798 convention that the free Negroes "in too many instances" were "given to Idleness, Frolicking, Drunkeness, and in some few cases to Dishonesty." But, as the New York Manumission Society noted in a similar report, "when we regard their opportunities of instruction, and their few motives to exertion, we rather wonder that they are not more depraved." [42]

[40] Leon F. Litwack, *North of Slavery* (Chicago, 1961) , *passim;* Jeremy Belknap to David Howell, June 14, 1790, in George H. Moore, *Additional Notes on the History of Slavery in Massachusetts*, December, 1866 (n.p., n.d.) , p. 12; François Alexandre Frederic duc de la Rochefoucauld-Liancourt, *Travels Through the United States of North America*, trans. H. Neuman (2 vols.; London, 1799) , I, 532; George H. Moore, *Notes on the History of Slavery in Massachusetts* (New York, 1866) , p. 225; Frances A. Kemble, *Journal of a Residence on a Georgia Plantation in 1838–1839* (New York, 1863) , p. 11.

[41] *1805 Convention Minutes,* pp. 32–33.

[42] Dunlap to Elizabeth Dunlap, January 17, 1806, *Diary of William Dunlap* (3 vols.; Collections of the N.Y. Hist. Soc., 1929–31) , II, 370;

Undoubtedly the failure of many of the freedmen to live up to the abolitionists' conception of proper conduct brought anguish to the abolition societies. In 1808 the New York Manumission Society was forced to view "with regret the looseness of manners & depravity of conduct in many of the Persons of Colour in this city." The society appointed a committee to draft a plan "for promoting a reformation among that part of the African race, who are dissolute in their morals, keep Houses of ill fame, and are otherwise pursuing a conduct injurious to themselves and others." The next year the manumission society told free Negroes that "their method of celebrating the abolition of the Slave Trade was improper, in as much as it tended to injure themselves and cause reflections to be made on this Society." At this point, however, the free Negroes balked, telling a committee of abolitionists that they had invested a great deal in the preparations for their parade and that "they could not think of relinquishing their proposed method of Celebrating the day." [43]

The Pennsylvania Abolition Society placed much of the blame for the increasing hostility of public opinion on the conduct of the free Negroes. Many of the state's free Negroes had come to Philadelphia, where they were joined by fugitive slaves from the southern states. "Freed from the shackles, but not from the vices of slavery those victims of inhumanity thronged our streets in search of pleasure or employment." Although some of them had found honest jobs, "too many served only to swell the list of our criminals and augment the catalogue of our paupers. As the burthen increased, the reputation of our institution diminished." [44]

The pioneer philanthropist, Benjamin Rush, came up with a novel solution for this problem. He noted that

It has long been a matter of regret among the friends of the free blacks that they are employed chiefly as servants and sailors, for which occupations many of them are but little qualified and in

---

"Report of the Acting Committee, Burlington Anti-Slavery Society" (Misc. MSS of the Pa. Abolition Soc.), V, 127–28; *1806 Convention Minutes*, p. 7.

[43] N.Y. Manumission Soc., "Minutes," II, 177–78, 181, 186, 223, 231.

[44] *1809 Convention Minutes*, pp. 15–16.

which they are peculiarly exposed to continue in the practice of such vices as have been contracted in slavery.

Moreover, "most of the black men who come to Philadelphia from New Jersey and the southern states are farmers." Therefore, Rush offered to donate a 5,200-acre tract for the resettlement of free Negroes as farmers. He appropriately proposed to call this agricultural community "Benezet." [45] But this plan was never pursued.

As free Negroes became more numerous, the prejudice against them increased. In 1821 the Massachusetts legislature, alarmed by "the increase of a species of population" that might "become both injurious and burdensome," appointed a committee to investigate methods of restricting the immigration of free Negroes. In 1834 a group of whites told the Connecticut legislature that the whites could not compete with Negro labor. "Whenever they come into competition . . . the white man is deprived of employment, or is forced to work for less than he requires." Thousands of white men had been forced to flee the state "for the accomodation of the most debased race that the civilised world has ever seen." [46] The influx of free Negroes and fugitive slaves into Philadelphia inspired several campaigns to restrict the immigration of Negroes, and in 1817 the New Jersey Assembly was asked to inquire "into the expediency of making more effectual Legislative provisions to prevent the introduction of people of Colour into this State." Although these efforts to prevent the immigration of Negroes failed, they did indicate an increasing hostility toward the freedmen, hostility that sometimes led to rioting and mob violence.[47]

The Negroes, freed by the abolition laws but hemmed in

[45] Benjamin Rush to the President of the Pennsylvania Abolition Society [1794?], in *Letters of Benjamin Rush,* ed. Lyman H. Butterfield (2 vols.; Princeton, N.J., 1951), II, 754–56.

[46] Moore, *Slavery in Mass.,* pp. 238–39. The Connecticut petition is quoted in Edward S. Abdy, *Journal of a Residence and Tour in the United States of North America . . .* (3 vols.; London, 1835), III, 246–47.

[47] *Ante,* pp. 207–8, 208 n.; *N.J. 41 Assembly 2,* pp. 91, 122, 145, 159–60, 190, 232; *N.J. 42 Assembly,* pp. 8, 9; *N.J. 43 Assembly,* pp. 8, 10; Litwack, *North of Slavery,* pp. 100–103.

by legal restrictions and prejudice, realized that emancipation had not been a panacea. Yet they valued their freedom. As one freed Negro put it, "I don't know much about freedom . . . but I wouldn't be a slave ag'in, not if you'd give me the best farm in the Jarsies." [48]

If abolition did not drastically alter the life of its Negro beneficiaries, neither did it seriously interfere with the daily life of slaveowners. Gradual abolition laws allowed masters to retain all their slaves; it was only some twenty years after their enactment, when the children of his slaves would demand wages or leave, that masters began to feel the real effects of the new policy. But whereas the immediate effects of gradual abolition were small, it ultimately forced northerners to rely on free rather than slave labor.

CONCLUSIONS

With the passage of the 1804 gradual abolition law by New Jersey, the principle of gradual abolition had triumphed in the North. Although abolitionists occasionally attempted to persuade northern legislatures to pass total abolition bills, their attention was increasingly focused on the South. At home, slavery was well on the road to extinction. But the hopes of abolitionists that the gradual abolition program would also triumph in the South were doomed to failure.

Why did peaceful and gradual abolition succeed in the North when it took a bloody Civil War to free the slaves of the South? The usual contention that slavery was simply not profitable in the North cannot withstand critical reexamination, for this assertion rests on the assumption that northerners believed that it was unprofitable. This assumption is incorrect. Throughout the period northerners continued to pay high prices for Negroes; slave prices remained relatively stable, showing no decline to reflect a growing conviction that slavery was uneconomical. Negro slaves continued to sell for high prices in the North because they filled an important role in the northern economy as skilled farmers, industrial workers, and domestics.

[48] William J. Allinson, *Memoir of Quamino Buccau* (Philadelphia, 1851), p. 16.

If slavery was seen to be a losing proposition in the North, there would have been no need for gradual abolition laws; abolitionists could have expected slaveowners to act in their self-interest and to manumit their Negroes as soon as they could without incurring any financial responsibility for their future care. Instead, masters strenuously resisted gradual abolition laws and fought freedom suits. If slaveowners believed slavery was unprofitable, they would not have petitioned the Pennsylvania Assembly to allow them to keep their unregistered Negroes in bondage; they would not have asked New Jersey to repeal its gradual abolition law, nor would they have attempted to evade New York's law prohibiting the importation of slaves.

It is true that slavery probably became less essential as European immigration increased in the post-Revolutionary period. But individual slaveowners continued to resist any attempts to deprive them of their property.

Why, then, did the North abolish slavery? One reason is that non-slaveholders regarded it as detrimental to their own interests and to the interests of the community. These feelings had led to several attempts to limit the importation of Negroes in the Colonial period. More important, however, was the intellectual ferment of the Revolutionary era. As John Jay put it, "prior to the great revolution, the great majority . . . of our people had been so long accustomed to the practice and convenience of having slaves, that very few among them even doubted the propriety and rectitude of it." Although the abolitionists had made a few converts, "the number of those converts compared with the people at large was then very inconsiderable." But, "their doctrines prevailed by almost insensible degrees, and was like the little lump of leaven which was put into three measures of meal." [49] The ideas of John Woolman and Anthony Benezet found a receptive audience during the controversy with England. The generation of the founding fathers was sincere in its espousal of a generous love of liberty and hatred of all forms of tyranny. The abolitionists could make an effective

[49] Jay to Granville Sharp, [1788], in Henry P. Johnson (ed.), *The Correspondence and Public Papers of John Jay* (4 vols.; New York, 1890–93), III, 342.

appeal to men who thought that taxation without representation was a step to slavery and ask them to consider the plight of their Negroes, doomed to perpetual servitude. Moreover, the late eighteenth century was a period of humanitarian reform throughout the Atlantic community. As men questioned the justice of harsh penal laws, imprisonment for debt, and other evils, they also attacked slavery. It was a period in our history when men were willing to reexamine their institutions and their ideas, a period that was auspicious for reformers.

At the same time, northern Negroes seemed more prepared for freedom than ever before. Since the slave trade had been cut off, almost all the Negroes were native Americans who had adapted themselves to the values of the masters' society, sharing their customs, language, and religion. Negroes who served northern masters rarely worked in large plantation gangs, and they not only had greater opportunity to integrate themselves into the white society, but their masters knew them better and feared them less than the planters of the South.

Nonetheless the progress of abolition was slow, especially in New York and New Jersey where slavery had been deeply woven into the texture of daily life. Not only was the abolition movement hampered by the sanctions of tradition and a widespread belief in the inferiority of Negroes, but the abolitionists were hampered by arguments based on the rights of property. For, ironically, just as the Revolutionary philosophy gave rise to a new concern for the Rights of Man, it elevated concern for man's right to property to new heights. The tenets of the philosophy of the American Revolution could serve slaveowners as well as abolitionists, and it was not until the abolitionists had worked out a compromise on the troublesome issue of compensation that they were able to persuade New York and New Jersey to adopt gradual abolition.

The ideas of the American Revolution and the new humanitarian concern had a profound effect on the South as well as the North. But southern abolitionists faced much greater difficulties. Slavery had already become deeply ingrained in the southern way of life. Even gradual abolition would have undermined the property rights of thousands of influential men and left the South to devise a new labor system. If northerners were afraid of a large population of free Negroes, the South had more reason to be afraid. If the inducements to end slavery were as strong south of Pennsylvania as they were to the north, the obstacles were so much the greater. Everywhere in the North slaveowners were in a minority, and ultimately they could be forced to yield to the humanitarian ideals of the age, providing that the program of gradual abolition would allow some safeguards for the rights of property.

TABLE I

SLAVE PRICES, NEW YORK, NEW JERSEY, AND PENNSYLVANIA [a]

appendix

Dates	Description	Price [b]
		1700–24
1709	man	40 (*current, Pa.*)
1710	man	65
1710	woman	35
1714	"new" Negro	17.10 plus 15.50 if he lives to the spring.
1717	woman	50
1720	30 yr household Negro, from Barbados	55
1720	field hand	50 ("*too high*")
1722/3	16–17 yr wench	45
1723	6 mo pregnant household wench	45
1723	wench, 3 yrs in this country, badly trained	50–51
1723	19–20 yr wench	55
1723	wench & 4 yr child	75 ("*very extraordinary price*")
1723	man	30
		1725–49
1725	woman	45
1725	child	15
1725	child	10
1725	child	5
1729	25 yr man	35
1730	50 yr woman	35
1730	25 yr woman & 15 mo child	40
1730	18 yr woman	45

[a] *This table is based on data collected from a great variety of sources, published and manuscripts. For an annotated version of this table, see: Arthur Zilversmit, "Slavery and Its Abolition in the Northern States" (Ph.D. dissertation, University of California, 1962), pp. 324–29.*
[b] *Price is in pounds, unless otherwise noted.*

TABLE I—Continued

Dates	Description	Price [b]
1735	men	45–50
1736	14 yr woman	45
1738	woman	48
1739	woman & infant	38
1740	woman & 2 yr boy	30
1745	woman	40
1748	26 yr woman	70
1748	woman	30
1748	7 yr girl	30
1748	5 yr boy	15
1748	2 yr girl	10
1748	6 mo child	5
1749	25 yr Mulatto woman	48
		1750–62
1750	man	64.10
1750	man	54
1751	Negro	46
1751	Negro	46
1752	man	50
1752	boy	40
1754	30 yr man	70
1756	good iron worker	30–40
1757	Mulatto woman	50
1758	man	75
1758	boy	45
1758	woman & child	60
1758	girl	30
1758	man	20
1759	25 yr man, carpenter	50
1759	man	75
1760	man	75
1760	boy	60
1760	old man	30

TABLE I—Continued

Dates	Description	Price [b]
1760	boy	20
1760	45 yr man, farmer & iron worker	50
1760	8 yr girl	40
1761	woman & child	50
1761	19 yr girl	51
1762	woman	50
1762	man	62.10
		1763–75
1763	42 yr woman	40
1763	3½ yr boy	25
1763	35 yr man	45
1763	19 yr man	120
1763	19 yr man	120
1763	26 yr man	120
1763	35 yr man, "subject to fits."	30
1763	40 yr man	45
1763	17 yr boy	100
1764	man	100
1767	6 yr boy	31
1767	forge man	100
1767	boy	60
1768	woman & boy	66 (York currency)
1770	man	75 (hard cash)
1773	6 yr girl	25
1773	5 yr boy	70
1775	household woman	100
		1776–83
1777	boy	65
1777	11 yr boy	40 (York money)
1778	woman & child	110
1778	30 yr man, plantation hand	$600

TABLE I—Continued

Dates	Description	Price [b]
1778	30 yr wench & 7 yr boy	$1200
1779	7 yr boy	50 bu. wheat & 50 bu. rye
1779	same boy	2,000 (Pa. money)
1780	15 yr girl	120 (species)
1780	15 yr girl	120 (species)
1780	26–27 yr farmer & tanner	130 (species)
1780	19 yr wench & child	100 (York currency)
1780	20 yr man	150 (species)
1781	8 yr boy	45
1781	22 yr man	swap for boy & girl, 10–14, or 5 tons bar iron
1781	15–16 yr boy	80 (gold or silver)
1781	46 yr wench, cook	60 (hard cash)
1781	girl	60
1781	19 yr man	10,000 (continental currency)
1783	household wench	100
		1784–1804
1785	woman	30
1785	24 yr woman	65
1787	man	100
1787	woman & 2 girls	120
1789	woman & 2 children	140
1790	slave	100
1790	40 yr man "complete coachman"	50 ("very low price")
1790	22 yr man	78
1792	30 yr man	106
1794	21 yr "boy"	90
1794	good male slave, 18–25 yr	100 (or $250)

TABLE I—Continued

Dates	Description	Price[b]
1794	good woman slave, 18–25 yr	70
1794	chimney sweep	85
1794	33 yr man	95
1795	18 yr girl	70
1795	14 yr boy	100
1795	10 yr girl	75
1796	wench	70
1796	8 yr girl	40
1796	14 yr boy	100
1796	man, tanner	120
1797	25 yr man, farmer	$250
1797	18 yr household boy	110
1797	20 yr boy, waiter	80
1798	man	$100
1799	18 yr boy, "compleat waiting boy"	80
1799	woman & 4 mo child	80
1799	14 yr waiter boy	60
1799	30 yr woman, cook	60
1799	22 yr woman	100
1800	13 yr boy	40
1801	woman & child	$200
1801	farm woman	50
1801	woman	$135.50
1801	woman & child	$200
1803	18–19 yr man	$262.50
1803	woman	$120
1803	woman	$120
1804	6 yr girl	$50
1804	6 yr girl	$50

TABLE II

NEW JERSEY SLAVE PRICES,
1750–60 (PRICES IN POUNDS)

Men	Women	Boys	Girls	Page [a]
	45			8
		50		29
50				42
40				51
30				69
60				73
55				77
	45			104
		35		108
	20	25		118
	45			125–126
	30			126
		35		128
40	55 [b]			133
45	35			142
45				159
55				162
	40 [b]			171–172
			27	203–204
60	40	30	30	228
40				228
40				228
50				245
		30		249
			42.10	250
	20			121
60				155
40				156
	60			166–167
50				170
25				183

[a] Calendar of New Jersey Wills, Administrations, Etc., Archives of the State of New Jersey, *1st ser.*, *XXXII*.
[b] *Indicates woman and child. A few male slaves, worth less than twenty pounds, and two women, worth less than two pounds, have been excluded.*

TABLE II—Continued

Men	Women	Boys	Girls	Page [a]
		11.12		184
	55 [b]			189
			35	192
50				194–195
	50			212
	30			217
70				221
	40	60		224
50	25			225
25				226
65				226
80				226
		25	25	15
		32		15
		40		16
25			40	25
			30	25
		65		34
60				38–39
50	40 [b]			55
35				58
40				60
	60			64
70	35	35		86
60	20			89
25			25	98
	45			104
		50		109
		35	25	113
	40			230
		40		252
	25			254

TABLE III

NEW JERSEY SLAVE PRICES, 1794–1801 (PRICES IN POUNDS, UNLESS OTHERWISE INDICATED)

Men	Women	Boys	Girls	Source [a] Book	Page
100				Monmouth wills	7206
100					
90	50 [b]	40			7239
100	50	40			
		77.10			
		77.10			
		60			7312
	55				7325
100		35	20		7404
100	60	38			
		12			
	20	30			7469
		75			7505
		75			
			45		7520
90	50		35		7547–48
20	70 [b]				7571
80	60				
100					
60					
50					
20					
	60				7591
	20		15		7641
40		40			7730
100	50	45			
	25	15			
100			20		7835
20					7839
35					7911

[a] *Will Books and Files, MSS in the Superior Court Clerk's Office, Trenton.*
[b] *Indicates woman and child.*
[c] *Woman and two children; aged and worthless slaves are excluded.*

Men	Women	Boys	Girls	Source Book	Page
		36	35.10	Monmouth wills	7942
		60			7885
100	60 c			Bergen wills	2543
	50	30	20		2550
60	40				2593
110			40		2625
120		80	34		2644
120		80	34		
100					
100					
100					2644
35					
35					
90	50 b	50			2651
100		35			
		20			
75	65	15	10		2825
35		60	35		8297–99
100			25		
100			10		
100			10		
		60	35		8389–90
40	10				8425
60	50				
80	60				
45	65				
70	45				
	35				8425
	30				
	25				
	20				
	15				
	70				8560
	49 b	50	3	Essex wills	8154

TABLE III—Continued

Men	Women	Boys	Girls	Source Book	Page
	40 [b]				
100	60	60	35	Essex wills	8209
60					
40	55	10	55		8262
			10		
75			35		8280
	20 [b]				8292
85					9164
80	40				9189–91
80.11	60	10	20		
40					9253
75	60	40	35		9262
		100			9433
	30		30		9542
95				Middlesex wills	9010
	45	80			9016
55					9025
50	60	10	10		9069
60	50 [c]				9102
80					9128
90					9164
20	20	120	60		9197
120		100			
	50				9213
	50				
100	50				9228
100	50				
40					9239
	35				9261
	35				
60		45			9264
		110	60		9352
	60				9397
90	50	30			9421
		20			

TABLE III—Continued

Men	Women	Boys	Girls	Source Book	Page
		15			
80	32			Middlesex wills	9453
		80	40		9490
		80	40		
100					9510
70	40		20		9605
	60				9629
	65		19		
120	50 [b]		20		9641
	50	15			9659
		$150	$55		9735
		$50			
		$125			9767
	60		10		9801
			8		
			4		
75		65	26.5		9823
		41.11.3			
	45 [b]				9833
100	65	90			8973
	45	65			
		35			8983

Men	Women	Boys	Girls	Source County	File
	30			Morris	963N
	40 ($100)			Hunterdon	1910J
	28 ($70)		$40		1910J
30	50 [b]				1781J
80			40		1781J
	50 [b]	80		Somerset	1137R
		80	25		1137R
	25				1067R
$250	$110		$125		1134R
	55				1034R

TABLE IV

MANUMISSIONS IN NEW YORK WILLS [a]

Period	Wills Mentioning Slaves	Wills Manumitting Slaves	Percentage of Manumissions in Wills Mentioning Slaves
1744–1753	59	3	5%
1754–1760	37	4	11%
1766–1771	55	5	9%
1777–1783	44	6	14%
1784–1786	32	2	6%
1786–1796	32	4	13%
1796–1800	34	20	59%

[a] *Figures derived from:* Abstracts of Wills on File in the Surrogate's Office, City of New York (Collections of the New-York Historical Society, 1895–1906), *IV, V, VII, IX, XIV, XV.*

TABLE V

MANUMISSIONS IN NEW JERSEY WILLS [a]

Period	Wills Mentioning Slaves	Wills Manumitting Slaves	Percentage of Manumissions in Wills Mentioning Slaves
1781–1785	23	3	13%
1796–1800	40	16	40%

[a] *Figures derived from:* N.J. Archives, *1st ser., XXXV, XXXVIII.*

TABLE VI

NUMBER OF SLAVE MANUMISSIONS, NEW YORK COUNTY [a]

1746–1750	1
1751–1755	2
1756–1760	1
1761–1765	2
1766–1770	3
1771–1775	—
1776–1780	—
1781–1785	1
1786–1790	3
1791–1795	6
1796–1799 [b]	8
1799–1800	15

[a] *Figures derived from: Harry P. Yoshpe, "Record of Slave Manumissions in New York During the Colonial and Early National Periods,"* Journal of Negro History, *XXVI (1941), 78–104.*

[b] *This does not include slaves manumitted after March 29, 1799 when the abolition law permitted masters to manumit old and sick slaves without posting bonds. These slaves are included in the period 1799–1800.*

bibliographical essay

I. NEGRO SLAVERY IN THE NORTH

There is no general history of slavery in the North. Ulrich B. Phillips, *American Negro Slavery* (2d ed., Gloucester, Mass., 1959), devotes a chapter to northern slavery. John Hope Franklin's survey of Negro history, *From Slavery to Freedom* (2d ed., New York, 1961), provides a good introduction to the subject. There are several valuable local studies, however, foremost among which is Lorenzo J. Greene's *The Negro in Colonial New England* (New York, 1942). George H. Moore, *Notes on the History of Slavery in Massachusetts* (New York, 1866), is still useful. Edgar J. McManus, *A History of Negro Slavery in New York* (Syracuse, 1966), is the most recent account of slavery in an important state and it supersedes previous studies. The standard account of slavery in Pennsylvania is Edward R. Turner's *The Negro in Pennsylvania* (Washington, D.C., 1911). Despite the importance of slavery in New Jersey, there is no adequate book on the subject. Henry S. Cooley, *A Study of Slavery in New Jersey (Johns Hopkins University Studies in Historical and Political Science,* XIV [1896]), provides the most complete account. It should be supplemented by Marion T. Wright, "New Jersey Laws and the Negro," *Journal of Negro History,* XXVIII (1943), 156–99. And for a thorough account of the legal status of northern Negroes see Emma L. Thornbrough's unpublished doctoral dissertation, "Negro Slavery in the North: Its Legal and Constitutional Aspects" (University of Michigan, 1946).

Newspaper advertisements describing slaves offered for sale or seeking the return of fugitives are valuable sources of information about slave skills. A convenient collection of these advertisements is found in "Eighteenth Century Slaves as Advertised by their Masters," *Journal of Negro History*, I (1916), 163–216. The volumes of newspaper extracts published as part of the series, *Documents Relating to the Colonial, Revolutionary, and Post-Revolutionary History of the State of New Jersey* (generally known by the binder's title, *New Jersey Archives*), contain a great number of advertisements describing slave skills. The earlier volumes, which produce advertisements in full, are especially valuable.

A general impression of the extent of slaveholding in the community and of the relative value of slaves may be obtained from a study of wills and estate inventories. Many volumes of the *New Jersey Archives* are devoted to a *Calendar of New Jersey Wills, Administrations, Etc.,* which include estate inventories. Like the newspaper extracts, the earlier volumes contain greater detail than the later ones that seem to have been edited primarily for geneologists rather than historians. The volumes of *Abstracts of Wills on File in the Surrogate's Office, City of New York,* published as part of the *Collections of the New-York Historical Society,* also include inventories and both the New Jersey and New York collections of wills are useful in determining the frequency of testamentary manumissions.

Negro education and Christianization is discussed in two excellent articles by Frank J. Klingberg: "The S. P. G. Program for Negroes in Colonial New York," *Historical Magazine of the Protestant Episcopal Church*, VIII (1939), 306–71, and "The African Immigrant in Colonial Pennsylvania and Delaware," *ibid.*, XI (1942), 126–53. "Rev. John Sharpe's Proposals, Etc.," (*Collections of the New-York Historical Society, 1880*), 339–63, is a contemporary account of early efforts to educate Negroes in New York. Marion M. T. Wright, *The Education of Negroes in New Jersey* (New York, 1941) has useful material on the early period.

Many local histories devote chapters to the place of slavery in the life of the community; they are especially rich in anecdotal material that contributes to forming a picture of Negro life. Travel accounts are an invaluable source for social history. The Duc de la Rochefoucauld-Liancourt, *Travels Through the United States of North America*, trans.

H. Neuman (2 vols.; London, 1799) is especially useful. Mrs. Anne Grant, *Memoirs of an American Lady* (2 vols.; New York, 1901) depicts slavery in pre-Revolutionary Albany, New York. Slavery in rural New Jersey in the late eighteenth century is described by Andrew D. Mellick, Jr. in *The Story of an Old Farm* (Somerville, N.J., 1889).

There are few accounts of slavery in the North from the view of the enslaved Negroes. "Sojourner Truth," who later took an active role in the abolition movement, was held in slavery in New York until she was freed by the abolition law of 1817. [Olive Gilbert], *Narrative of Sojourner Truth* (Boston, 1850) is marked by bitterness. The *Life of James Mars* (Hartford, 1864), is the story of a Connecticut slave. Although the *Memoir of Quamino Buccau* (Philadelphia, 1851), was written by a white man, William J. Allinson, it is based on the recollections of a slave who served in New York and New Jersey before the Revolution.

II. ABOLITION

The starting point in examining the early antislavery movement is Mary S. Locke, *Anti-Slavery in America* (Boston, 1901). Unfortunately, David B. Davis, *The Problem of Slavery in Western Culture* (Ithaca, N.Y., 1966) was published too late for me to use it as extensively as I would have liked. It provides an invaluable interpretive account of the intellectual context of the abolition movement in the colonial period. Professor Davis has promised to deal with the post-Revolutionary period in a subsequent volume. The standard account of the Quaker opposition to slavery is Thomas E. Drake, *Quakers and Slavery in America* (New Haven, 1950). Sydney V. James, *A People Among Peoples* (Cambridge, Mass., 1963) is an insightful interpretation of Quaker benevolent activities in the eighteenth century. *A Brief Statement of the Rise and Progress of the Testimony of the Religious Society of Friends Against Slavery and the Slave Trade* (Philadelphia, 1843), is still valuable for its extensive extracts from the records of Quaker meetings.

There are only a few biographies, memoirs, and collections of correspondence of early abolitionists. George S. Brookes,

Friend Anthony Benezet (Philadelphia, 1937) includes a great number of Benezet letters. Other Benezet letters are included in the manuscript copies of letters to Granville Sharp at the New-York Historical Society. Amelia M. Gummere's edition of *The Journals and Essays of John Woolman* (2 vo's., London, 1922), has a valuable biographical introduction. Mack Thompson, *Moses Brown* (Chapel Hill, N.C., 1962) is an excellent biography of an important Rhode Island abolitionist. *The Works of Samuel Hopkins,* ed. Edwards A. Park (3 vols., Boston, 1852) includes a long biographical sketch and reprints many of Hopkins' letters on slavery. David Cooper, a Quaker abolitionist who led several attempts to abolish slavery in New Jersey, recorded his anti-slavery activities in his journal. Extensive extracts from this valuable document have been reprinted in [William J. Allinson,] "Notices of David Cooper," *Friends' Review,* XV–XVI (1861–63), *passim.*

The manuscript records of the abolition societies are invaluable in determining the aims and methods of the abolitionists. The papers of the Pennsylvania Society for Promoting the Abolition of Slavery at the Historical Society of Pennsylvania are voluminous. The papers of the New York Society for Promoting the Manumission of Slaves are at the New-York Historical Society, and the papers of the New Jersey Society for Promoting the Abolition of Slavery are in the Quaker Collection at Haverford College. These records include not only minutes of society meetings but the records of committees, drafts of petitions, and correspondence. There is a manuscript history of the Pennsylvania Abolition Society by William J. Buck at the Historical Society of Pennsylvania. The published records of the conventions of antislavery societies which met periodically after 1794 are also useful. The minutes were published under various titles but are usually indexed under American Convention for Promoting the Abolition of Slavery, the organization's title after 1803.

A list of the important pamphlets and newspaper articles debating slavery and abolition is too extensive to include in this essay, but a guide to some of this material can be found in Dwight L. Dumond, *A Bibliography of Antislavery in America* (Ann Arbor, Mich., 1961). Unfortunately, this is simply an alphabetical list, without any description or division by topics or by chronology.

Abolition in the northern states during the Revolution is discussed by Benjamin Quarles, *The Negro in the American Revolution* (Chapel Hill, N.C., 1961). See also: Jeffrey R. Brackett, "The Status of the Slave, 1775–1789," *Essays in the Constitutional History of the United States,* ed. J. Franklin Jameson (Boston, 1889); George Livermore, *An Historical Research Respecting the Opinions of the Founders of the Republic on Negroes as Slaves, as Citizens, and as Soldiers* (3d ed., Boston, 1863); and William C. Nell, *The Colored Patriots of the American Revolution* (Boston, 1855).

Records of the colonial and state legislatures are the most important source for tracing the political progress of abolition. Although these records indicate the nature of petitions and amendments and show the important votes on abolition bills, they do not report the substance of the debates. Indexes are poor, especially in the earlier period. In three cases, however, the texts of debates on abolition are available. Thomas Lloyd, a pioneer in the art of verbatim reporting, recorded the debates of the Pennsylvania legislature on the revision of the abolition law in 1788: *Proceedings and Debates of the General Assembly of Pennsylvania* (4 vols., Philadelphia, 1787–88). Part of the heated debate on the revision of the New Jersey slave code and the unsuccessful attempt to amend it to include a gradual abolition plan was reported in the *State Gazette* (Trenton, N.J.) January 23 and April 10, 1798. There are two reports of the debate on abolition at the New York constitutional convention of 1821: *A Report of the Debates and Proceedings of the Convention of the State of New-York,* L. H. Clarke, reporter (New York, 1821) and *Reports of the Proceedings and Debates of the Convention of 1821,* Nathaniel H. Carter and William L. Stone, reporters (Albany, 1821). Letters published in newspapers during and after debates on abolition bills hint at the political maneuvering and give some indication of the tenor of the debates.

The abolition of slavery in Massachusetts is illuminated in two important articles: William O'Brien, S.J., "Did the Jennison Case Outlaw Slavery in Massachusetts?" *William and Mary Quarterly*, 3d ser., XVII (1960) , 219–41; and John D. Cushing, "The Cushing Court and the Abolition of Slavery in Massachusetts: More Notes on the 'Quock Walker Case,' " *American Journal of Legal History*, V (1961) , 118–44. Jeremy Belknap, "Queries Respecting the Slavery and Emancipation of Negroes in Massachusetts . . . ," Collections of the Massachusetts Historical Society, 1st ser., IV (1795) , 191–211, is extremely useful. In preparing this essay, Belknap consulted several prominent Massachusetts citizens; their replies to his questions are printed in "Letters and Documents Relating to Slavery in Massachusetts," Collections of the Massachusetts Historical Society, 5th ser., III (1877) , 373–442.

The abolition of slavery in New Jersey is discussed by Simeon Moss, "The Persistence of Slavery and Involuntary Servitude in a Free State (1685–1866) ," *Journal of Negro History*, XXXV (1950) , 289–314. This article also has other valuable material on slavery in that state.

For discussions of abolition in other states see: Leonard W. Labaree, "Introduction," *The Public Records of the State of Connecticut*, VIII (Hartford, 1951) , xvii–xx; Edgar J. McManus, "Antislavery Legislation in New York," *Journal of Negro History*, XLVI (1961) , 207–16; and Edward R. Turner, "The Abolition of Slavery in Pennsylvania," *Pennsylvania Magazine of History and Biography*, XXXVI (1912) , 129–42. The impact of abolition on the Negro is described in Leon F. Litwack's definitive, *North of Slavery* (Chicago, 1961) .

index

INDEX

tions for laws to protect
Negroes, 208–10, 212; on prospects for abolition, 176, 179–80;
protects abused slaves, 23; protects free Negroes, 162–64

New York Provincial Congress,
considers abolition, 139–40

New York slave code: allows deportation as punishment, 161,
210; allows masters to punish
slaves, 13–14; on assault, 14; on
baptism, 9; gives compensation
for executed slaves, 16; on free
Negroes, 15, 16–17, 18–19; on
fugitive slaves, 12; manumission
procedures, 150, 180 n, 181, 213;
prohibits meetings, 12; on murder, 14; as reaction to slave rebellion, 15; revisions of, 151–52,
212; severity of, 13; on slave testimony, 14; on theft, 14; on trial
procedures, 14, 15, 16, 150

Nisbet, Richard, pro-slavery writings of, 95

Norris, Isaac, opposes Quaker abolitionists, 63

Northern slavery, contrasted with
slavery in South, 32, 228

Northern states, slave population
of, 222

Otis, James, on slavery, 98

Paine, Ephraim, supports abolition, 147, 148

Paine, Thomas, antislavery writings of, 96

Pemberton, James, antislavery activities of, 159, 160

Pennsylvania: duty on imported
slaves, 47–48, 90, 92; duty on
imported slaves disallowed, 62;
enacts abolition, 130–31; need
for slaves in, 34; opposition to
slave trade in, 90; prohibits
slave trade, 157–58; revises abolition law, 158–59; slaveowners

oppose slave baptism, 8; slave
population of, 6; slavery in, 6

Pennsylvania abolition law, 1780:
provisions of, 128–29, 131; revisions of, 158

Pennsylvania Abolition Society,
174; on character of free
Negroes, 224; decline of, 206;
helps found New Jersey Abolition Society, 173; institutes freedom suit, 204–5; lobbying activities of, 164; opposes restrictions
on free Negroes, 207; petitions
Congress, 164–65; protects free
Negroes, 162–64; revived, 159,
162; on total abolition bill, 204

Pennsylvania legislature, considers abolition: 1717, 62; 1722, 64;
1778–80, 126–28, 130–31, 133,
136–37

Pennsylvania legislature: considers prohibiting importation of
Negroes, 90, 126, 127; considers
restriction of free Negroes, 127,
128–29, 207–8; considers restriction of free Negro immigration, 225; considers revision of
manumission procedures, 93;
considers total abolition, 202–4,
205–6, 207, 208 n

Pennsylvania Provincial Convention, petitions for end of slave
trade, 125

Pennsylvania slave code, 6; compensation for executed slaves,
16; on free Negroes, 19; legal
rights of slaves and free
Negroes, 127, 128; on manumissions, 18, 77; prohibits meetings
and carrying arms, 16; on rape,
16; on separation of slave families, 158–59; on theft, 13; on
trial procedures, 16, 127

Philadelphia, as center of Enlightenment thought, 93

Pittsfield, Massachusetts, supports
abolition, 112

Political parties, role of in aboli-